Balzac's
Comedy of Words

Portrait of Balzac, by Bertell, courtesy of the Maison de Balzac Museum, Paris. Photograph by R. LaLance.

Balzac's
Comedy of Words

By Martin Kanes

Princeton University Press
1975

Publication of this book has been aided by a grant from
The Andrew W. Mellon Foundation
This book has been composed in 10 point Linotype Baskerville
within a format planned by Bruce Campbell
Printed in the United States of America
by Princeton University Press,
Princeton, New Jersey

Acknowledgments

Sections of the book have appeared in somewhat different form as articles in various journals. I must thank the following publishers for permission to reproduce previously printed material: Syracuse University Press, for parts of chapter seven published in *Symposium* (Fall-Winter, 1969) as "Balzac and the Problem of Expression"; Editions Garnier Frères for parts of chapter one published in *L'Année balzacienne* (1969) as "Balzac et la psycholinguistique"; and the Società Editrice Internazionale for parts of chapter two published in *Studi francesi* (1970 and 1972) as "Logic and Language in *La Peau de chagrin*," and "The Mythic Structure of *La Peau de chagrin*."

Too many persons and institutions have provided help over a number of years for me to be able to list them all here; a general acknowledgment of what all scholars owe each other must suffice. However, I must particularly thank the Guggenheim Foundation, the Fulbright Commission and the Committee on Research of the University of California, Santa Cruz, for material help without which this undertaking could never have been completed. My wife's role as benevolent critic has been indispensable at every step in the way.

|v|

Contents

List of Abbreviations

The abbreviations used are essentially those employed by Ferdinand Lotte in his *Dictionnaire biographique des personnages fictifs de la Comédie humaine* (Paris, 1952). I have added a few symbols to refer to several of the *Oeuvres diverses*.

AS	Albert Savarus	EHC	L'Envers de l'histoire contemporaine
B	Béatrix	EM	L'Enfant maudit
Be	La Cousine Bette	Ep	L'Epicier
Bou	Les Petits Bourgeois	EtF	Etude de femme
BS	Le Bal de Sceaux		
		F	Ferragus
CA	Le Cabinet des antiques	FF	La Femme comme il faut
CB	César Birotteau	FA	La Femme abandonnée
Ch	Les Chouans	FE	Une Fille d'Eve
ChO	Le Chef-d'oeuvre inconnu	Fir	Madame Firmiani
CP	Le Cousin Pons	FM	La Fausse Maîtresse
CS	Le Catéchisme social	FP	La Femme de province
CSS	Les Comédiens sans le savoir	FT	La Femme de trente ans
		FYO	La Fille aux yeux d'or
CT	Le Curé de Tours		
CV	Le Curé de Village	Gam	Gambara
DA	Le Député d'Arcis	H	Honorine
DAr	Des Artistes	HA	Un Homme d'affaires
Des	Une Passion dans le désert		
DG	Du Gouvernment moderne	IG	L'Illustre Gaudissart
		IP	Illusions perdues
DL	La Duchesse de Langeais		
Do	Massimilla Doni	LA	Lettre adressée aux écrivains français
E	Les Employés	Let	Lettres sur le théâtre
EB	Etudes sur M. Beyle	LL	Louis Lambert
EG	Eugénie Grandet	Lys	Le Lys dans la vallée

ABBREVIATIONS

Balzac's
Comedy of Words

Introduction

To put himself in the place of God and totally describe the world: such was the ambition of Honoré de Balzac. Who can help but admire the magnitude of the goal and the tremendous act of will that drove him toward it? Yet who can fail to see that it also had to culminate in a work whose drama lay, like that of life itself, in unresolved issues, incoherent circumstantiality, incomplete portraits, unfinished adventures, and unfulfilled destinies? To such an undertaking there were no frontiers.[1] Even if a certain "objective" content were always there, verifiable though constantly expanding, its aesthetic significance could not be quantified or determined a priori. Within the imaginative structure we call the *Comédie humaine* there is, therefore, a continuous double movement of exploration and interpretation. Balzac may indeed have met a miserly barrelmaker who eventually suggested the character of old Grandet; but there was always the interpretive "transformation" of which Proust spoke, and hardy indeed is the critic who would undertake to unravel a skein that an author himself must leave entangled.

Not only hardy, but perverse. For the question is not solely what is "real" or "true" in a novel. The question is in the nature of the interpretive process. Here the *balzacien* can make a useful distinction between two kinds of assumptions on which the narrative is built: the assumption of that which is known, as against that which is knowable. This is not at all the distinction between the everyday acceptations of "true" and "imaginary," for both may be true or both imaginary in common-sense meaning. By that which is known, I mean those concepts concerning which the nar-

[1] For interpretations of the *Comédie humaine* as a drive toward unity, see H. U. Forest, *L'Esthétique du roman balzacien* (Paris, 1950); and André Allemand, *Unité et structure de l'univers balzacien* (Paris, 1965).

|3|

rator can assume a certain community of views with his reader. By that which is knowable, I mean those concepts that are problematical or empirically unverifiable, but nevertheless possible. The full test of the "realism" of a Balzacian novel, if one really needs one, lies in the success with which it induces us to accept this, too, as "known." Balzac himself set this process up as the major problem of his creative life, when he agonized in the *Dissertation sur l'homme* on the difficulties of moving from "propositions démontrées" to "propositions à résoudre."[2] In Mikel Dufrenne's words, "l'oeuvre de prose parle de l'homme . . . non pas l'homme réel, ni non plus un homme imaginaire, mais l'homme possible, dont la possibilité réside dans la Nature comme foyer de tous les possibles."[3]

To call oneself the "secretary of society," even in half-jest as Balzac did, is to assert that society—the data of the *Comédie humaine*—preexists; that one has but to record. The city of Tours, of which his narrator writes so lovingly so many times, is an unproblematical part of human experience described with the voice of logic and analysis. But there is also that range of the Balzacian narrative which cannot rely on a community of experience: the Tours of the abbé Troubert and the Tours of the abbé Birotteau are two quite different places, and the Tours we as readers perceive in the text is partially the result of that contradiction. The voice of logic and analysis must here fall to silence, and the narrative must now substitute all the devices through which language records its own explorations, and imagination its own discoveries.

Yet I should not like to suggest in the least that the shift from the known to the knowable takes place sequentially. Balzac's narrator moves back and forth between what he knows we know, and what he wants us to accept as knowing. His task is to absorb what is possible into what verifi-

[2] The text of the *Dissertation sur l'homme* is given in the appendix. For a detailed analysis, see chapter one.
[3] Mikel Dufrenne, "Critique littéraire et phénoménologie," *Revue internationale de philosophie,* xviii (1964), 205–206.

ably is, and to mask that transition through the manipulation of his narrative voices. And to such an extent is he successful in the enterprise that he has been accused of creating in the *Comédie humaine* a self-fulfilling prophecy: *que la France est balzacienne!*

The main thrust of the interpretation of the *Comédie humaine* I propose is that there was a contradiction between the empiricism Balzac inherited, mainly from Locke and Condillac (and which he never really relinquished despite later massive doses of a dubious mysticism obtained largely second hand), and the necessities of creative writing. Yet for all its shortcomings, empiricism persisted as a kind of permanent obstacle to be negotiated and bypassed. I am not suggesting that empiricism was an attitude that he "overcame" at some point in order to become a great novelist, nor even that he was a visionary rather than a realist; but simply that the texts themselves are marked by the urgent necessity of passing beyond a type of narrative description inherited from post-Cartesian empiricism. The *Comédie humaine* can be viewed as the ongoing attempt to resolve a continually unsatisfactory state of affairs.

For historical reasons, this process tends to center around the problem of language itself. It is the role of language *in,* not the language *of,* the *Comédie humaine* that asks for our attention. Peculiar as it may seem, there has been no major study of the theory or theme of language, nor of linguistic techniques used as narrative devices in Balzac's work. What examinations do exist are usually limited to negative judgements of Balzac's style, a subject to which I shall pay scant attention.[4]

---

[4] The only substantial work done in this connection is a course given by Charles Bruneau at the Sorbonne many years ago. He found the language of the *Comédie humaine* to be basically middle-class, with appropriate excursions upward and downward as characterization required. (Charles Bruneau, *La Langue de Balzac* [Paris, 1953]). One might also mention Mario Roques' brief essay "La Langue de Balzac," in *Le Livre du centenaire* (Paris, 1952), pp. 246–57. Will G. Moore also published a note on the subject entitled "Une Question mal posée: le style de Balzac," in *Langue et littérature,* CLXI (1961), 275–76. A more searching analysis is to be found in

But the importance of language as such in the imaginary world of the *Comédie humaine* is obvious to anyone who has read more than a few pages. In the post-Cartesian world in which Balzac grew up, language was seen as primarily mimetic, but also as a necessary part of the process of knowing, since its universals were viewed as those of thought itself. In this sense, language is one of the great themes, if not the greatest theme, of Balzac's work. For anyone committed to a secretaryship to society, the subject was unavoidable.

Educated in an Oratorian school, Balzac was inevitably exposed to the classical interest in language. From Aristotle's *Rhetoric,* through Plato's *Republic,* via Cicero's *De Oratore,* and on through medieval writers on eloquence and rhetoric, the idea that language is power can be traced in clear and unbroken descendance. Developments in the eighteenth and nineteenth centuries did not so much abolish as transform these traditions. For Locke, as well as for Cicero, language was an instrumentality of power. When Balzac wrote of Napoleon, "ce qu'il n'a pas achevé par l'épeé, je l'accomplirai par la plume," he was not merely expressing his youthful admiration for a legendary figure: he was also attaching himself to a train of thought that goes back to antiquity.

By the same token, it is quite natural that he should ultimately have tied his work to Dante, although there is no indication that his knowledge of Dante's work was anything but superficial.[5] Contemporary critics, when they made the comparison, usually saw Balzac's work as an *Inferno* without

---

Henri Mitterand, "A propos du style de Balzac," *Europe,* nos. 429–30 (1965), pp. 145–61. There have also been a few compendious studies of detailed facets of Balzac's style, chief among which are J. M. Burton, *Honoré de Balzac and His Figures of Speech* (Princeton, 1921); Gilbert Mayer, *La Qualification affective dans les romans d'Honoré de Balzac* (Paris, 1940); and Olli Välikangas *Les Termes d'appellation et d'interpellation dans la Comédie humaine d'Honoré de Balzac* (Helsinki, 1965).

[5] For some general comments on Dante's influence see Kurt Wais, "Die *Divina Commedia* als dichterisches Vorbild im XIX und XX Jahrhundert," *Arcadia,* III (1968), 37–38.

a *Paradiso*.[6] But there are several reasons why Balzac might have tended to see a predecessor in Dante. He undoubtedly took "comedy" in its older sense of "performance," which still survives in the word "comédien," an actor. His work was to be theatrical, a dramatic setting-forth. Theatricality implies certain techniques with which we shall be concerned at some length, especially the way man exteriorizes inner drives. In this approach, he was supported by the ideas of Lavater, who provided a framework that, typically, was both useful and restrictive.[7] But what kind of performance was at issue in Dante? In his tenth letter to Can Grande della Scala, Dante discusses and rejects the idea that comedy must deal only with humble people, but he does maintain that it is couched in "lax and humble speech." The Dantesque tradition thus invites us to reject conventional rhetoric, and suggests a trend that was to culminate in the linguistic realism of the nineteenth century. Nor does "lax and humble speech" relate only to characterization. It raises the problem of the stance adopted by the narrator toward his own prose: not as a matter of style, but of the very functioning of language. Putting all this together turned out to be one of Balzac's major tasks, and a terse remark in the *Physiologie du mariage* gives a hint of how he viewed the process: reading, he notes, is "two people creating together."

The essence of the *Comédie humaine* does not, therefore, lie exclusively in the accuracy of its descriptions, the correctness of its social theorizing, the perspicuity of its psychologizing, or indeed, in any perfection of "style." Such virtues and faults Balzac shared with a dozen forgotten contemporaries. The value of his creation lies squarely and directly in the pact established between the narrator and the reader, in the authenticity of the joint creation that

[6]*Ibid.*, p. 38. See also Fernand Baldensperger, *Orientations étrangères chez Honoré de Balzac* (Paris, 1921), p. 166; Vittorio Lugli, *Dante e Balzac, con altri Italiani e Francesi* (Napoli, 1952), p. 34; René Guise, "Balzac et Dante," *Année balzacienne* (1963), pp. 297–319.
[7]For a full discussion of Lavater, see chapter 5.

leads us mysteriously, yet inevitably, to see in it a work of "literature." It is striking that in this invited alliance between author and reader, Balzac should have anticipated one of the major theses of contemporary phenomenology. It is we who, in the words of Dufrenne, bring a text into existence, we who take it from its author and confer upon it its being.[8] It should be clear, then, that I am not addressing myself to any of the current quarrels over the possible contributions of linguistics to literary analysis, but merely using certain concepts from linguistics when they appear to be handy tools for an exercise in literary interpretation.[9]

Although he planned a *Pathologie de la vie sociale,* which was to study human life through "la démarche et par la parole," it does not appear that Balzac ever wrote a sustained theory of language beyond the very early *Dissertation sur l'homme.*[10] The invitation is, nevertheless, clear: if the *Comédie humaine* proposes words and gestures as persuasive devices of imaginary wholeness, then surely we can look to see if they really operate as such. Whether all this will lead us to conclude, with Pierre Barbéris, that Balzac viewed language as an instrument of liberty,[11] or with Charles Affron, that he saw it as an instrument of failure,[12] is a typical Balzacian paradox that our readers, like his, will be left to resolve for themselves.

The study that follows is thematic, and primarily concerned with the text rather than with history or biography.

[8]Dufrenne, "Critique littéraire," pp. 197–98.

[9]The bibliography of mutual anathema between purely literary critics and convinced linguistic critics is enormous; let me merely mention that my own inclination is toward a prudent distinction between the two. Knud Togeby has set out the case for separation in a brief but trenchant article, "Littérature et linguistique," *Orbis litterarum,* XXII (1967), 45–48; in a lighter but equally effective statement, D. H. Stewart points out the generally obfuscating effects of strictly linguistic analysis on the purposes of literary texts. See his "Linguistic Limits," *Rendez-vous,* III (1968), 1–13.

[10]Balzac describes these projects in a note to the *Traité des excitants modernes* in *Oeuvres complètes,* edited by Marcel Bouteron and Henri Lognon (Paris: Conard, 1912–40), XL, 769.

[11]Pierre Barbéris, *Balzac et le mal du siècle* (Paris, 1970), II, 1767–68.

[12]Charles Affron, *Patterns of Failure in the Comédie humaine* (New Haven, 1966), pp. 113–31.

But the rigorous limitation of analysis to what happens in a text, so tempting and even so obvious on the surface, assumes that one knows clearly and precisely what the text is. In the case of the *Comédie humaine* there is a well-known problem: we are dealing with a linguistic structure that was constantly being altered as it was being added to, with alterations being made as a function of additions, new additions made because of alterations carried out, and the whole enterprise ended by the arbitrary fact of Balzac's untimely death. One of Balzac's chief intentions was that the *Comédie humaine* should constitute a totality and be read as such. Yet the organization of the *Comédie humaine* has nothing to do with the order of its composition, the chronological order of its events, or even the progressive development of its themes. Along with the incompleteness of the whole, nonsequentiality is a basic characteristic of the *Comédie humaine*.[13] Both qualities introduce a randomness in our perception of the entire *Comédie humaine* that is strangely at variance with the proclaimed determinism of the author.

In an attempt to circumvent these difficulties and still provide an interesting and meaningful reading of the *Comédie humaine,* I shall begin with certain historical considerations. It has been pointed out a number of times that the French novel progressed through a series of transformations from approximately 1630 to 1830, when it achieved a recognizably modern form.[14] The development was fundamentally away from a concept of conventional verisimilitude based primarily on flattering the reader's inher-

---

[13] Barbéris touches in passing on this point, which should really be of fundamental importance to his political interpretation of the *Comédie humaine*. Rejecting Balzac's own arrangement according to philosophical principles, he argues for an arrangement according to the chronology of the narrative, on the grounds that Balzac was at some pains to make the parts of the whole as internally consistent as he could. Yet Barbéris admits that Balzac rejected straight historical chronology, and he is thus left in a dilemma that leads nowhere *(Balzac et le mal du siècle,* II, 1496).

[14] See Georges May, *Le Dilemme du roman au XVIIe siècle* (New Haven, 1963); and Elwyn F. Sterling, "The Theory of Verisimilitude in the French Novel prior to 1830," *French Review,* XL (February-May 1967), 613–19.

ent sense of reality, toward a more sophisticated notion of verisimilitude as being coextensive with and internal to the novel. The effect of this shift was to focus attention on the techniques of the novel as such, and came about at precisely the time when linguistics and psychology also reached critical turning points. The decade from 1820 to 1830 might be said to have seen the emergence of a "new" novel, along with a new linguistics and a new psychology, and all were central to Balzac's concerns.

But history has its limits, and we must ultimately turn to the texts themselves. The characteristic randomness of the *Comédie humaine* will allow us to isolate the theme of language in the work as a whole, ranging back and forth among the texts, seeking echoes and resonances, and making connections I believe Balzac would have recognized as valid. The reasons for this are several. It does not appear to me that Balzac's ideas on language changed very much after the late 1820s, and I have found that there is little to gain, at least in this connection, in differentiating between "early" and "late" texts, or indeed between the various stages in the evolution of a given text. For the same reason I shall examine certain themes and novels several times from varying points of view. In taking the work as a whole, I have also put aside problems of sources. If, for example, Balzac did not really come under the influence of Bonald until about 1840, as Bernard Guyon has argued, the theories of the Catholic thinker were nevertheless widely disseminated long before then, and Balzac could hardly have failed to note what an important role Catholic traditionalists assigned to the theory of language.[15] Moreover, Balzac's habit of backtracking and rewriting makes the chronological pinpointing of influences an extremely risky business—a game really not worth the candle

---

[15] Bernard Guyon, *La Pensée politique et sociale de Balzac* (Paris, 1947), p. 691. On the other hand, Henri Evans maintains in his *Louis Lambert et la philosophie de Balzac* (Paris, 1951), p. 201, that Balzac rejected Bonald's theories of language about 1840. From our point of view, it does not much matter one way or the other.

in this instance. I have preferred, therefore, to interpret the *Comédie humaine* in terms of the widespread general speculations about language and psychology that characterized the late eighteenth and early nineteenth centuries.

A final word about editions. The primary edition to which my references will be made is the Conard edition.[16] All quotations have been collated with the Pléiade edition and with other critical editions as necessary. Variants are recorded in footnotes. I make no apologies for my long-standing affection for the Conard edition, with its creamy paper, its generous margins, its marvelous engravings. As it turned out, the variants that concerned me were practically nil, and I can only say that I am delighted that my explorations of the *Comédie humaine* took me through the pages of a set that Balzac's printery, I am sure, would have been proud to have turned out.

[16]Page numbers to the relevant volumes accompany each quotation. Volume numbers are given only where a text occupies more than one volume.

Approaches and Theories

CHAPTER I

Contemporary Theory and the *Dissertation sur l'homme*

The *Dissertation sur l'homme,* written in 1819, is a text of highest importance in the development of Balzac's thought.[1] Although it is juvenile and pretentious in conception and execution, it attempts to deal with problems of staggering complexity that had been discussed for centuries: the mind-world relationship, the thought-word relationship, the soul-body relationship. It clearly emerges from the young man's voracious reading in philosophy, and can be viewed as his first attempt at serious theoretical writing. The difficulties were many. Psychology (or what would be so called today), was traditionally barely distinguished from "philosophy." It was marked by no scientific conceptions, and as a defined field of disciplined inquiry it hardly existed. The very word was a neologism at the beginning of the nineteenth century.[2] In the innumerable dictionaries and compendia of the period, psychological material was distributed under the rubrics of philosophy, metaphysics, and ethics, and was usually treated in terms of such abstractions as will, memory, imagination, and above all, soul.

Less amorphous but more stultified, linguistics was in an equally parlous state. It was practically indistinguishable

[1] The title *Dissertation sur l'homme* is not Balzac's, but is a convenient way of referring to folios 4, 5, 7, 8, and 9 of dossier A 166 in the Spoelberch de Lovenjoul Collection of the Chantilly archives. It was jointly deciphered by M. Henri Gauthier and myself, and published by him in *L'Année balzacienne,* 1968, pp. 94–103.

[2] According to Littré, the word "psychologie" was used for the first time by the German philosopher Wolff, "pour désigner l'étude que l'on fait du moral et de l'intelligence." The *Encyclopédie* has no article on psychology as such, although the word appears in the "Discours préliminaire," precisely in reference to Wolff.

|15|

from some aspects of what is today called psychology, and in some quarters tended to blend into theology.[3] Grammar was one of the queens of pedagogy, to be sure, but it was normative grammar. The *Dissertation* is thus situated in a multiple and somewhat confused tradition.

How was Balzac's interest in psychology and linguistics first aroused? Where did he find his material? To what extent is the *Dissertation* a reworking of prior notions, and to what extent is it a piece of original thinking? In order to orient our analysis of the *Dissertation,* we must go back to Balzac's stay in Vendôme, and review briefly the education he received in the Mareschal and Dessaignes establishment. More liberal than most educators, even considered slightly subversive, the Oratorians used comparatively advanced methods. Many subjects were taught in French rather than in Latin, and the study of French itself, as a language, was developed to a relatively high degree.[4] Mareschal was considered an expert in such matters, and a document in local archives describes him as a specialist in *grammaire générale.*[5] His reputation rested to a great extent on his *Essai d'une grammaire latine élémentaire et raisonnée,* published in 1808— that is, during Balzac's residence at his institution. This primer permits us to see how language was studied when Balzac began his serious education, for it reflects the two principal influences on Mareschal: the Port-Royal theory of *grammaire générale,* and its modification by post-Cartesian sensualism.[6]

One can say without exaggeration that the Port-Royal

[3] The term "linguistics" should not be taken here in a modern technical sense. It hardly appeared at all in the philosophical works of the eighteenth century, for the excellent reason that it existed as an independent domain of inquiry only as of about 1820. I am using it here for lack of another convenient term, to indicate the ensemble of eighteenth-century theories on the origin and nature of language.

[4] Georges Snyder, *La Pédagogie en France aux XVIIᵉ et XVIIᵉ siècles* (Paris, 1965), p. 365.

[5] Cited by J. Martin-Demézil and Charles Portel, *Balzac à Vendôme* (Tours, 1949), p. 26.

[6] The book has been analyzed, but from the point of view of theological doctrine, by Philippe Bertault, *Balzac et la religion* (Paris, 1942), pp. 46–49.

Grammaire had made it almost impossible to maintain the distinction between thought and word. Arnauld and Lancelot had formulated the principle of an immutable logic translated by a language whose perfection was determined by its conformity with thought. To speak well meant that one thought well, language being but the carbon copy of a universal logic.[7] Words then would signify the objects of thought that are, in their turn, either real things (substances), or manners of being (accidents). This implies, of course, that the original element of the thought-word-object triad is thought itself, and that the operations of the mind are projected outward toward the world.[8] The primacy of thought also implied that a knowledge of selfhood might be experienced without the mediation of language—what André Cresson has called "l'intuition interne, immédiate."[9] This was seen as a process by which the thinking being "cessera même de croire à l'apport du langage."[10] This aspect of the original doctrine came to interest second-generation Cartesians very much indeed; one has merely to think of Malebranche, so often cited in Balzac's *Notes philosophiques,* and his interest in "pure understanding."[11]

[7] At the beginning of the nineteenth century, a chair of General Grammar replaced the traditional chair of Logic in the Ecoles centrales—an indication of the extent to which the one subject was seen as coextensive with the other.

[8] Antoine Arnauld and Claude Lancelot, *Grammaire générale et raisonnée de Port-Royal,* edited by M. Petitot (Paris, 1803), p. 273.

[9] André Cresson, *Descartes, sa vie, son oeuvre* (Paris, 1957), p. 33.

[10] Henri Lefebvre, *Descartes* (Paris, 1947), p. 113.

[11] A complete analysis of Cartesian doctrine on this point would be impossible here, and not directly relevant to our purposes. Nevertheless, it might be pointed out that Descartes himself spoke of language as such only very briefly in Part v of the *Discours de la Méthode,* where his remark that animals lack speech because they lack thought again underscores the primacy of thought over words. In a letter to Mersenne (November 20, 1629), he explains the diversity of human languages as being the result of "la corruption de l'usage," implying an ideal former state in which a single language was a perfect reflection of thought. He never pursued this tack, and what one might call the "Babel" question remained to plague his followers. The position of Port-Royal on the matter of usage is hotly debated. The most thorough discussions can be found in Roland Donzé,

Many of these original Cartesian positions were reflected in Mareschal's book. He begins, with a ceremonious salute to Port-Royal and a succinct statement of its basic doctrine: "Nous parlons pour exprimer nos idées; nos idées s'expriment par des mots; il y a donc autant de sortes de mots qu'il y a d'espèces d'idées."[12] The statement is characteristically categorical. The human mind proceeds in a straight line; human reason is unchangeable. And so Mareschal writes, quite naturally, that nouns, adjectives, verbs, and adverbs, and the ideas they represent exhaust all the possibilities of all languages, "parce que nous ne pouvons pas avoir d'autres sortes d'idées."[13]

Nevertheless, Mareschal was writing in the early years of the new century, when the views of Arnauld and Lancelot had undergone modification. His deference to Port-Royal is counterbalanced by the acknowledgement of debts to Condillac, to Court de Gébelin, to Domergue, to Lemarre, and to the abbé de l'Epée. Although Mareschal makes no direct reference to John Locke, it is clear that one of his major sources is Condillac's volume of *Grammaire* from the *Cours d'études écrit pour le prince de Parme,* and, through this, Locke's *Essay on Human Understanding.*[14] The Lockian dou-

---

La Grammaire générale et raisonnée de Port-Royal (Berne, 1967); and Keith Percival, "The Notion of Usage in Vaugelas and in the Port-Royal Grammar," *Papers from the Fourth Regional Meeting of the Chicago Linguistic Society* (Chicago, 1968), pp. 165–176. The notion of usage raised the possibility of linguistic relativism, and may account for some of the later uneasiness about the ability of language to represent.

[12]Lazare-François Mareschal, *Essai d'une grammaire latine elementaire et raisonnée* (Paris, 1808), i, 1.

[13]*Ibid.,* i, 3. This view is, of course, highly conventionalistic. Many post-Cartesians held that reality suscitates identical representations in the minds of men, which are then labelled by linguistic signs that vary from language to language only in their phonic "rind," but not in their semantic "core." For an examination of this trend of thought, see Tullio de Mauro, "Giambattista Vico: From Rhetoric to Linguistic Historicism," in *Giambattista Vico: An International Symposium,* Edited by G. Tagliacozzo and Hayden V. White (Baltimore, 1969), p. 286.

[14]Balzac was later to read Locke himself, and his reaction can be found in the *Notes philosophiques,* which are most easily consulted in Vol. XXV of the *Oeuvres complètes* issued by the Société des études balzaciennes (Paris, 1962). One important passage is a discussion of the existence of God (fols.

ble source of ideas—external sensation and internal combinations of sensation—was well known to Mareschal. "Un objet se présente à nous, il fait une impression; nous en conservons une image, l'idée,"[15] he writes, and he easily derives language from sensory impressions, apparently not perceiving any contradiction with the Cartesian principle of innate ideas: "Quand nous voyons un objet, quand nous pensons à un objet, nous en avons l'image ou l'idée: pour exprimer cet objet, nous lui donnons un nom . . . c'est un *substantif.*"[16] After the substantive, which is the direct designation of the object, Mareschal discerns its modes, thus obtaining the adjective, the verb, and the adverb. This is all he needs to establish human language in all its complexity. His book, of course, is but an elementary manual, which simplifies and often deforms quite subtle theories. But it was exactly here—in the domain of the practical—that Cartesian and sensualist theories could most easily be reconciled. Whether ideas were innate or derived from sensation, everyone agreed that words should translate ideas as precisely as possible, and that when the former were not clear the latter were also confused. If one were to believe Mareschal's book, the ability to write was merely a matter of training and perseverance; Balzac was soon to learn that the truth was not quite so simple.[17]

As one looks at the *Dissertation*, it becomes quite apparent that it could not have been derived solely from the teaching

---

56–57). The most widely disseminated translation of Locke in France at the time Mareschal was writing (and even at the time Balzac was composing his *Dissertation*) was one published in Amsterdam by Pierre Coste in 1700 under the title *Essai philosophique sur l'entendement humain.* All my quotations from Locke will be from the fourth edition (1750).

[15] Mareschal, *Essai,* ii, 1.

[16] *Ibid.,* ii, 1. One notes that he also assigns language the function of designating objects rather than ideas, an idea we shall explore more fully under the name of naive realism.

[17] Let us note, before leaving Mareschal, that despite his reputation this grammarian was rather behind the times in his knowledge of contemporary theories. He seems not to have been familiar with the works of Leibnitz, who had already cast doubts on the supposed universality of linguistic structures; not does he seem to have known the work of Maine de Biran, whose psychological theories opened a number of new paths.

at the school; and if the reservations expressed by the abbé Bertault on Balzac's supposed omnivorous reading in the school library are correct, then clearly the young man had to reeducate himself from the ground up at a later date.[18] But the *Dissertation* is distinctly eighteenth-century in tone, suggesting that what Balzac did was to take the simple notions acquired in his childhood, and explore them at much greater depth. In order to judge the significance of the *Dissertation* and the *Notes philosophiques* in the context of linguistic theories, therefore, we must briefly reconstruct the various theoretical positions that Balzac must certainly have examined in detail at the end of the second decade of the century.

One of the first things he must surely have observed in his reading of John Locke is that Locke discusses language as a kind of afterthought.[19] Like the Cartesians, Locke considers that words are signs of ideas,[20] but he insists that they are arbitrary, not natural.[21] Locke also insists on an extremely close tie between idea and word, since the latter can refer only to the former: "personne ne peut les appliquer immédiatement comme signes à aucune autre chose qu'aux idées qu'il a lui-même dans l'esprit."[22] Here, Locke is taking a strong position against what we shall designate as "naive realism," the principle that the word is the sign of the object. Within the mind, moreover, language is the medium whereby complex ideas are created and preserved.[23] This leaves open the possibility that complex ideas can arise without reference to reality, and Locke cites the problem of the translator who cannot find in a given

[18]Bertault, *Balzac et la religion*, p. 30.

[19]R. I. Aaron has justly observed that Locke became aware of the need for a theory of language only after having written at least part of the second book of the *Essay*. R. I. Aaron, *John Locke* (Oxford, 1955), p. 193.

[20]Locke, *Essai philosophique*, III, 48.

[21]*Ibid.*, p. 54.

[22]*Ibid.*, p. 55.

[23]*Ibid.*, p. 126. Or, elsewhere: "Quand une fois on y a attaché un nom dans lequel les parties de cette idée complexe ont une union déterminée et permanente, alors l'essence est, pour ainsi dire, établie, et l'espèce est considérée comme complète" (p. 128).

language complex terms corresponding to those in another language. There is even a great danger, according to Locke, in supposing that because we name an object, it exists outside of our minds.[24] This is the essence of "naive realism," and leads, according to Locke, to all kinds of philosophical problems. For Balzac, it led to the preoccupations of the *Dissertation* and ultimately to *La Peau de chagrin*, which is largely concerned with this very problem.

In France, sensualism was chiefly expounded by Condillac, sometimes called the French John Locke.[25] The great distinction between the two thinkers, and one that must have struck Balzac strongly, was that Condillac saw the question of language as primordial. His chief complaint about Locke was the Englishman's relative inattention to linguistic theory.[26] Condillac saw that even if thought were anterior to words, a theory of language was an absolute prerequisite to any systematic philosophy, since only language enables us to reconstruct processes of thought. In this way, we approach the perplexing notion that language both reflects thought and creates it. Compared to the Port-Royal conception of language as the static mirror of a perfect logic, Condillac's conception was extraordinarily dynamic.

Condillac's thesis thus contains the possibility that language systems can *create* thought; that is, that they can determine world views.[27] Had he pursued this tack more vig-

[24]These names are the celebrated "mixed modes," discussed in Book III, chapter v, para. 4.

[25]Etienne Bonnot de Condillac, *Essai sur l'origine des connaissances humaines* (Paris, 1798), pp. 13–14.

[26]Subsequent thinkers, such as Tracy, credited Condillac with being the discoverer of the real relationship between word and idea: that language is both the condition and vehicle of thought. For an account of the eighteenth-century debate over the passivity or activity of the mind in receiving sensation, see H. B. Acton, "The Philosophy of Language in Revolutionary France," *Proceedings of the British Academy,* XLV (1959), 199–219.

[27]"L'art de parler n'est donc que l'art de penser et l'art de raisonner, qui se développe à mesure que les langues se perfectionnent." Etienne Bonnot de Condillac, *Cours d'étude pour l'instruction du prince de Parme: la grammaire* (Paris, 1798), p. xxxvii. For an excellent discussion of the matter of

orously, he might have circumvented many problems in sensualist linguistic theory, and, at the same time, have suggested alternatives to its literary counterpart of naive realism. The crux of the matter was, of course, to explain how language could determine the development of the "art de penser." Such terminology might, after all, be simply a metaphorical way of avoiding the difficulties of the mind-world relationship. Other dissatisfactions with the sensualist position quickly developed as well. By proposing the concept of the mind as a passive recipient, Condillac found himself unable to explain the mechanisms of perception. This point interested Balzac very much, and he speculated upon it in some detail in the *Dissertation*.[28]

Perhaps more important than any theories Condillac could have brought to Balzac is the distrust of language with which his work is riddled. If, in Locke's system, words signify only ideas, in Condillac even this relationship is placed under suspicion. If words can *create* ideas, they can be deceptive. This is the chief accusation leveled by Condillac against Descartes and Leibnitz. He criticizes Leibnitz's notion of force, for example, as a word empty of meaning.[29] Condillac had put his finger squarely on the problem of naive realism; indeed, on worse—on freewheeling language that covers an intellectual void: "Il semble que, pour soutenir nos conversations, nous soyons convenus tacitement que les mots y tiendront lieu d'idées . . . chacun peut

institutional signs in Condillac, see G. Leroy, *La Psychologie de Condillac* (Paris, 1937), p. 60.

[28]If the mind were literally a *tabula rasa,* obviously, perception would not be an activity of mind, but merely the distinction between the dominant and recessive qualities of the impinging stimuli themselves. Although Condillac did not see the difficulty, such a situation would have rendered language impossible. In a series of debates at the Institut national des sciences et arts, the question was discussed at length, and Degérando attempted to save Condillac's system by arguing that the mind possesses a certain measure of intentionality, which distinguishes perceptions from sensations, and thus renders possible the use of signs. Degérando's work led straight to Maine de Biran's "puissance motrice" to which we shall shortly refer. For a discussion of Degérando, see Acton, "Philosophy of Language," p. 209.

[29]Etienne Bonnot de Condillac, *Traité des systèmes* (Paris, 1798), pp. 176–77.

impunément parler sans avoir appris la valeur des mots. Voulez-vous apprendre les sciences avec facilité? Commencez par apprendre votre langue."[30]

Rousseau, whom Balzac had also read, was a thinker scarcely to be avoided around the year 1820, and he was hung as securely as others on the horns of the word-thought dilemma. About halfway through the first section of the *Second Discourse,* he enigmatically remarks that language seems to have been necessary for language to have been invented (a paradox later picked up by his archenemy Bonald).[31] Bonald used Rousseau to attack the sensualists, of course, but he turned Rousseau's paradox to account by observing that if thought and word were one, man could not have conceived of inventing speech—which had, therefore, to be of divine origin.[32] From the divine origin of language, Bonald derived the infallibility of scriptural writing, and ultimately a whole theocratic political system. Although Balzac did not discuss Bonald's theories until much later, Catholic emphasis on the- centrality of language ("l'homme, intelligence fine, *n'est connu que par sa parole,*" in Bonald's words), was a basic ingredient in his intellectual formation.[33]

[30]*Ibid.,* p. 406. Many forthcoming Balzacian ideas are contained in this passage: the word-idea relationship that underlies *La Peau de chagrin,* the "varnish" effect, the theme of "conversation," and others. All of these are "logical" concepts, of course; and they are expressed in an eighteenth-century mode. One thinks, obviously, of Diderot who, in the *Lettre sur les sourds et les muets,* accepts both logic and intuition in order to distinguish between the arbitrary and nonarbitrary aspects of language. (Interestingly, he assigns aesthetic factors to the domain of the nonarbitrary). See Robert L. Politzer, "On Some Eighteenth Century Sources of American and German Linguistic Relativism," *Weltoffene Romanistik: Festschrift Alwin Kuhn,* edited by G. Plangg and E. Tiefenthaler (Innsbruck, 1963), p. 29.

[31]Louis de Bonald, *Législation primitive,* 3d ed. (Paris, 1829), p. 49. Was this a form of Vico's contention that language and writing emerged simultaneously? Ernst Cassirer argues for Rousseau's debt to Vico on this point, and on the general concept of the development of language from the passions. See his *Philosophie der symbolishchen Formen* (Darmstadt, 1953; repr. 1964), I, 93. Jacques Derrida, in his *De la Grammatologie* (Paris, 1967), p. 156, makes a similar point.

[32]This aspect of Bonaldian doctrine is clearly analyzed by Henri Moulinié, *De Bonald* (Paris, 1916), p. 211.

[33]Bonald, *Législation,* p. 49.

Rousseau himself was of no help to Balzac in this connection. A theory of divine origin seemed the only one that could satisfactorily account for the existence of human speech. Rousseau sagely declined to take up a definitive position, preferring to scrutinize the mechanism of language rather than its source.[34] But he did emphasize an idea that was to become increasingly important in the stream of European linguistic speculation. This was the idea that language had its roots not in reason but in irrationality and the passions. According to this view, love, fear, hate, and other emotions first led men to verbalize, and clear articulation followed only when interpersonal persuasion became necessary. Rousseau thus took issue with the dominant eighteenth-century view that logical ideas preceded words, and underscored the then quite novel idea that language might not only be arbitrary, but irrational.[35]

There were, finally, certain aspects of German linguistic thought that we must mention, not so much because they were specifically known to Balzac at this time, but because they were "in the air" and foreshadowed certain developments in his own work. His precise knowledge of German philosophy at this early date is difficult to establish, but was probably very sketchy and derived from handbooks and compendia. The *Dissertation* itself mentions no important German thinkers, although other manuscripts of this period do refer to Spinoza, Leibnitz, Kant, and Fichte.

[34]See Pierre Juliard, *Philosophies of Language in Eighteenth Century France* (The Hague, 1970), p. 29; and John Viertel, "Concepts of Language Underlying the 18th Century Controversy about the Origin of Language," in *Problems in Semantics,* edited by F. P. Dineen (Washington, D.C., 1966), pp. 115–18. Derrida justly underscores the way in which the progress of the written language ("écriture") was linked in Rousseau's mind with the corruption of mores *(Grammatologie,* p. 240). This connection also would tend to deny the possibility of divine origin, unless one were to conceive of a divinity putting into man's hand the instrument of his self-degradation.

[35] The nonrationality of language is also connected with the very long tradition of mystical speculation. Saint-Martin, Boehme, Fabre d'Olivet, Court de Gébelin, Madame Guyon, and others had proposed various forms of divine (though not necessarily orthodox) origin, and had also variously emphasized transcendental links between sound and meaning,

Sténie, written shortly after the *Dissertation,* makes a few knowledgeable allusions to Spinoza and Fichte, and it is not improbable that Balzac gleaned something of these thinkers from Madame de Stael's *De l'Allemagne.*[36] On the other hand, he seems not to have been direcdy familiar with the thinker who might have been most suggestive: Wilhelm von Humboldt.

Humboldt's linguistic speculations were close to Rousseau's: that man is man only because of language, and yet must already be man in order to discover language.[37] Humboldt was concerned, of course, to act vis-a-vis Kant in much the same way as Condillac vis-a-vis Locke: that is, to point out the failure of the older man to account for language. Humboldt transformed Kant's a priori categories into linguistic ones, but since Kantian categories were themselves qualities of mind, Humboldt's transformation led directly to the doctrine of linguistic relativity.[38] It also led to the concept of language as a determining factor of consciousness, to its "Funktionsfähigkeit." This was embodied in Humboldt's celebrated principle of *energeia,* the inner form of language, which was not "forma formata" but "forma formans," an expression of the inherent power to create forms.[39] The drive toward form was, in Humboldt's view, the basic operation of language. Neo-Kantians, of course, saw *energeia* as the projection of the world by the mind, thus establishing the primacy of language over thought.[40]

---

word and object; indeed between Word and God. I am persuaded that although Balzac used some of their vocabulary, he never, even in *Séraphita* and *Louis Lambert,* exploited or even understood their doctrines.

[36] Albert Prioult, *Balzac avant la Comédie humaine* (Paris, 1936), pp. 16 and 37. Prioult asserts (p. 47) that Balzac read various popularized histories of philosophy, and possibly discussed German philosophy with his friend Barchou de Penhoen, who was an expert in the field.

[37] This position is still held by contemporary neo-Humboldtians, such as Helmut Gipper. See his "Wilhelm von Humboldt als Begründer moderner Sprachforschung," *Wirkendes Wort,* xv (1965), 7.

[38] Politzer, "Eighteenth Century Sources," p. 27.

[39] Gipper, "Wilhelm von Humboldt," p. 15.

[40] Gipper makes the important observation, however, that Humboldt is in no way speaking of Saussurian "parole" within the framework of

At times, recondite eighteenth-century arguments over the origin and nature of language seems to lie rather far from Balzac's ultimate concerns. Yet in the years from 1817 to 1820, when he had serious ambitions as a philosophical thinker, they were the main focus of his work. These issues will appear later, transformed as literary themes in the *Comédie humaine*, where their accuracy as linguistic theories will not be at stake. It is important that this distinction be kept in mind: we will be dealing not with a second-rate philosopher, but with a first-rate novelist.[41]

Against these general points of view, the young Honoré Balzac began the redaction of the *Dissertation*. It opens with a sentence that encapsulates almost everything he inherited from eighteenth-century sensualism: "Le langage est un art par lequel l'homme dépeint à l'homme tous les objets qu'il aperçoit, toutes les sensations qu'il éprouve et tous les rapports qu'il peut découvrir entre les sensations et objets." But it also adopts traditional Cartesian ahistoricity by setting aside the question of origins ("Il est inutile pour la question qui nous occupe de suivre l'homme pas à pas . . .") and taking up a highly synchronic, descriptive attitude ("Prenons le langage tel qu'il est . . ."). Balzac subscribes to Mareschal's theory about the development of nouns before all other parts of speech, and then clearly distinguishes, as did Port-Royal, between the "matérialité réelle" of words and their function as signs. Because nouns seem to him to have a more direct relationship to objective reality, he ascribes to them a greater "materiality," indeed physical existence as vibrations in the air. Out of this was to come, many years later, one of his basic linguistic metaphors—the

---

"langue," but of the total speech experience, which makes articulated sound an expression of thought. *Ibid.*, p. 12.

[41] It is obviously impossible, and unnecessary in the present context, to present a complete history of European linguistic theory. For a good summary of the nonrationalist trend, see George A. Wells, "Vico and Herder," in Tagliacozzo and White, *Giambattista Vico,* pp. 96–97; and also Karl Otto Apel, "Die Idee der Sprache in der Tradition des Humanismus von Dante bis Vico," *Archiv für Begriffsgeschichte,* VIII (1963), 337–80.

word-event.[42] In addition to their materiality, nouns are composed, in his view, of "collections" of relationships; chiefly those between themselves, the ideas they represent, and the sensations that provoke the ideas. He then distinguishes proper nouns (indicating material objects) from modifying words (indicating qualities or relationships); and both of these from a category of more abstract words "qui ont d'autres idées pour mères." The first two groups seemed clear enough to him, but the "mots abstraits" presented the most difficult problems of definition. With the courage of the young, he pressed on undaunted.

What follows is a simplified version of Lockian sensualism and French empiricism, through which Balzac tries to define his "mots abstraits." To do so, he translates the linguistic concept into a conceptual one, proposing the possibility of the "idée composée" or "seconde idée," which he derives not from sensation or from perceptible relationships among sensations, but from an awareness of the change in our minds brought about by sensations—that is, from the consciousness of thinking itself. Balzac was, of course, by no means capable of anticipating or developing the complex psychology of Maine de Biran, but he was obviously on the track of a very subtle phenomenon. In *La Peau de chagrin* he was to find a name for this phenomenon, which he conceived to be both the subliminal stream of psychic energy that made thought and language possible, as well as the stance of self-awareness that enabled the mind to be aware of the whole complex function.

The *Dissertation* itself however, remains a logical, not an intuitive document. And in order to try to work out some understanding of the object-thought-word relationship, Balzac organized the main body of his essay around four key concepts: "puissance," "espèce," "collection d'idées," and "langage" itself.

In referring to his "seconde idée," Balzac noted that it is "la sensation de [la] puissance même." "Puissance" was a

[42]See chapter 6.

|27|

term he could have picked up from the peripatetic philosophers, for whom it indicated the capacity of the mind to perceive exterior sensation. In this context, "puissance" was almost synonymous with "mind," since it distinguished sensible from insensible matter.[43] In addition, he might well have encountered the term in the mystical traditions of France and Germany. In both, "puissance" was used to signify some vaguely divine principle; but the very real questions that surround the extent of Balzac's knowledge of these writers seems to me to place this source in a very subsidiary position (although these traditions did contain some elements pertinent to Balzac's later theory of creativity).[44] On the other hand, the Cartesians themselves used "puissance" to signify the innate nature of ideas. Indeed, the word "puissance" appears in Descartes' *Meditations* precisely in this context: "Peut-être qu'il y a en moi quelque faculté ou puissance propre à produire ces idées

[43] A handbook of Aristotelian philosophy popular in France in the eighteenth century describes "puissance" in terms that strongly anticipate certain passages of *Louis Lambert:* "Comme l'expérience nous apprend que l'objet externe n'entre point en notre corps pour se joindre aux puissances de notre âme et que nous savons d'ailleurs que ces puissances ne sortent point de leurs organes pour aller s'unir aux objets extérieurs, il faut bien dire que cette union n'est point immédiate." Pierre Chanet, *Traité de l'esprit de l'homme et de ses fonctions* (Paris, 1649), p. 57. There is no direct indication that Balzac knew this little work; Chanet, however, reflected a very widespread point of view and used a very common terminology.

[44] Madame Guyon speaks of "les puissances et les sens," although she takes a curiously sensualist stance by dividing "puissance" into "entendement," "mémoire," and "volonté." Jeanne-Marie Guyon, *Moyen court et très facile pour l'oraison* (Grenoble, 1685), p. 48. The term is also used extensively in her *Cantique des cantiques* (Lyon, 1689), but her terminology generally remains hopelessly vague. Saint-Martin speaks of three kinds of "puissance": productive, sensitive, and vegetative, which recalls the ancient doctrine of the three souls. He maintains, moreover, that the animal (or animated) soul is the product of the "puissances actives et créatives de la nature." Louis-Claude de Saint-Martin, *L'Homme de désir* (Lyon, 1790), pp. 56 and 228). Jacob Boehme sees "puissance" as movement and procreation, united in the "corps de Dieu," and collectively constituting all the possibilities of Becoming. For him, "Puissances" are rooted in the heart, for "c'est là la source de toutes les Puissances, et d'où la Parole elle-même tire son ascension." Jacob Boehme, *L'Aurore naissante* (Paris, 1800), I, 12, 15–16, 74.

sans l'aide d'aucunes choses extérieurs,"[45] which seems to be connected with Balzac's conception of "seconde idée." Among the neo-Cartesians, "puissance" variously signified the intellectual potential of the brain or its real and actual power, but they were uneasy about it. Malebranche reproached the orthodox Cartesians with its vagueness: "Ils sont englobés par la critique générale de la notion de *puissance,* qui ne réveille point dans l'esprit d'idée distincte et particulière."[46] Perhaps Balzac adopted the term because it had lost so much of its precision. We know that the word occupied him greatly at this point, for he made a note on it in the contemporary *Notes philosophiques:* "Et si vous balancez encore, je puis prononcer le mot de puissance, du principe éternel qui a créé l'univers."[47]

It is surprising, in view of the importance of the term and the debate that raged around it, that the *Encyclopédie* had no article on it. It was, perhaps, too touchy. But it is clear that for Balzac "puissance" was not an orthodox concept. Rejecting theology, he attempted to develop the concept by treading a fine line between Cartesian innateness and mechanistic sensualism. At stake, in his view, was some way of understanding the operations of mind. To accomplish this, the *Dissertation* divides "puissance" into five operations: memory, will, imagination, judgement, and relation-making. These operations are grouped under the

[45]René Descartes, *Oeuvres,* edited by Charles Adam and Paul Tannery, IX: *Méditations* (Paris, 1905; repr. 1964), p. 31.

[46]Cited by G. Rodis-Lewis, *Nicolas Malebranche* (Paris, 1963) p. 179. Malebranche considered "puissance" too close to the concept of innateness for his purposes. (Nicolas Malebranche, *De la recherche de la vérité,* edited by G. Rodis-Lewis [Paris, 1945], III, 175).

[47]"Notes philosophiques," in *Oeuvres complètes* (Paris, Société des études balzaciennes, 1962), XXV, 543. In such passages Balzac is clearly trying to find some understanding of the mind apart from theological explanations. Locke himself had distinguished in man a certain "power," which he classified among the simple ideas arising from reflection. He claims that man observes in himself the ability to think, and from this derives not his sense of existence but his sense of "power." (*Essai philosophique,* I, 248). Condillac criticized Locke for what he nevertheless considered to be a return to Cartesian endogenism, and manifestly avoided using the term himself.

rubric of "espèces," the second important term used in the *Dissertation.*

Once again, Balzac adopted an Aristotelian term with singular offhandedness. The Peripatetics saw "espèces" as subtle emanations from physical bodies, which made perception possible. But Balzac's "espèces" have nothing to do with such emanations. He is simply talking about what the eighteenth century called "faculties" of the mind, except that he created a new one, relation-making. No prior writer mentions such a faculty, although it was implicit in Cartesianism and sensualism. And, of course, until the question of relation-making was understood, "puissance" itself remained a mystery. Ultimately, the "espèces" did not solve the problem of "puissance" but merely postponed it. Yet none of this was mere word play. There is something quite understandable in the fact that Balzac did not simply adopt the traditional term "faculty." Although eighteenth-century writers obviously understood the word "espèce," they did not use it themselves; consequently it was free of both Cartesian and sensualist colorations. And Balzac was manifestly trying to find a line of thought that would allow him as much independence as possible from prior systems. None of the well-known tableaux of the mental faculties corresponds to the "espèces" proposed by Balzac.[48] The *Dissertation,* at least in this respect, is an attempt to produce an original piece of thinking. If he still used the old vocabulary, and to some extent the old categories, Balzac did not copy. He struck out in new directions with his unexplained and undefined faculty of relation-making, as well as with the quite peculiar association he set up between two of his "espèces": memory and imagination. He accepted none of the orthodox views of image-making and image-storing, but maintained that memory is a function of

[48]A list of all the eighteenth-century tableaux of the faculties would be endless. Of Balzac's five, memory, will, imagination, and judgement all appear here and there in various schemas ranging from Descartes himself through Port-Royal, Locke, Condillac, Bonnet, La Mettrie, D'Alembert, Helvétius, Destutt de Tracy, Cabanis, and Cousin.

simple ideas, whereas imagination is a function of complex ideas. Imagination, not memory, supports the creative aspects of mind that derive from the "idées secondes." The *Dissertation* thus clearly rejects the classical association of memory and the Muses.[49] Creativity, one is forced to conclude from the *Dissertation,* has more to do with the self-observance and self-consciousness of mental processes, than with copying the world. Even more significant, perhaps, is Balzac's statement that although "puissance" is composed of the five "espèces," the former is not merely the sum total of the latter, which he likens to imaginary lines inscribed for convenience on the globe. The metaphor suggests that none of these terms should be taken with the literalness that characterized eighteenth-century terminology. There is ultimately such a difference between the Balzacian "espèces" on the one hand, and eighteenth-century faculties and Aristotelian species on the other, that one is led to concede to the young author much more originality of thought than the juvenile tone of his essay would seem to justify.

The third key concept of the *Dissertation* is that of "collections." Again, self-awareness is a critical issue. Although Locke had not decided whether ideas are representations of exterior reality or states of mind, he leaned heavily in favor of the latter. Condillac, especially in his later writings, opted for a more representational theory,[50] and he was followed in this by the *Encyclopédie* and all the intellectual currents that derived from it.[51] But it is clear that neither

---

[49]Memory had already been transformed in the seventeenth century from a purely mnemnotic device, reflecting the world, into a tool for the *discovery* of new knowledge. But the consequence was a link with the Ratio, which Balzac, aligning himself with emergent romanticism, rejects. See F. Yates, *The Art of Memory* (Chicago, 1966), pp. 368–89.

[50]Leroy, *Psychologie de Condillac,* pp. 42–44.

[51]Jean Le Rond d'Alembert, "Discours préliminaire des éditeurs," *Encyclopédie ou dictionnaire raisonné des sciences, des arts et des métiers,* 3rd ed. (Geneva and Neuchâtel, 1778–1779), i, x. The great exceptions were, of course, Rousseau and Maupertuis. Balzac's much-admired Charles Bonnet also remained loyal to Locke on this point, maintaining against Condillac that the idea is "une manière d'être de l'âme dont elle a la conscience

Locke's mathematically couched formulations nor the arid presentation of Condillac could satisfy Balzac.[52] He tried to break away from mechanistic approaches, not in the *Dissertation* itself, but in the contemporary *Notes philosophiques*. There he distinguishes words that correspond to perceptible objects from those that do not. The "collections" of the former are easy to identify, but those referring to abstractions are inductive, reflexive, and difficult to pin down.[53] By admitting the latter category in the *Dissertation,* Balzac departed emphatically from the sensualist position. He did not, however, move to outright idealism. A few decades after the composition of the *Dissertation,* the notion of "collections" was replaced by the truly complex idea, in which primary unities lose their identity in a concept which, like "puissance," is qualitatively different from the "sum of its parts." Theories of mind were thereby rendered less mechanistic, and Balzac was not alone in condemning, barely ten years later, the sterile game of "analyse." The transformation was largely the work of Maine de Biran, whose delicate psychology replaced, in France, the eternal

---

ou le sentiment." Charles Bonnet, *Oeuvres,* Vol. xiv: *Essai analytique sur les facultés de l'âme* (Copenhagen, 1760), 30.

[52] Locke writes typically: "je dis que les idées spécifiques que nous avons des substances ne sont autre chose qu'*une collection d'un certain nombre d'idées simples, considérées comme unies à un seul sujet*" (*Essai,* ii, 313). The italics are Locke's. The same attitude returns in the conclusion to Book ii: "Toutes les idées que nous avons des différentes espèces de substances ne sont que des collections d'idées simples avec la supposition d'un sujet" *(Essai,* ii, 344).

[53] "Notes philosophiques," in *Oeuvres complètes* (Paris, Club de l'honnête homme, 1962), xxv, 554. A few lines further on in the "Notes philosophiques," Balzac rather obstinately maintains that Locke admitted collections of both simple and complex ideas: "Il n'y a pas de vide à cet égard dans la Métaphysique. Locke le comble; ce n'est pas sur cette partie qu'on peut le contredire." Which makes one wonder just what reservations Balzac did have. The manuscripts are silent on the point. Condillac was of little help, insisting mainly upon the need for logical deduction. In discussing Locke's "collection de l'idée qu'il appelle *homme*" Condillac specifically rejects the notion that reflexive ideas could constitute collections *(Traité des systèmes,* p. 40). He was mainly concerned with being sure that each simple idea entering into a collection was clearly and accurately determined *(Essai sur l'origine,* pp. 389 and 479).

dusty debates on faculties. At the same time, philology replaced "grammaire générale" in a shift that finally responded to Condillac's insistence on the central role of language.[54]

One of the surprising things about the *Dissertation* is that it fails entirely to deal with materialist speculation that saw direct and necessary connections between complex thoughts and objective reality. Among the materialists, Helvetius perhaps went to greatest extremes when he observed that it is impossible to conceive of words that do not apply to specific objects.[55] La Mettrie also conceived of mental processes in the most simplistic, mechanistic terms: "Rien de si simple," he wrote, "comme on voit, que la Mécanique de notre Education! Tout se réduit à des sons, ou à des mots, qui de la bouche de l'un passent par l'oreille de l'autre, dans le cerveau, qui reçoit en même temps par les yeux la figure des corps, dont ces mots sont les Signes arbitraires."[56] Along with Helvétius and La Mettrie, Turgot took up a strong stand of this sort. Although Turgot admitted the arbitrariness of signs,[57] he insisted that words,

[54]Locke, too, had stressed the fact that the existence of collections depended almost entirely on language: "Chaque mode mixte [est] composé de plusieurs idées simples. . . . Ce qui est la marque de cette union . . . c'est le nom qu'on donne à cette combinaison d'idées. Car c'est sur les noms que les hommes règlent ordinairement le compte qu'ils font d'autant d'espèces de modes mixtes; et il arrive rarement qu'ils reçoivent ou considèrent aucun nombre d'idées simples comme faisant une idée complexe, excepté les collections qui sont désignées par certains noms." (*Essai philosophique*, ii, 274–75). A few pages further on, he reiterates his conviction that only collections to which men "donnent certains noms" have any real existence (ii, 276). Despite all this, however, Locke did not endow language with that central and original position that it occupied in Condillac's system, and which undoubtedly accounted for so much speculation on language in France.

[55]Claude-Adrien Helvétius, *Oeuvres complètes*, Vol. iii: *De l'Homme, de ses facultés intellectuelles et de son éducation* (Liège, 1774), 136.

[56]Julien Offroy de La Mettrie, *Oeuvres philosophiques*, Vol. ii: *L'Homme machine* (Berlin, 1764), 32. Needless to say, the word "mécanique" plays a large part in all such materialist speculation, and will be important in *La Peau de chagrin*.

[57]For a brief exposition of Turgot's theories of language, see Juliard, *Philosophies of Language*, p. 31.

once "established," referred not to our mental perceptions but to reality itself. Turgot founded language not on "la raison présente à elle-même," but on action—that is, on the mind-in-the-world. Language, he held, refers primarily to objects; only secondarily does it refer to perception. He returns frequently and categorically to the point.[58] In short, Turgot saw the origin and end of language in external reality; he denied the role of self-consciousness except as a very secondary process having little to do with the essential functioning of language.

In one way or another, these men were talking about the problem of "naive realism," which could mean either the presence of the word as a real object in a real world, or the word as a direct and necessary label for aspects of reality. Locke had already condemned the latter attitude in the *Essay*,[59] and Maupertuis had, in his turn, accused his contemporaries of falling into the former error.[60] The simplicity, not to say the childish reductionism, with which Turgot and his faction elaborated their theory left them open to all kinds of criticism; especially to the charge that they eliminated from language all but the most mechanical, analogical operations.[61] The striking absence of any allusion what-

[58]Anne Robert Jacques Turgot, "Remarques critiques sur . . . Maupertuis"; cited in Ronald Grimsley, *Maupertuis, Turgot et Maine de Biran sur l'origine du langage* (Geneva, 1971), pp. 66 and 78.

[59]Book III, Chapter 10 of *An Essay Concerning Human Understanding* contains some especially strong statements about the dangers of supposing that words stand for the reality of things.

[60]Pierre-Louis Moreau de Maupertuis, "Reflextions philosophiques sur l'origine du langage"; quoted in Grimsley, *Maupertuis, Turgot et Maine de Biran*, p. 6.

[61]One could, of course, interpret the debate in social, if not quite political terms. It was not too many years later that Marx, in the *German Ideology*, observed that the dominant conceptual categories of an age, as well as its language, are those of the dominant class. That fairly obvious insight was developed, in its turn, by Sartre, who pointed out that those who find themselves in revolt against the dominant social categories are handicapped from the outset by having their words "stolen" from them: "As soon as the ideologist speaks, he says more and something different from what he wants to say; the period steals his thought from him. He constantly veers about, and the idea finally expressed is a profound deviation; he is caught in the mystification of words." Jean-Paul Sartre, *Search for a*

ever to this position in the *Dissertation* suggests that Balzac did not perceive it at that time as a problem of much consequence. But a transformation took place between approximately 1820 and 1830, for around the latter date *La Peau de chagrin* dealt directly with this question.

Meanwhile, these various debates left as their legacy a century of uncertainty and doubt about the role and function of language in human consciousness and culture. It was perhaps inevitable that a group of thinkers, including such diverse minds as Rousseau and Turgot, should breed disquietude in an age of reason. Add to this the elitist condescension toward popular usage and the "damage" it was considered to have done to language, and it is not surprising to see a large body of writing devoted to the dangers and pitfalls of language. The kernel of distrust can be found in Descartes himself; later Locke complained about the "imperfection" of words.[62] Condillac accused idealist philosophers of imprecise vocabulary; Voltaire and Diderot stressed the "inadequacy" of language; Malebranche suffered from quite similar misgivings;[63] and Helvétius spoke at great length of the abuse of words.[64] Behind all these concerns was a fundamental question about the nature of mind and man's relationship to the exterior world. Descartes had already seen that the mind—although it could exist—would remain forever undiscoverable to others without language as an instrument of analysis and of manifestation in the world. Closer to Balzac and to the mood of the period in which the *Dissertation* was composed

---

Method, translated by Hazel Barnes (New York, 1967), p. 113. Seen in this way, Turgot's "naive realism" is the logical consequence of middle-class mercantilism, and his theory of language is simply the counterpart of an ideology that regarded material reality as a substance to be manipulated for the greater enrichment of the manipulator.

[62]This is the title of Book III, chapter 9, of the *Essai philosophique.* Chapter 10 is entitled "De l'abus des mots."

[63]Most interesting are his protestations against misuse of such words as "puissance," "faculté," and "espèce." See *De la recherche de la vérité,* edited by G. Rodis-Lewis (Paris, 1945), II, 196.

[64] Helvétius, *De l'Esprit,* in *Oeuvres* (Liège, 1774), I, 43.

was Victor Cousin, who saw a vicious circle in Condillac's system: if language is not of divine origin, it must be born in the mind, of which it is also said to be a source. The paradox was not unlike Rousseau's. Cousin attempted to break out of it through temporality, suggesting that if one ignores the question of origins, language can perfectly well be cause and effect *successively*, acting as a simple version of "feed-back."[65] For all its eclecticism, Cousin's work sets a typically French stamp of reasonableness on speculations about creativity, and avoids recourse to the metaphysical propositions of German philosophers.

But it was Maine de Biran who made the most significant. moves in this direction. He saw the mind as inherently possessing notions of unity and causality through the simple fact of existence.[66] In his essay on "L'Origine du langage," directed against Bonald and the theory of divine origin, Biran maintained that some kind of language is necessarily a prerequisite to the existence of mind ("l'entendement"); but by "language" he meant not merely verbal signs, but all those acts by which the *moi* becomes self-conscious. For Biran this constituted the very definition of intuition, and justified the identification of language as the central capacity of the mind. He thus took to its radical extreme the liberation hinted at by Cousin, by making the word independent of ideas and objects. With Maine de Biran, Cartesian deduction as well as sensualist impressions find their philosophical end. And with this change, "grammaire générale" also expired. Language as such, independent of all other phenomena of mind, was seen as an autonomous activity, and became a valid subject of study. This development gave rise to philology on the one hand, and to romantic and symbolist (not to say, eventually, surrealist) verbal experimentation on the other.[67]

[65] Victor Cousin, *Cours d'histoire de la philosophie moderne* (Paris, 1846), I, 106–10.

[66] "Note sur les Reflexions de Maupertuis et de Turgot . . ." Quoted in Grimsley, *Maupertuis, Turgot et Maine de Biran*, pp. 99 and 103.

[67] François-Pierre-Gonthier Maine de Biran, *Oeuvres*, edited by Pierre Tisserand, Vol. XII: *Défense de la philosophie* (Paris, 1939). Biran's main text

The split opened the way for ideas that had been cir-
culating in Europe for some time, but which until about
1820 had failed to breach the wall of *grammaire générale.*
The distinction between the latter and the newly-emergent
philology was not merely a distinction between synchrony
and diachrony in the study of language; it was also, and
more importantly, a distinction between the Cartesian ideal
of a logically formed, clearly constructed language, and the
concept of language based upon imagination, emotion, and
above all, reflexivity. Slowly but surely a new model—the
metaphoric, romantic model—emerged as an alternative to
the Cartesian ideal of syllogism. Much of this took place
just as Balzac was working on the *Dissertation,* and if he was
too close to these events to see their implications immediately, they nevertheless turn out to be quite strikingly
present in the *Comédie humaine* itself.[68]

But the breaking of the sensualist word-idea link raised
problems in its turn. Chief among them was the description
of thought itself. For Descartes, as for Locke and Condillac,
the description of mental processes posed no particular
problem. But if consciousness is primarily averbal, as Biran
and others were beginning to say, then how could language
describe consciousness? What kind of metaphors are there
whose first terms are inexpressible? We recognize here one
of the chief problems of European romanticism, which Biran formulated most directly in France. His own solution
(the theory of "métaphores primordiales") is not important
here; what is important is the fact that the question of

---

on the subject of language, "L'Origine du langage," occupies pp. 167–203
of this volume.

[68]Many of these concepts have now been traced as far back as Vico, for
whom language was fundamentally poetic and imagistic. The question of
Vico's influence on the romantic movement has been widely debated. In
addition to the works already cited, see Stuart Hampshire, "Vico and the
Contemporary Philosophy of Language," in Tagliacozzo and White,
Giambattista Vico, pp. 477 and 479; also Alain Pons, "Vico and French
Thought," *ibid.,* pp. 165–185. It appears extremely difficult to sustain an
argument for Vico's influence in France before about 1825, which
perhaps accounts in part for the slow development of the new ideas in
Balzac's intellectual milieu.

language became, through his work, extraordinarily visible, and extraordinarily problematical.[69]

The importance of the question of language for Balzac, and the essential role the subject was to play in the *Comédie humaine,* is therefore historically accounted for by the fact that he was situated at an intellectual crossroads, at a critical turning point in western philosophical speculation. And we can understand why, with both discouragement and ambition, he scribbled the following paragraph in the *Notes philosophiques:* "Quel serait le moyen de substituer aux mots de la Métaphysique un langage de signes conventionnels et faciles qui puissent, comme dans les sciences exactes, empêcher les erreurs de s'y glisser et qui pourraient, en le faisant marcher de propositions démontrées en propositions à résoudre, de vérités en vérités, lui donner l'espérance d'atteindre les choses les plus inconnues et de déchirer les derniers voiles de la nature?"[70]

"Déchirer les derniers voiles de la nature." It was the same as saying "découvrir un nouveau langage." Clearly the veil was a veil of language; and at the heart of all Balzac's early writings was an immense yearning to discover some area of philosophical certitude, some confidence about the place of man in the world, some language by which to move from "propositions démontrées" to "propositions à résoudre." At the same time, Balzac clearly felt the need to pass beyond mechanistic concepts of mind with which centuries of speculation had failed to solve any problems. It is, of course, basic to everything that was to follow that he chose to direct all these speculations toward an attempted analysis of "genius." In fact, the definition of "genius" is the

---

[69] For an astute analysis of Biran's work on metaphors of mind, see Maurice Bémol, "La Représentation imagée de l'esprit et l'expression de l'inexprimable," *Revue d'esthétique,* xv (1962), 139–65. Biran's place in the development toward modern psychology and phenomenology has been most clearly described by Colin Smith, "Destutt de Tracy and the Bankruptcy of Sensationalism" in *Balzac and the Nineteenth Century: Studies in French Literature Presented to Herbert J. Hunt* (Leicester, 1972), pp. 205–207.

[70] "Notes philosophiques," in *Oeuvres complètes* (Paris, Club de l'honnête homme, 1962), xxv, 555.

excuse he gives for composing the *Dissertation* in the first place. He was specifically interested in the literary genius, the genius of words. With just a suggestion of ambition, he remarks in the *Dissertation* that whole books had been written to explain genius; and although he admits to trembling in approaching such a question, he maintains that the subject has attracted his attention. Well might he tremble, for he was in effect trying to express concepts his eighteenth-century categories could not handle. Condillac had observed that the success of intellectual geniuses depends upon the language they have available to them;[71] and conversely that nations could have geniuses only after their languages were highly developed.[72] The Balzac of the *Dissertation* found himself in just such a quandary, but Condillac offered little help in its solution.[73]

And so, in the end everything came down to the question of language. And that question will remain central for Balzac. We shall have many things to say about the linguistic elements in the *Comédie humaine,* including abstract speculations on the nature of language, the mind-world question, the portraiture of characters, and the position of the narrator. The "coloration" of Balzacian prose is not nearly as simple—or as dishonest—as Roland Barthes would make it out to be.[74] Already in 1954, Robert Dagneaud had ob-

[71]Condillac, *Essai sur l'origine,* p. 439.

[72]*Ibid.,* p. 442.

[73]*Ibid.,* p. 443. Condillac encounters here a thinker with whom he otherwise had very little in common: Humboldt. The German philosopher held that although the early stages of linguistic evolution were the work of entire nations, the later and more sophisticated stages were the work of individuals of genius. (See Gipper, "Wilhelm von Humboldt," p. 7). The vagueness of the term did not help matters much: "genius" could be either the endowments of an individual or the qualities *sui generis* of a language system; that is, a nonrational criterion of acceptability that varies from one language to another. See S. A. Leonard, "The Philosophical Basis of Eighteenth-Century Language Theories," reprinted in *Classics in Linguistics,* edited by D. E. Hayden, E. P. Alworth, and G. Tate (London, 1967), p. 37 ff. Leonard is mainly concerned with English philosophy, but his observations can be applied to Continental thought as well.

[74]Roland Barthes, *Le Degré zéro de l'écriture* (Paris, 1965), p. 69.

served that Balzac understood the importance of endowing his creatures with their own language.[75] But what Dagneaud did not grasp was that Balzac's concerns with language were by no means limited to problems of characterization and dialogue.

After the *Dissertation,* the *Notes philosophiques,* and the other juvenilia, Balzac entered a paradoxical period of feverish activity, but also of intellectual quiescence. The writings of the 1820s constituted a workshop in which he learned the basic—and sometimes grubby—techniques of the writer's craft. But the instrument he was fashioning was, obviously, a linguistic one; and many of the techniques he evolved were to underpin the great works of the 1830s and 1840s. In these early novels, however, they are cruder, more simply used, and consequently more easily observed.

[75] Robert Dagneaud, *Les Elements populaires dans le lexique de la Comédie humaine d'Honoré de Balzac* (Paris, 1954), p. 9.

CHAPTER II

From the *Dissertation* to *La Peau de chagrin*

The important achievement of the years roughly from 1818 to 1820 was Balzac's adoption of a more or less sensualist stance, pragmatically oriented, although colored by doubts and uncertainties. This development is most clearly seen in Balzac's juxtaposition of Descartes and Locke, in which Locke is clearly the winner in the young essayist's mind.[1] The adoption of such a point of view has two important implications for language: first, it tends to favor a theory of human rather than divine origin; second, it implies some form of linguistic mimeticism, since the word, in Locke's view, is so strongly linked to idea and sensation. Of the two, the second consequence was by far the more important to a budding novelist. In its purest form, any theory of linguistic mimeticism stresses primarily the descriptive function of language and the writer's task of seeing that his descriptions are accurate. Locke's strictures on the subject were numerous and well known to Balzac. But mimeticism cannot account for what some theoreticians call the "creative" (nowadays, "generative") aspects of language. Mimeticism reduces the aesthetic aspects of language to devices of style, and tends to assimilate fiction to ordinary discourse "plus decoration." This trend can be clearly seen in Balzac's early novels. They share with the gothic novel, the boudoir novel, the "bibliothèque rose," and all other fashionable genres narrators whose hallmarks are strained self-consciousness, coyness, clichés, and bombast—in short, all the rhetorical devices that reach for "literariness" over and beyond the conceptual content of

---

[1] The political importance of this development has been minutely studied by Barbéris, *Balzac et le mal du siècle;* here I am concerned only with its literary implications.

|41|

what is being said. In all Balzac's early novels, without exception, we can observe the narrator busily engaged in applying to his stories various layers of varnish—a term Balzac was later to use himself—to a series of humdrum and occasionally downright silly stories.

For the sake of convenient discussion, I have divided these novels into three natural chronological groups: 1) *Falthurne* and *Sténie;* 2) *L'Héritière de Birague, Clotilde de Lusignan, Jean-Louis, Le Vicaire des Ardennes,* and *Le Centenaire;* and 3) *Annette et le criminel, La Dernière Fée, Wann-Chlore,* and *Le Corrupteur.* There is some debate over early texts of which Balzac may have been partially or entirely the author. These, however, seem sufficiently his own for the kind of literary cross section we need to make.[2]

Falthurne and *Sténie* mark the transition from purely philosophical essay-writing to the composition of novels. *Falthurne* is a strange text, fragmented and unfinished, with a disconnected plot and perplexing events almost impossible to summarize.[3] Two texts go under this title, the first dating from 1820, and the second probably from 1823 or 1824. In the first, Falthurne, the heroine, appears as a woman endowed with supernatural powers of science, which enable her to cross time and space at will. She takes several forms, including Agathise, "la fille de la montagne," and the witch of Sommaris. On the other hand, her powers

[2]For major investigations of the early novels, see André Le Breton, *Balzac, l'homme et l'oeuvre* (Paris, 1905); Baldensperger, *Orientations étrangères;* L. J. Arrigon, *Les Débuts littéraires d'Honoré de Balzac* (Paris, 1924); Pierre Barrière, *Honoré de Balzac, les romans de jeunesse* (Paris, 1928); A. Prioult, *Balzac avant la Comédie humaine* (Paris, 1936); and especially Pierre Barbéris, *Aux Sources de Balzac: les romans de jeunesse* (Paris, 1965). Such general works as Maurice Bardèche, *Balzac romancier* (Paris, 1940), or André Wurmser, *La Comédie inhumaine* (Paris, 1964), obviously pay some attention to this early period.
[3]A detailed study of *Falthurne* can be found in the introduction to the edition by P. G. Castex (Paris, 1950). The differences between the two texts that go by this title have been most clearly set out by him. All quotations are taken from this edition. *Falthurne* can also be consulted in the edition prepared for the "Cabinet romantique" series of the Bibliophiles de l'originale (Paris, 1961–63), by J. A. Ducourneau. These volumes reproduce the format of Balzac's own copies.

in the second *Falthurne* appear to be mystical and contemplative. The connection between the two forms of the character can be seen most clearly in the second *Falthurne,* where the heroine is described with one of the key terms of the *Dissertation:* "Une dignité inconnue l'entourait comme d'un nuage et imposait tellement silence que nul n'osa l'interroger ni le contempler, car un seul de ses mouvements semblait être la Puissance même."[4] The joining of the mystical and the rationalist elements of "puissance" in a single symbolic character suggests that Balzac saw the two trends as complementary rather than antithetical. If, as P. G. Castex quite rightly points out, Falthurne represents the "génie de l'homme," it is because she unites in herself two sides of the human psyche.

But the significance of *Falthurne*—and shortly thereafter of *Sténie*—is that the linking is attempted in terms of fictional narration. In *Falthurne,* one must observe, the link is tenuous: the text falls into two distinct parts, apparently composed at several years' interval. But both parts are organized in terms of a dual narrator. The story of Falthurne is recorded by an "abbé Savonati," a materialistic Italian priest whose tale is in its turn "translated" and edited by a M. Matricante. Matricante's observations about Savonati, about his own ignorance of Italian, about the help his nephew gives him, and so on, form a running commentary in a series of footnotes from which he emerges as much more than a translator. He is the true narrator of the tale, since despite—or perhaps because of—his crass ignorance and incredible insensitivity, he blithely forges ahead with translation from a language he hardly knows, works through his not-too-intelligent nephew, and freely edits what comes out of this strange cooperation. His chief endeavor is to get the reader to admire Savonati, and he succeeds, oddly enough, by establishing a striking contrast between Savonati's intelligent, penetrating—and subversive—thought on the one hand, and his own fatuous-

---

[4]*Falthurne,* p. 163.

ness on the other. Yet Matricante, through his very blindness, does arouse our amused indulgence. In later Balzacian texts, the appeal to the reader's sympathy will move up from the footnotes into the narrative itself, but the essential maneuver—cooption of the reader—will remain constant through the very last texts of the *Comédie humaine* itself.[5]

Despite the structural weakness of *Falthurne,* there is serious concern in it for problems of language and thought. When the abbé Savonati laments, for example, that human language is incapable of expressing the operations of genius, he is registering a common contemporary complaint. If ordinary men can not penetrate the secrets of nature, it is because in his view a curtain of words hangs between reality and the mind. Here the language of *Falthurne* comes straight from the *Dissertation:* "Celui-là qui lève le voile de plomb dont une puissance jalouse enveloppa le sanctuaire des causes primaires, celui-là dompte la terre" (p. 11). Savonati has no suggestions as to how the process will take place; but his linking of voice, gesture, and glance, and especially the description, in the second *Falthurne,* of a remote village where a kind of perfect language is spoken (p. 162), suggest that the lifting of the veil has less to do with metaphysics than with the fidelity of expression to conception, of the concrete to the abstract.

But that, of course, was merely to restate the problem, not to solve it. *Falthurne* offers only a few suggestions on how to circumvent the veil, and these are fairly rudimentary. The most important is the role of presentiments. These were the stock in trade of the exaggerated romanticism mocked by *Falthurne,* and at least one of Savonati's functions is to debunk and deflate this kind of wild rhetoric. The abbé therefore explains presentiments as physical emanations similar to odors (p. 9). He talks in terms of purely mechanical processes, although he calls them "indefinissables." The closest he comes to any other kind of explanation is when he calls them "pensées involontaires"

[5] For possible sources of Balzac's interest in maneuvering the reader, see Bardèche, *Balzac romancier,* pp. 1–52; and *Falthurne,* pp. lxvii–lxviii.

(p. 23). Only once does Savonati—or Matricante, one cannot really tell, since we see the former through the translation of the latter—use presentiments seriously as a device of characterization, when describing the disappearance of Falthurne and Rosadore (p. 26). "Voices," too, are mentioned, but just once, when a female protagonist explains how she was forcibly married to a man she did not know: "trois fois mon coeur m'avertit de mes malheurs par une voix secrète; jusque-là je fus innocente, hélas!" (p. 102).[6]

Compared to *Falthurne*, *Sténie ou les erreurs philosophiques* is a model of reasonableness.[7] Yet it is so given over to arcane disputations among its characters that interest in the plot (sorely tried, as a matter of fact, by the epistolary form), just about disappears. Its main concern is the quandary of Sténie, who is married to a man she does not love, and of Del Ryés, whom she loves and who loves her. A more traditional situation could hardly be imagined, but here it is complicated by an interminable exchange of letters among various characters who seek to discover philosophically whether or not Sténie and Del Ryès should fling convention to the winds and consummate their love. This discussion is conducted chiefly between Del Ryès (a romantic) and his friend Vanehrs (a convinced rationalist). The question of *whose* errors are indicated in the title is much debated,[8] but the nature of one error is absolutely clear: Sténie and Del Ryès are held back from uniting with each other by all kinds of social imperatives. There is great discussion about the existence of God, the relativism of moral judgements, and other issues. These can all be re-

[6]Certain familiar Balzacian techniques of linguistic characterization make their appearance in *Falthurne:* Bongarus, exmonk and now knight's squire, is addicted to Latin interjections; Savonati never fails to allude to the murderous Cardinal Huberdully as "le grand Cardinal, lumiere de l'église." But this is still phraseology, having little to do with inner motivation.

[7]Prioult has provided an excellent edition of this novel (Paris, 1936). All references are to the Prioult edition.

[8]For a succinct account, see Bernard Guyon, "Sur la première philosophie de Balzac," *Revue d'histoire de la philosophie et d'histoire générale de la civilisation,* no. 20 (15 October 1937), pp. 369–92.

duced to a simply stated problem: do reason and analysis (here taken broadly to mean syllogistic thinking) provide adequate tools for understanding the world and the self ? Or must one sometimes renounce them in favor of arational modes of thought? Furthermore, which kind of thinking is language best able to convey?

Del Ryès' position is traditionally romantic. He argues from premonitions and dreams, insisting that he is the champion of revery and a believer in the significance of dreams (p. 8). This is an old argument, and it is important to note that Del Ryès does not regard dreams as the traces of some ulterior world, but, like Savonati's premonitions, as the "shadow" of nature (p. 8). Dreams are for him a kind of "vue interne" (p. 8), which enable man to perceive things hitherto unseen or not yet seen in everyday life (p. 8). In other words, while a romantic, Del Ryès is not a mystic, which makes his dialogue with Vanehrs possible in the first place. In fact, he quite energetically rejects anything that smacks of idealism. Existence is a fact, he writes to Sténie, and he attacks Fichte for denying the reality of the perceived world (p. 178). True, Del Ryès is more or less forced into this position because he is trying to convince Sténie to consummate their love. He comments tartly on the philosophies of Malebranche, Kant, Fichte, Wolff, and Spinoza, and although he does not quite deny the existence of God, he does seem to be saying that since God has permitted their passion to exist, any "evil" inherent in it must derive from purely human criteria.

It is his friend, Vanehrs, who gradually leads him to this position, and who constantly urges him to press for a conclusive act with Sténie. Vanehrs represents a highly sensualist concept of mind, taking even the extreme position that since one cannot avoid receiving impressions from the world, one cannot avoid thinking: "Presque toutes nos idées premières . . . sont malgré nous, nous ne pouvons que les diriger . . . il est évident que nous ne sommes pas maîtres de ne pas apercevoir" (p. 30). Man is consequently not really free; he constantly experiences "pensées composées" other than those he would like to be thinking (p. 30). Again, we encounter a key term from the *Dissertation,* and in a context that tends to devaluate rational control of the processes of mind. How these "pensées composées" arise is, of course, not specified; although they clearly lie at the basis of the irresistible love felt by Del Ryès and Sténie. "Mais ma pensée est malgré moi," writes Sténie, "je n'en suis pas la maîtresse, elle t'appartient, te cherche, te désire, toujours" (p. 160). However such ideas arrive, they represent in her eyes "true" reality. In such thoughts, and the words that express them, the veil between expression and conception is removed; conversely, the source of evil, the installer of the veil, so to speak, must be society. And so one of the things Vanehrs continually urges upon Del Ryès is that he must give up playing with the words of the world: Sténie is worth infinitely more than "ces caractères que l'on nomme éloquence" (p. 75). As a rationalist, Vanehrs is not suggesting a retreat into mysticism; for him, the rejection of "éloquence" is merely the acceptance of one's desires and of the pain of ratiocination (p. 142). Here we encounter for the first time in Balzac the theme of the burden of thought; and, significantly, in connection with the problem of language. In Vanehrs' view, rational man should act, not deviate into the labyrinths of language.

Wandering in these labyrinths is, of course, exactly what Del Ryès and Sténie do. They ordinarily find little satisfaction in it, since it proves inadequate to their thoughts and desires. They mostly take refuge in the romantic topos of "inexpressibility" which, when *Sténie* was being written, was surely not as shopworn as it appears today. Del Ryès writes to Vanehrs that the word "love" is "trop faible pour exprimer ce que je sens" (p. 53); for her part, Sténie confides to a friend that "aucun mot n'exprime ma pensée" (p. 103). Having thus converted their passion into rhetoric, Sténie and Del Ryès reap nothing but frustration. Little wonder, then, that their experience leads them, if not to the physical consummation of their love, at least to an awareness of the inadequacies of language. "J'estime bien peu l'amour loquace," remarks Sténie (p. 190). Something about "explanation" misses the central truth about desire and emotion. Sténie quite naturally tells Del Ryès, that she cannot fully render in words the thoughts that besiege her (p. 115); he, quite as naturally, responds that he shares with her "un tacite langage" (p. 152).

There are, of course, ways of getting round the inadequacies of language. The protagonists resort especially to gesture[9] and to music.[10] But these options are not open to the narrator, who has only words at his disposal. The romantic topos of inexpressibility inevitably leaves the narrator hung on the horns of a dilemma. In *Sténie* the problem is well hidden, for the epistolary form allows Balzac to escape from the necessity of "placing" a narrative voice. It is not really until *La Peau de chagrin* that the matter is faced head on.

The next group of novels, roughly clustered around the year 1822, demonstrate a great improvement over *Falthurne* and *Sténie*. Their plots are hackneyed and their rhetoric sometimes tired, but their language has a new ease, and at moments an attractive "flow" that contrasts strikingly with the painful and stilted narration of the two earlier works.[11] Some of them show, moreover, considerable self-awareness, at least in the sense that a piece such as *L'Héritière de Birague* contains a good deal of satire on the pseudomedieval novel. If the whole of *L'Héritière de Birague*

[9]Del Ryès writes, at one point: "Ma démarche, suivant ce qui m'agitait, était tantôt lente, tantôt rapide" (p. 77).

[10]Del Ryès' performance of the popular *Songe de Rousseau* on the piano, and especially his improvisations on the melody, are the subject of a lengthy letter by Sténie, who underscores its nonverbal communicative qualities: "il contraignait ses auditeurs, hors d'haleine, de penser profondément, enfin il fesait mal" (p. 115).

[11]*Sténie* is dated by various critics from 1820, 1821 or 1822. Without worrying too much about exactness, we are justified in placing it just after *Falthurne* and before the other youthful novels. A number of other fragmentary texts, contemporary with *Sténie,* have been preserved and have been most conveniently assembled in Ducourneau's edition of the *Oeuvres complètes,* Vol. 24: *Romans et contes* (Paris, 1972). References to the other early novels will be to the Ducourneau reprints in the Cabinet romantique series (Paris, Bibliophiles de l'originale, 1961–1963).

is intended as a satire, then it is such a good one that it comes perilously close to being indistinguishable from the real article. The question is a puzzling one, especially when one compares any one of Balzac's published potboilers with such a fascinating, well-written fragment as *Une Heure de ma vie,* which also dates from 1822.[12] It may well be that Balzac is already making—perhaps unconsciously—a distinction between literary hackwork and work that was of genuine importance to him. Yet it is precisely in the inferior works that one can see most clearly themes, motifs, and rhetorical devices that will eventually become part of the technical equipment of the narrator of the *Comédie humaine.* Here language obtrudes itself ceaselessly on the reader's consciousness through sheer artificiality and exaggeration. One example will suffice, the musing of a character in *L'Héritière de Birague* after he has caught a glimpse of the Italian villain of the story: "Ouais, se dit-il en lui-même, que signifie la présence de ce coquin dans un lieu qui semble fait exprès pour devenir un véritable coupe-gorge? Le drôle est entré à l'auberge où j'ai couché avec un air inquisiteur. . . . Sa hideuse figure exprimait une maligne joie lorsqu'il a vu le vieillard grondeur arriver. . . . Il a voulu lier conversation avec lui. . . . Chassé par la crainte de la correction que je lui préparais, il a pris les devans, et je le retrouve ici comme en embuscade; cet ultramontain damné méditerait-il quelque noir forfait? Le brusque mais bon vieillard aurait-il éveillé, par quelque action imprudente, la cupidité du bandit qui le guette? . . . Ventre-singris! tout ceci me paraît furieusement louche! Je prétends l'éclaircir."[13] Yet one wonders how seriously this kind of exaggeration is to be taken when one encounters such teasing narrative self-awareness as the following: "Depuis longtemps Villani ne l'écoutait plus, par cinq raisons: la première, parce qu'il soupçonna le bonhomme d'avoir la tête timbrée, vu son grand âge, et qu'ainsi il

---

[12] Reproduced in the Ducourneau edition, *Romans et contes,* pp. 213–26.

[13] *L'Héritière de Birague* (Paris: Bibliophiles de l'originale, 1961), I, 100–101.

pouvait fort bien ne pas se souvenir du nom de l'étranger; la seconde, parce qu'il réfléchit que Géronimo lui donnerait des renseignements plus sûrs; quant aux autres, elles nous manquent; le marquis pensa trop bas."[14]

On the other hand, the 1822 group does show considerable continuity in the development and extention of previously used techniques. Characterization by linguistic tic now really comes into its own. Captain de Chanclos, in *L'Héritière de Birague,* invariably refers to his son-in-law as "Comte Mathieu, *mon gendre"* and to Henri IV as *"L'aigle de Béarn mon invincible maître."* The abbé Gausse, in *Le Vicaire des Ardennes,* speaks almost exclusively in proverbs, and the schoolmaster Tullius Lesecq has the unconquerable habit of larding his speech with obscure Latin quotations. In *Le Centenaire,* the mysterious old man is always narratively "tagged" by his habit of addressing others as "enfant d'un jour" or "homme d'un jour," a superfluous underscoring of his own superhuman status. These methods are heavily repetitious, ultimately monotonous, and in the end remain unconnected with any other aspect of characterization.

Along with the linguistic tic, we find the first use of the phrase "laisser échapper"—an expression and a concept that were destined for great development in Balzac's later, mature novels. "Laisser échapper" appears first as a hyperbolic crutch for summary psychologizing. At moments of crisis—and they are legion in these texts—"laisser échapper" is sure to appear. When the young heroine of *Le Centenaire* first catches sight of General Beringheld, who is to influence her life so profoundly, she recoils "en laissant échapper un mouvement de surprise" (I, 24–25). The marquis de Rosann confronts his wife and her supposed lover "après avoir laissé échapper un mouvement convulsif " (III, 122), and parallel occurrences can be found in the other novels of this group. None of this, however, is connected with real psychological analysis, or even with the kind of generalized speculation on human nature that was to be so

[14]*Ibid.,* I, 144.

characteristic of the *Comédie humaine.* "Laisser échapper" remains here entirely external, and in itself signifies very little as far as the development of the narrative is concerned. In the years of the *Comédie humaine,* however, we shall see how it becomes closely associated with the theory of "inner and outer man" and how it acquires an altogether richer and deeper significance. There are numbers of rhetorical devices of this sort that can be traced in literally unchanged form from the earliest to the latest novels but which, by reason of their increasing interconnections with the rest of the text, acquire complex and fascinating resonances.

Language itself now emerges as a center of power in ways that had not been possible in the epistolary form of *Sténie,* or through the split narrative voice of *Falthurne.* The marquis de Monbard is literally betrayed by his words into a confession of love for Aloise (*L'Héritière de Birague,* I, 61); the Italian villain is forced to flee from an important encounter by the words "gants parfumés" (*ibid.,* I, 66); and the mysterious Jean Paqué repeatedly threatens to punish all the novel's malefactors by merely pronouncing a few crucial words (*ibid.,* II, 124). When Argow the pirate holds Mélanie de Saint-André in his power, he tortures her by slowly revealing that her husband Joseph is a priest, and the text underscores the physical nature of his assault by italicizing the key words *nul, prêtre, concubine (Le Vicaire des Ardennes,* IV, 225). *Le Centenaire* provides Balzac's first fictional explanation of the physical power of words, when an old crone tells a fantastic tale by the flickering fire in her grate: "cette lueur voltigeait dans la chambre comme les paroles de la sage-femme dans l'imagination de ses auditeurs: elle les avait lancées une à une, et le peu d'idées qu'elles contenaient contribuait à donner à l'âme une espèce de vague et de rêverie pesante" (I, 231). Perhaps the most striking instance of the narrator's interest in the power of words occurs in *Le Vicaire des Ardennes,* when Joseph prepares to tell Mélanie that they can safely be married after all, and, fearing for her sanity in the excess of joy that he anticipates, wishes he could convey the information "sans que mes lèvres formassent des paroles" (*Le Vicaire des Ardennes,* IV, 105). The notion is something like Sténie's yearning for nonverbal communication, and of course is directly connected to the problem of the "veil." In some of these novels, the by now familiar recourse to music seems to provide a solution: only through music can Marianine give some relief to her father from his strange disease (*Le Centenaire,* I, 48–49).[15]

With the exception of Marianine's use of music to calm, if not cure, her father, descriptions of language in the 1822 group derive ultimately from a mechanistic conception of the structure of language and consciousness very close to that of the *Dissertation.* In *Le Centenaire* the mechanistic quality is quite explicit. The old man himself, we are told, might be taken for "un homme factice" created by some latter-day Pascal (I, 81); and he is referred to as a "bizarre machine" (I, 118), or as a "vaste machine" (II, 78). The hero's mother is described as a "machine féminine" (II, 122), and young Tullius himself seems at one point to be "une machine qui se meut par un mécanisme ingénieux" (II, 226). The motif reaches its climax when Tullius finds himself an orphan, possessor of an immense fortune and limitless power; in such circumstances and for such a person as he, "la vie n'était plus qu'un mécanisme sans prestige, une décoration d'opéra dont il n'apercevait que les ressorts et les machines" (III, 92). The same position will be occupied by Raphaël de Valentin, by Gobseck, and by Castanier, all of whom are literally condemned to understand the "machinery" of life. This kind of approach, used as plainly as it is in *Le Centenaire,* has the advantage of simplifying problems of characterization: for one thing, it renders the rapport between "inner and outer man" neat and easily intelligible, because it abolishes the problem of

[15]The situation is not exactly parallel to that of Wanda in *L'Envers de l'histoire contemporaine,* but the connection between music and suffering is already underscored. It will appear again, among other places, in *La Duchesse de Langeais.* Generally, music is an antidote to pain, in accordance with long-standing tradition.

the "veil." But in *Le Centenaire* such mechanistics are used for what one might call "gothic" effects, and the result is not happy. Logical improbabilities stand elbow-to-elbow with quite precise explanations of mysterious events. The disjuncture is most visible at the end, where the story of a nineteenth-century vampire dribbles off to an ending so vague that an extra "conclusion," an exchange of letters between certain characters and the editor, as well as two "notes de l'editeur" are necessary; all of which maintain that objections are nul and void because truth—his novel—is stranger than fiction. In his first supplementary "note," the "editor," Horace de Saint-Aubin oddly remarks that his brother is an "esprit mathématique, qui va de preuve en preuve et qui ne marche qu'avec *l'Analyse*"; whereas for himself, "depuis longtemps j'ai pris à gauche, et . . . j'ai tout donné à l'imagination" (IV, 212). The terminology comes almost literally from the *Notes philosophiques,* and the nostalgia for something other than mechanistics is parallel to that of Del Ryès. But now the yearning for imagination seems to be more acute, for it is hard to see how he could otherwise justify his tale about centenarians and vampires.

The 1822 group consequently seems to develop some serious narrative alternatives. Alongside "sensualist" metaphors of language, such images as "voices" are greatly expanded. "Voices" really come into their own in *Le Vicaire des Ardennes.* What, asks the hero of himself, is sinful about his love? Nothing, he concludes, for "aucune voix secrète ne nous a arrêtés" (II, 99). As in *Sténie,* "voices" tend to appear when the inner conscience, guided by some as yet undefined instinctual urge, comes into conflict with society and with the language society provides. Horace puts it succinctly to Mélanie, whom he believes to be his sister, when he cites the "voix secrète" which tells him that society's laws do not determine sinfulness (II, 115). In such a situation, the words of society are clearly the words of reason and order, whereas the "voices" represent some kind of suprasocial and suprarational principle. Often, then, characters disbelieve what they perceive in surrounding reality in order to obey what their "voices" tell them is a higher truth. The marquise de Rosann never believes that her son is dead: "Un secret pressentiment me crie que mon fils existe!" (*Le Vicaire des Ardennes,* II, 225); and she maintains her irrational stance against all evidence until circumstances prove her right. Although there are no "voices" in *Le Centenaire,* there are multiple allusions to presentiments that operate in almost exactly the same way—one of the most important being the presentiment that causes General Beringheld to break his word, put his honor in question, and consequently get the story under way (I, 62).

These rhetorical maneuvers imply, once again, the old attempt to tear away the veil, to match mind and world as closely as possible. But now we encounter the serious possibility that there might be danger in the endeavor. The clownish capitaine de la Vieille-Roche "ne pensait à rien, c'est-à-dire à rien qui pût troubler sa digestion" (*L'Héritière de Birague,* I, 94), using a formulation that echoes *Le Vicaire des Ardennes* and anticipates *La Peau de chagrin.* The same expression occurs a number of times in *Clotilde de Lusignan,* where Dr. Trousse inveighs against the dangers of thought. "You think too much," he cries to his mistress the princess; "si je me porte bien, c'est que je ne pense jamais" (I, 75). As with capitaine de la Vieille-Roche, the context is farcical, for Trousse, as his name indicates, stands in the long tradition of comic doctors reaching back to Molière. Yet we must pay attention to what he says, for within a very few years, the problem of thinking will become a decidedly critical and even potentially tragic matter. Even in 1822, as a matter of fact, the potential peril of thought has serious overtones; the Intendant Robert, privy to the dreadful secret of the Morvans, tries at one point to escape the pain of thought: "Monseigneur . . . je crois . . . nous ne sommes pas maîtres de nos pensées. . . . Voyez-vous, monseigneur . . . la pensée. . . . Ah! c'est une grande calamité" (*L'Héritière de Birague,* II, 65).

The increasingly apparent danger of thought lends new urgency to the topos of inexpressibility, which is now tied directly to the emotions: "plus les passions sont vives, plus elles nous jettent dans la méditation et dans cette oisive rêverie dont le délire a tant de charme," says the Marquise de Rosann (*Le Vicaire des Ardennes*, II, 176). At its extreme, the inexpressibility topos leads the narrator to the curious idea of nonthinking thought, or perhaps more accurately and less curiously, to arational thought: "Aujourd'hui," writes Mélanie in her diary, "je suis restée pâle, immobile, sans penser à rien, et sans éprouver aucune fatigue à l'âme. . . . Quel charme! . . . qu'on m'explique comment il se fait que l'on sente la pensée sans penser réellement? . . . *Il me semble que je suis nuage!*" (*Le Vicaire des Ardennes*, IV, 7–8) Clearly we have moved beyond the conventions of the gothic thriller.

All this suggests that buried in the extraordinary stage property of these novels is a new awareness of thought processes as something more complex than the mechanistic procedure of the sensualists. And it is of some significance that alternatives to naive realism seem to have been suggested by *the experience of writing fiction*. The problem of expression itself, the possibility that one could think without expressing, or express without thinking, bizarre as these may have seemed, all led the Balzacian narrator to a startlingly acute sense of the complexity of thought.

That complexity found its fullest expression thus far in *Le Centenaire*, which, by virtue of its very subject, led the narrator out of the usual paths of elementary realism. The bizarre incidents of the story are all somewhat apologetically presented, with a number of "editor's footnotes" disclaiming responsibility for vagueness of expression and gaps in ideas (IV, 53). One long note in effect asks the reader to accept the idea of a centenarian without requiring proof (IV, 194–95). Some discussion, however, simply had to be incorporated into the body of the tale, and we consequently find several passages in which the centenarian attempts to explain the conditions of his existence. One speech in particular, where he is enticing a victim into his lair, has tonalities that strongly anticipate *Louis Lambert*: "Tu entreras dans l'atmosphère pur et vide de la pensée, tu parcourras le monde idéal, ce vaste réservoir d'où sortent les *Cauchemars,* les *Ombres*" (IV, 46). The old man kidnaps his victims "par la pensée" (IV, 16), and he takes Marianine on a long voyage through space and time to see her beloved Beringheld (IV, 55–62). Toward the end of the story, when she is entirely in the power of the old man, Marianine is shown all the efforts of Beringheld to rescue her, although she is far distant from her beloved general (IV, 190–207). These episodes are, basically, fumbling attempts to bypass sensualist psychology and naive realism. When Marianine first comes into the centenarian's lair, her brain is paralyzed, unable to receive sensations or handle ideas other than those allowed by the old man (IV, 54). Once the sensualist chain has been broken there is nothing left but reflexivity—the solution hinted at in the *Dissertation*—and the room turns out to be nothing but a projection of herself: "Mais cette chambre est le cerveau de Marianine, *elle se regarde en elle-même*" (IV, 56; italics in text). Even more strikingly "Lambertian" in tone is the narrator's question whether, in such experiences, "les lieux s'approchaient et comparaissaient en *elle,* ou si c'était elle qui se transportait à cet endroit" (IV, 200). The answer seems to be that both alternatives come down to the same thing: when the veil disappears, mind and world become one.

Le *Centenaire* proceeds, then, to its vague and unsatisfactory ending. In some way not clearly specified, the vampire is finally defeated and Marianine marries her true love. That is how it must be in such fantastical tales. But important questions had been raised, however awkwardly, and they were questions whose answers were to be the object of that vast inquiry called the *Comédie humaine.*[16]

[16]Parallels between *Le Centenaire* and *La Peau de chagrin* are many and striking: Marianine, like Raphaël, meets an old man when she is on the verge of suicide; both old men possess a private chamber that contains a chaotic collection of artifacts representing signal moments of human history; they also possess an inner sanctum, one of science (the centenarian's), one of art (the antiquarian's); both inner sanctums contain documents covered with magic language. In both stories, the heart of the problem of existence is language and the veil it might or might not interpose between the mind and the world.

The 1825 group of novels continues many of the same themes and techniques, but the approach seems to have become in general much more reasonable. Gone are the incredible gothic exaggerations, the horrors, the cardboard decor. Instead the plots, while still hyperbolic, tend to deal with problems of real life. *Wann-Chlore* tells of a traditional love-frustration wherein the heroine Chlora is kept from marrying her beloved Horace through the perfidy of a treacherous friend. *La Dernière Fée* picks up the magical themes of *Le Centenaire*, but instead of wandering off into a vague and inconclusive ending, explains all the supernatural events through the device of a wealthy duchess secretly playing fairy godmother to the hero. Again, the plot involves a very ordinary situation in which a youth is loved by two women, a duchess and a peasant girl, at the end of which the duchess wins out by reason of her supposed "enchantments." *Annette et le criminel* involves us in no supernatural or extraordinary events at all. The theme is the conversion of Argow from a merciless pirate into a model of virtue through the pure love of a young woman.

The language of these novels can still make one smile. But it is no longer a matter of bolstering tottering plots. The florid rhetoric is now derived, in various ways, from a more "ordinary" drama—not from a need to overcome our disbelief with hyperbole. The situations in these stories are the reverse of those in the earlier group, where horror and terror did not prevent hero and heroine from living happily ever after. The drama of everyday life, we now discover, provides far fewer chills, but also far fewer neat conclusions. Chlora and her lover die; Annette and Argow die; the peasant girl, Catherine, dies; Abel dies, although to be resuscitated as Count Osterwald. The 1825 novels are quite clearly making the transition from the world of sheer fantasy to what one might already call a kind of realism.

This transition inevitably involved the problem of the veil. The narrator of *Wann-Chlore* reiterates the old position: "c'est le cas de remarquer ici que plus on sent moins on exprime" (I, 102); but how then is he to express what his characters cannot, without either making a god of himself or ignoramuses of them? Omniscience was not quite the answer, for the narrator then would find himself verbalizing emotions he concurrently claims are inexpressible. His answer—and he arrives at it in terms of narration—is the key concept of *homo duplex,* separating the "inner" self of emotion from the "outer" self of overt action. In telling the story of his past for the heroine's benefit, the hero of *Wann-Chlore* distinguishes an "outer" biography from the "inner" emotional history of his life (II, 172). Horace never describes this "vie intérieure"; his account of his emotional life is, at best, merely oratorical: "je marchais comme marche l'Ombre, l'Esprit" (III, 107). This suggests that the Balzacian narrator is now beginning to realize that the faithful rendering of extreme emotion might require something other than verbal hyperbole; the theory of *homo duplex* emerges as one of the main bridges to the mature characterization of the *Comédie humaine.* Eugénie of *Wann-Chlore* is forced by circumstances to repress her true emotions, which, "ne se déversant sur aucun objet extérieur . . . devaient se répandre avec effusion sur le premier être qu'elle jugerait digne d'etre son protecteur" (I, 197). "Déverser," "répandre," and "effusion," instead of something like "s'exercer" or "manifester," indicate the beginnings of a more sophisticated approach to the description of emotions. Unfortunately, it is not developed further. For that, we shall have to wait for Eugénie Grandet, among others. But one can see what the narrator is driving at by contrasting Eugénie's reactions with those of her mother and grandmother, who are intent on trapping Horace into marriage. The two ladies try to force the girl into calculating her responses to Horace, "les graduer comme les *crescendo* d'une sonate" (II, 131). The narrator, by now, knows better than this: true love, in his words, is a slow mixing of emotions that "s'infusent en quelque sorte, et deviennent une seule âme" (II, 211). Effusion becomes infusion; and the narrator quietly observes that in cases of true love everything, including language, disappears "pour faire place à des rapports nouveaux" (ii, 133–34). The same theme, in almost the same terms, is developed in *La Dernière Fée,* when the narrator describes the budding love between Abel and the "fairy" duchess. It is a passage worth quoting not only for its thematic contents, but as an example of the excellent writing beginning to show up in this group of novels:

"Connaît-on rien de plus délicieux que ce langage de l'âme? cette puissance sympathique qui, sans le secours incomplet de la parole humaine, vous fait pressentir ce que pense, ce que souhaite, désire, l'objet chéri que l'on aime? Dans cette région pure de la pensée, dégagée des grossières sensations du corps, règne un charme subtil que nulle parole humaine ne peut rendre, puisque nulle parole humaine ne peut donner l'idée d'un mystère qui ne doit être que *senti* par l'âme; il semble qu'en ces moments trop rares, une flamme légère aille d'un coeur à l'autre, y porter successivement *le jour* de *la pensée* et une fraicheur, un délice indicibles; enfin peut-être est-ce ainsi que s'entretiennent les anges des cieux!" (ii, 145–46). The precise nature of the "rapports nouveaux," of the "langage de l'âme," remains in prudent shadow, of course; that exploration was to be the substance of entire novels in the *Comédie humaine,* whose intermingling of "truth" and "fiction," if we may anticipate, will be one of the chief strategies of attack on the "veil."

Infusion, effusion, expressibility, and the riddle of language come together most dramatically in *Annette et le criminel,* where the drama of expression is directly tied to the character of the heroine. Annette, although not repressed by social conventions (she has, on the contrary, a pair of indulgent and understanding parents), is nonetheless the sort of person who keeps her emotions under tight control—and this serves to explain her unexpected and explosive response to Argow. She also looks for the small, telltale signs of the "inner" self in others, which explains her rejection of her cousin's suit (although his offense—the seduction of an actress before Annette's very eyes—is hardly subtle). She is the most assiduous student of the "inner-outer" relationship we have yet encountered in the early novels. And the most interesting way the inner-outer distinction manifests itself in this novel is through "talismanic" words; that is, through words of tremendous force representing at the surface of the self a concentrated accumulation of vast inner energies. The most striking instance of this phenomenon is Argow's conversion itself. Annette tells him "Je vous crois un être bon, un honnête homme," whereupon "ces deux phrases . . . prononcées par cette jeune fille en larmes, lui soulevèrent le rideau qui lui cachoit sa vie passée, et il se regarda avec horreur" (II, 135). This is the only instance in the early novel where the veil is actually lifted, and it is lifted between two characters through the agency of language; the narrator's problems are still not involved.

When psychic energy is not sufficient to bring internal mental activities to the surface in the form of words, the result is often the occurrence of "voices." In *Annette et le criminel* "voices" represent the most deep-seated desires of the heroine. She hears voices as she moves toward marriage with Argow (I, 216; II, 135–36; III, 135); and after his conversion they assure her of his ultimate salvation (II, 166; III, 101; IV, 147). But *Wann-Chlore* is the novel of this group where "voices" play their most important role. Here, two conditions are necessary for the emergence of "voices": first, the character must be a virtuous one; second, there must be a question of conscience. Horace Landon is particularly involved in these issues, since he must decide whether or not to marry Eugénie despite his unflagging love for Chlora: "Depuis son retour à Paris, Landon avait été poursuivi par le souvenir d'Eugénie; une voix intérieure lui reprochait sa conduite envers elle" (II, 86). There is even a strikingly modern description of what one might almost call schizophrenia when Horace listens as a disinterested spectator to the "deux voix contraires" that argue within him (II, 31). But the narrator is not able to sustain the implications of this approach, and the passage ends on a flatly parliamentary note: "L'orage fut terrible, le combat animé, pénible; mais Landon écoutait la dernière voix [et] obéit à l'idée tyrannique du moment" (II, 32). Landon having made the wrong choice, the novel proceeds for two more volumes, but the rich potential of the device itself remains entirely unexplored.

Such voices are obviously connected with the voices we have observed before, in that they provide a convenient metaphor for all those levels of mental life—instinct, intuition, passion—which are apart from our rational dealings with the world, and for which Balzac had no ready vocabulary. They are connected, furthermore, with another conception that first appears in *Wann-Chlore*, and which will become celebrated under Balzac's pen: the so-called "don de seconde vue." The Scottish heroine Chlora can foresee disaster because "les Ecossaises ont le *don de seconde vue*" (IV, 121); and although Eugénie herself is not Scottish, she gives Horace some much needed advice "poussée par cet instinct particulière que l'Ecossais appelle *une seconde vue*" (I, 212). There is no stated connection with the "seconde idée" of the *Dissertation*, nor is there yet even any suggestion that *seconde vue* might have creative possibilities or be an instrumentality of art. Awaiting further development, it remains simply the instinctive behavior of the mind, breaking through the veil by some unexplained operation other than rational analysis.

One must not assume, on the other hand, that the early novels are exclusively concerned with the problem of handsome heroes and exquisite heroines laboring to communicate ineffable emotions. The increasingly "realistic" trend of the 1825 group involves the narrator in a host of other issues, mostly political.[17] One of these, however, is connected with the themes we have been discussing; this is the matter of "psychic energy."

[17]The most exhaustive study of the early period from this point of view is of course that of Barbéris, *Balzac et le mal du siècle*, Vol. I.

Psychic energy had, of course, already been involved in the theory of *homo duplex,* and in the forcefulness of talismanic words.[18] But in the 1825 group, the notion acquires an altogether new dimension—that of the relationship of mind to world, or of self to society. In *La Dernière Fée* some words are said to possess a kind of original energy, perhaps something akin to the indescribable subtlety sought after by lovers in their speech. The hero, Abel, living in a Rousseauesque paradise far from other men, tries to explain to Catherine (the only woman he knows), how he feels about the "fairy" with whom he has fallen in love: "à chaque instant, les phrases les plus énergiques des hommes que le frottement de la civilisation n'a pas encore altérées, et qui restent dans leur *neuf,* arrivaient sur ses lèvres enflammées" (I, 165). The narrator refrains from actually reproducing Abel's flaming words, thus underscoring his own dilemma; nevertheless, he has now identified his problem with civilisation, suggesting perhaps that the veil has something to do with the conventions of society. Towards the end of the novel, the "fairy" duchess writes a letter to a friend, describing the hero in similar terms: "son langage est exalté, et tient à celui des orientaux, avec cette différence toutefois, qu'il est souvent énergique et concis, comme celui d'un homme de la nature qui n'exprime que des idées" (II, 194). Is it mere coincidence, then, that both the centenarian of *Le Centenaire,* and the antiquarian of *La Peau de chagrin* should possess documents covered with "oriental" writing? And is it merely warmed over Rousseauism that the ideal of "energetic" language should be described here as the most direct link between expression and idea?[19]

Although the presence of Rousseau is obvious, the ques-

[18]The "energy" at issue here is that of words, considered as vehicles for the more general "energy" or will power that characterizes many Balzacian creatures. On the latter, see Ernst-Robert Curtius, *Balzac,* translated by Henri Jourdan (1933), pp. 69–94.

[19]Very much like Abel, young Joseph in *Le Vicaire des Ardennes* possesses an "énergie terrible" (II, 14), presumably because he has spent his childhood and youth in the tropical jungles, far from civilisation.

tion goes far beyond the old clichés about the Noble Savage. In *Annette et le criminel* "energy" very nearly gets out of hand. It is associated not with lovers seeking their essential selves under the shell of civil convention, but with characters in total opposition—social and political—to constituted society. The case of Argow turns the argument of Rousseauism upside down: rather than implying that separation from society creates or at least preserves the "energy" of language, Argow's situation implies that "energetic" individuals reject society and challenge its assumptions. Argow's energy *causes* his apartness; whereas Abel's and Joseph's energy had been *derived* from their apartness. Argow's energy is compared, appropriately enough, to Satan's (I, 119); Annette is haunted by his "yeux énergiques" (I, 143), by his "tête énergique" (I, 145), and by the appearance of his companions of whom "nulle n'étoit sans énergie" (I, 166). Their language and gestures betray barely contained force. None of Argow's band are children of the forest; they are children of society who have rejected its conventions. And the narrator is merely emphasizing again the force of language when he tells us that the energy of Annette's talismanic words can overcome this powerhouse. After Argow's conversion, his "énergie" literally disappears: "Cette figure énergique et audacieuse prenoit tous les caractères de la timidité" (II, 8); and towards the end of the story, society's approval of his transformation is made quite explicit: "Cette figure avoit contracté un tel caractère de sublimité et de grandeur, il régnoit une telle sérénité sur ce front, où jadis brilla tant d'énergie, qu'il y eut généralement une tendance à l'admiration" (III, 239).

"Energie" was destined for great developments in the major novels of the *Comédie humaine,* and especially in Argow's transubstantiation into Vautrin. Both, we note, will ultimately accept society's dicta, and that in its turn may suggest that the "veil"—if indeed it turns out to be a creation of society—cannot be pulled aside. But we are not yet there. The challenge of society to the individual, not merely in his "outer" life, but also in his most intimate selfhood, will be the central issue in many a coming work. From Vautrin himself down to such pathetic characters as Z. Marcas, the struggle of the individual to maintain his own authenticity, even in his very language, will be unavoidable. And flowing from that will be the equally unavoidable issue of the narrator himself and his problems in putting into words things other—perhaps—than what society wished those words to convey. For the Balzacian narrator, one thing can already be said: his indulgence in theorizing was a necessary and suggestive first step in the grand enterprise of tearing down the veil. But theorizing alone could not suffice. Such solutions as came to him came in the process of narration. He spent the decade of the 1820s creating his tools; now, with the composition of *La Peau de chagin*, he made a visible leap to an altogether different level of discourse.[20]

[20]Certain texts that were to become part of the *Comédie humaine* were written in the last years of the decade, and contemporary with, or slightly before, *La Peau de chagrin*. But it is this story in particular that pinpoints both the problem and what the Balzacian narrator thought might be its solution.

CHAPTER III

La Peau de chagrin and the Problem of Creativity

"L'expérience et l'exemple de la vie humaine en tant que vie et que mécanisme"—so Balzac refers in his *Album* to *La Peau de chagrin.*[1] Mechanism was, as a matter of fact, quite a natural word for him to use, in view of the *Dissertation sur l'homme.* It is a key concept of the first preface to the story, which adopts a distinctly sensualist attitude by viewing art as a better or lesser reflection of reality. The word "mécanisme" involved not only art, but an entire conception of the human condition; and many post-Cartesian thinkers found Descartes' attempts to link the physical and the spiritual by way of the pineal gland to be unconvincing, to say the least.

In this connection, the word "mécanisme" raised the question of language: for Descartes saw in language the final proof that human beings were not merely most perfect mechanisms, but possessed mind or "soul." Language was, consequently, the point where art and mind had to meet. Indeed, as a function of the mind, art remained inexplicable unless one could understand how, through language (taken in its widest sense), the mind came to grips with reality. Art, being a process "ayant pour objet de reproduire la nature par la pensée," as Balzac's preface put it, the great temptation of mechanics can be seen. Despite the momentary insights of the *Dissertation,* memory and decoration still seemed the most reliable foundations for serious art: "il ne s'agit pas seulement de voir, il faut encore se souvenir et empreindre ces impressions dans un certain choix de mots, et les parer de toute la grâce ou leur com-

---

[1] *Pensées, sujets, fragmens,* edited by Jacques Crépet (Paris, 1910), p. 95. This notebook will be referred to hereafter as the *Album.*

muniquer le vif des sensations primordiales."[2] Yet "mécanisme" seems an odd word for Balzac to have used in connection with *La Peau de chagrin* as we know it today.

The *Album* indicates abundantly that *La Peau de chagrin* gave its young author many difficulties. Of over one hundred fragments identified by Crépet in his edition, no fewer than twenty-eight relate to this novel. This is many more than the number of fragments pertaining to any other work mentioned there.[3] Yet despite the obvious thought lavished on the novel, Balzac was unable to answer the wits of 1830 who desired to know why Raphaël did not simply wish the skin to stretch, and thus eliminate his problem at a stroke? The question was malicious but not idle, and the difficulties persist to this day.[4] Through almost a century and a half since its publication, *La Peau de chagrin* has been a bit of an embarrassment to Balzacians, and there is a tendency to treat at least the symbolism of the skin as little more than regrettable romanticism.

Yet real difficulties arise not so much from whatever interpretation of the magic skin we prefer, but from the

[2] Echoes of the virtues of "primitive" words found in the early novels are clearly discernible here. The passage is reproduced in the Pléiade edition, XI, 173–74. Even during the Restoration, style as decoration was one of the more common clichés of literary criticism. Marguerite Iknayan, in *The Idea of the Novel in France* (Geneva, 1961), gives some interesting examples of the type (pp. 146–48). Parallel to these discussions were the line versus color debates in painting and the melody versus harmony debates in music, both of which were to find their place in the pages of the *Comédie humaine.*

[3] The works most frequently mentioned in the *Album,* aside from *La Peau de chagrin,* are *Le Curé de village, L'Histoire des treize, Illusions perdues, Les Ressources de Quinola,* and *Un Début dans la vie.*

[4] Varied interpretations of *La Peau de chagrin* are part of every major interpretation of Balzac as a whole. P. G. Castex excludes it from his classification of fantastic tales *(Le Conte fantastique en France de Nodier à Maupassant* [Paris, 1951]); Le Yaouenc accounts for Raphaël's illness in purely medical terms *(Nosographie de l'humanité balzacienne* [Paris, 1959], pp. 203–204); Maurice Allem denies that the skin is necessary to the story at all in his edition of the work; Henri Evans doesn't even mention the skin in his discussion of the novel *(Louis Lambert et la philosophie de Balzac* [Paris, 1951, p. 64); Pierre Barbéris calls the skin symbolic but logical *(Balzac et le mal du siècle,* II, 1474); Linda Rudich sees it as purely symbolic ("Une Interpretation de *La Peau de chagrin," Année balzacienne* [1971], pp. 205–33).

difference between the attitude implicit in the remark on mechanism, and the shape and form of the novel as we have it today. If the skin represents the "life principle," that curious eighteenth-century conception of human existence that assigned to each person a specific amount of life energy to be spent, then the skin is central and the myth is obvious. We can marshall to support this point of view all of Balzac's own declarations that "la pensée tue," that desire is the tragic destiny of man, forcing him to spend his precious energy. And critics have taken him at his word. H. J. Hunt writes that " 'pensée' is for Balzac a generic term"; M. Bardèche writes that "par *pensée* Balzac entend toutes les opérations intellectuelles, la volonté, la passion, les idées."[5] It is true enough that Descartes had used precisely this word to indicate the totality of mental processes, but the question is how Balzac used it and if, indeed, he was not in the process of trying to free himself from precisely such gross and unsatisfactory concepts. If we skip ahead for a moment and look at some of the psychological concepts of *Louis Lambert,* we can see that Balzac has given us the elements of a terminology that would begin to deal more efficiently with the psychological, linguistic, and philosophical issues he had been interested in ever since the *Dissertation.*

Louis Lambert distinguishes an interior from an exterior consciousness, or what might be called in modern terms the mind-in-itself from the mind-in-the-world. The former, he holds, cannot be known to the outside world, whereas the latter can be known to others. The mind-in-the-world is divided, according to Lambert's theory, into *volonté* and *volition,* (p. 91). *Volonté* is abstract and inchoate, although intentional; *volition* is composed of the shaped and definitive acts of the mind's encounter with the world. Balzac variously described *volonté* as a milieu, a soft mass, or a fluid, but it always represents the sensation of absolute intention or desire, independent of its ultimate fate and form

[5] Herbert J. Hunt, *Balzac's Comédie humaine* (London, 1959), p. 42; Maurice Bardèche, *Une Lecture de Balzac* (Paris, 1964), p. 16.

in the world exterior to the mind. *Volition,* as the result of the mind's encounter with the world, is a translated, altered, sometimes degraded form of *volonté,* converted into the acts of the mind-in-the-world. In purely psychological terms, Balzac talks of two kinds of mental activity: *Pensée,* which corresponds to *volonté,* and *Idée,* which corresponds to *volition. Pensée* is a flow of psychic energy, the stream of self-conscious intentionality that composes our innermost selfhood; *Idée* is the specific concretion of that energy in our encounter with reality.[6] The typical model of mental activity, according to Lambertian theory, is then for thought to move "de son état abstrait à un état concret, de sa génération fluide à une expression quasi-solide, si toutefois ces mots peuvent formuler des aperçus si difficiles à distinguer" (LL, 91). It follows that although Balzac's terminology may not have been the most precise possible, *Pensée* is not a global term for all mental phenomena. It represents only that original state of absolute desire, the intuition of what the Self might be in its purest intentionality.[7] *Idée,* on the other hand, represents what might be

[6] Many varieties of modern psychology recognize similar distinctions. D. W. Harding describes the creative process as one of "emergent definitions of interest, awareness of task or intention, perceptual discrimination, images, half-grasped similarities, shades and contrasts and conflicts of attitudes" D. W. Harding, *Experience into Words* (London, 1963), p. 172. He also describes, in connection with Blake, a process much like Balzac's *Idée* (p. 34). Even Bergson, surprisingly, spoke of concepts "formed on the model of solids." (See L. L. Whyte, *The Subconscious before Freud* [New York, 1960], p. 33).

[7] One catches here echoes of efforts to escape from the stultifying passivity of the mind that resulted from orthodox sensualism. Whether he knew it or not, Balzac was adopting a distinction that Descartes had made in a surprisingly similar context. The third Meditation contains the following passage: "Entre mes pensées, quelques-unes sont comme les images des choses, et c'est à celles-là seulement que convient proprement le nom d'idée; comme lorsque je me représente un homme, ou une Chimère, ou le Ciel, ou un Ange, ou Dieu mesme. D'autres, outre cela, ont quelques autres formes: comme lorsque je veux, que je crains, que j'affirme ou que je nie, je conçoy bien alors quelque chose comme le sujet de l'action de mon esprit, mais j'adjouste aussi quelque autre chose par cette action à l'idée que j'ay de cette chose-là; et de ce genre de pensées, les unes sont appellées volontez ou affections, et les autres jugemens." René Descartes, *Méditations,* p. 29. Among contemporary critics, only Curtius has noted this complex nature of thought in Balzac. See his *Balzac,* p. 74.

called rational cognition—the mind dealing analytically with the data of the real world, and proceeding syllogistically from origins to goals. But two great questions were unavoidable: did the movement from *Pensée to Idée* involve the "expenditure" of life-energy; and by what process did thought proceed from its fluid to its solid state? Both questions lie at the heart of *La Peau de chagrin,* and place it squarely in the tradition of philosophical speculation that leads from Humboldt's "forma formans" versus "forma formata" to Merleau-Ponty's "parole parlante" versus "parole parlée." Ponty's terminology in particular points to the basic issue in *La Peau de chagrin:* the movement from *Pensée* to *Idée* was somehow a function of language, and was involved with the "veil" theme that had been haunting Balzac since the *Dissertation.* [8]

Some of Balzac's concerns in *La Peau de chagrin* may have come to him from Bonald, who distinguished between "imaginer" and "idéer," and who argued that while words do not create ideas, they call forth ideas from obscurity into consciousness. Bonald, then, made language the very vehicle of mental life, and could not conceive of a kind of thinking that would remain nonverbal.[9] Bonaldian or not, the *Pensée-Idée* opposition is clearly associated in *Louis Lambert* with the problem of liberty and free creativity. But this, as we shall see, involved Lambert in the dilemma of expression: for *Pensée* to resolve itself into *Idée,* it must sacrifice the possibility of being anything other than what it becomes.[10] Lambert does indeed try to use the tools of *Idée,*

[8]On Merleau-Ponty, see the useful summary by Eugene Verstraelen, "Language Analysis and Merleau-Ponty's Phenomenology of Language," *Saint Louis University Research Journal,* iv (1966), 325–42. But the matter is of widespread concern to many branches of contemporary psycholinguistics. R. F. Berg, for example, describes a doubled mental life, which he characterizes as "preverbal" and "verbal." See R. F. Berg, "On the Origin of Verbal Thinking," *Linguistics,* xxviii (December 1966), 13.

[9]See Moulinié, *De Bonald,* p. 235.

[10]Pierre Barbéris argues *(Balzac et le mal du siècle,* ii, 1765–1772), that Lambert is victim of a "volition" tied to the historical realities of the July Monarchy. Although this is true enough, it does not explain how the mind struggles to free itself from the prior linguistic framework imposed by society. Sartre has treated the problem, in addition to the *Search for a*

which he calls *analyse,* but his terrible fate tells us just how far it got him.[11] The dilemma of *Louis Lambert* and the dilemma of *La Peau de chagrin* are of a single piece: both stories attack the problem of creativity and ask whether or not the creative mind can ever fully express itself without simultaneously destroying itself; whether the creative mind copies or generates a world; whether the veil of language is real or imaginary.

In *La Peau de chagrin* we find the same terms used in the same way as they were later to be explicated in *Louis Lambert.* The narrator of *La Peau de chagrin* uses the term *Pensée* to talk about dreams, revery, and above all, imagination—not memory—conceived as a mode of creativity and exploration. *Idée,* on the other hand, refers to the realm of cognition, of encounter with the world—the "objective" world, we may add, that Raphaël finds himself born into. It was clearly much easier for the narrator to talk about the phenomena of *Idée* than about those of *Pensée,* especially as one of the points at issue in *La Peau de chagrin* was to discover whether *Pensée* lay within the possibilities of language at all. *Idée* derived directly from the "mécanisme" first discussed in the *Album,* and was obviously involved with the symbolism of the magic skin. For we must ask ourselves whether Raphaël's phrase: "Valet! *valet* cela veut dire: il se porte bien, parce qu'il ne pense à rien" (p. 182), can be taken at its face value. Does failure to deal with the "objective" world equal "not thinking"? Even though we have moved far beyond the comic contexts of this theme in the early novels, can we accept the narrator's interpretation of thought as a drive toward death? Would this make sense in the young Balzac of 1830, just approaching intellectual

---

method, in *Situations I* (Paris, 1947), pp. 200–201.

[11]*Louis Lambert,* edited by Jean Pommier and Marcel Bouteron (Paris, 1954), p. 106. One can compare Lambert's effort to "express" his philosophy with the processes described by Berg, for whom verbal thinking always operates through logic (Berg, "Origin of Verbal Thinking," p. 11).

maturity and sensing himself to be on the threshold of vast achievements? Or should we say, as Emile Zola did much later, "ne l'écoutez pas, il se ment à lui-même"?[12]

For us it is obviously simplest to begin with what is most easily objectified: with the phenomenon of *Idée,* and its relationship to mechanistics, rationality, and the symbolism of the magic skin. The hero of the novel, Raphaël de Valentin, is described as a disciple of Gay-Lussac and Arago (p. 30), as a sympathetic reader of Descartes (p. 28), and of Voltaire (p. 30). Rigorously brought up by an empiricist father (p. 80), he belongs by training and background to the intellectual domain of *Idée.* Even in the face of his inexplicable experience with the magic skin he remains faithful to the power of reason: "Quoi! . . . dans un siècle de lumières où nous avons appris que les diamants sont des cristaux de carbone . . . je croirai, moi! à une espèce de *Mané, Thekel, Pharès?*" (p. 223). His appointment as editor of an opportunist newspaper emphasizes (in view of the narrator's well-known attitude towards journalism) this side of his character; and so when he first examines the magic skin it is as a "jeune incrédule" who claims to explain it "mathématiquement" (p. 34), who considers its magical powers to be mere "superstition" and its inscription "caractères mensongers" (p. 35).[13] And to ensure that there is no misunderstanding, Raphaël's friend Emile announces with much fanfare the device on the Valentin escutcheon: *"Non cecedit animus"* (He never faltered) (p. 54).[14]

[12] E. Zola, "Causerie," *La Tribune,* 31 October 1869. This newspaper article is reproduced in my *Atelier de Zola* (Geneva, 1963), pp. 202–206.

[13] It may seem odd that an empiricist should conclude a "Faustian" pact, but there is really no satanism involved at all. The narrator merely describes the all-too-human choices Raphaël faces, here principally whether or not to commit suicide: "Oui, j'ai besoin d'embrasser les plaisirs du ciel et de la terre dans une dernière étreinte pour en mourir" (p. 40).

[14] Barbéris observes justly that this escutcheon appears only in the 1845 reedition of the novel *(Balzac et le mal du siècle,* II, 1444). Reading *La Peau de chagrin* as a political novel, he sees this as a change in Raphaël's characterization. From our point of view, however, the addition of the escutcheon only reinforces the earlier portrait. Although there are no manuscripts or notes pertaining to the composition of *La Peau de chagrin* extant

Raphaël is therefore in the first instance a product of "Mécanisme," and he reveals a good deal about the operations of *Idée*. He views ideas not only as acts directed at objects in the world, but as tangible and negotiable objects in themselves. In the opening scene of the story he enters a gambling hall where he literally wages one *Idée* against another; at Taillefer's party he hears political principles, historical judgements, and moral opinions valorized and devalorized like so many stocks and bonds. Raphaël eventually discovers, as will Lucien de Rubempré, that "la patrie est une capitale où les idées s'échangent et se vendent à tant la ligne" (p. 44).[15] *Idée*, furthermore, is dense, and tends to have physical effects if not actual substance. Raphaël contemplating suicide is described as laboring under "le fardeau de son intelligence et de ses souvenirs" as well as under the "pesante idée du suicide" (p. 12). When he is faced with the problem of escorting Foedora without having cab fare, the potential embarrassments sting him "comme autant de dardes" (p. 139); and on at least one occasion the thought of the magic skin pierces his mind like a dagger (p. 219). Thus *Idée* is always a structured entity; one "has" an *Idée*, it arrives at specific moments and with specific effects. It seems quite natural, then, that in *Les Aventures administratives d'une idée heureuse*, Balzac should fantasize about a human being existing solely as the embodiment of an *Idée*.[16]

---

other than the fragments in the *Album*, it appears that Raphaël was first conceived of as a complete materialist; that is, the symbol as well as the victim of *Idée*. On this obscure bit of textual history, see Madeleine Fargeaud, "Dans le sillage des grands romantiques: S. H. Berthoud," *L'Année balzacienne* (1962), pp. 213–43.

[15]This phrase was added to the text in the *Furne corrigé*, once again underscoring the continuity and consistency of the theme over many years.

[16]Two points about Balzac's vocabulary must be made here: first, he did not consistently distinguish between the words *Pensée* and *Idée*, although the distinction between the two kinds of mental activity is clear enough; second, he tends to interchange, as he had already done in the *Dissertation*, the concepts of "word" and "thought," which only underscores the extent to which, in this perspective, the two things coincided.

All of this lies behind the symbolism of the magic skin. Sometimes hard and sometimes pliable, it is in the first instance a physical object. It can be manipulated and negotiated. Above all it has a precise—and important—shape, which pinpoints Raphaël's commitment to empiricism. Mechanistic quantifier that he is, he inevitably sees the functioning of *Idée* as the disbursement of that fixed amount of psychic energy which represents his life-force. For such a man as Raphaël, desire takes possession of the world through language. He is literally pushed into his initial gambling adventure by a sentence from Rousseau that the narrator calls the philosopher's "most logical" (p. 5).[17] His first response on seeing the skin is to mock it (p. 34); but when he later realizes the desperation of his situation, he immediately identifies his problem as linguistic: "Le *oui* et *non* humain me poursuit partout!" (p. 253). Ironically, the good Bianchon interprets to Raphaël the doctors' inability to cure him: "ils sont logiques," he observes (p. 254). But the point is lost on Raphaël. When he finally retires to a mountain hut, he experiences very real improvement, until he accidentally hears his hostess speaking of his poor condition to his servant Jonathas (p. 280), whereupon he takes a dramatic and inexplicable turn for the worse. The following day, the effect is repeated when he hears another set of "fatales paroles" (p. 281).

The malicious power of words is, of course, nowhere but in his own mind. Committed to the logic and literalness of language, he is caught in a trap of his own making. Having consulted the naturalist Lavrille, he comes away with the only thing he sees in science: "une nomenclature," with which, the narrator observes, he was content (p. 299). Planchette's explanation of mechanics is equally significant and equally lost on him: "Quelle immense vanité cachée sous les mots! Un nom, est-ce donc une solution? Voilà pourtant

[17]The sentence alluded to is "Oui, je conçois qu'un homme aille au Jeu; mais c'est lorsque entre lui et la mort il ne reste plus que son dernier écu." The Pléiade edition gives the quotation as "il ne voit plus que son dernier écu" (IX, 13).

toute la science" (p. 231). Japhet similarly admits the confusion of words and things when Raphaël accuses him of inventing words because he cannot invent things (p. 239). But again, Raphaël is unable to understand the significance of what he learns from the scientists he consults.

The scientists of *La Peau de chagrin* are undoubtedly caricatures,[18] but the point they make in the story is not in the least humorous. They are telling Raphaël as plainly as they can that their language is gratuitous. Their "science" leads them not to the world, but merely to their own language. And they admittedly do exactly what Raphaël does: they take their language to be the world. They are the heirs of naive realism, but their situation is lost on Raphaël. Having concluded his pact, Raphaël is convinced that when he verbalizes, *vouloir* becomes *pouvoir;* "saying makes it so," and he is the most naive realist of them all.

Yet the *shrinking* of the skin can represent nothing other than the possibility that language skews the relationship of the mind to the world. If all that language can accomplish is the sick world of Raphaël de Valentin, then language is indeed a terrible betrayer. And a *skin* as symbol of this view, is, of course, one of Balzac's great fictional inventions.

The magic skin is, then, the embodiment of *Idée,* and because *Idée* arises through the mediation of language, its behavior is governed by the act of verbalization. Whenever psychic energy is impelled into the world by language, the skin shrinks. But it does so only when desire or will are thus "materialized" for the first time. At Taillefer's orgy, the skin shrinks when Raphaël expresses the desire to be a millionaire (p. 188), although he has actually been one without knowing it since the death of his uncle O'Flaherty; when Raphaël is inadvertently led by Porriquet's babbling to verbalize an *Idée* which he has been thinking for some time (*"Je souhaite bien vivement* que vous réussissiez" [p. 200]), the skin immediately shrinks. Later, in a duel, Raphaël is able to escape injury and cause his opponent's death

[18]Victor Brombert, "Balzac and the Caricature of the Intellect," *French Review,* XXXIV, no. 1 (October 1960), 3–12.

through the enunciation of the wish (p. 270); and while escaping toward Paris he disrupts a joyous village fair because he is unable to repress an exclamation (p. 284). As in the case of the duel, we are not told what Raphaël says, although we can guess; the mere *fact* of verbalization is enough, and in both cases the wish is fulfilled, and the skin shrinks. In the final scene of the novel, Raphaël dies as he attempts to verbalize the most overpowering, all-consuming desire of his life—his love for Pauline: "Pauline! . . . je te veux . . . !" In this last burst of words, Raphaël finally expresses what he has felt for a long time; the expenditure of energy is such that he dies as both language and life-energy are exhausted: "le moribond chercha des paroles pour exprimer le désir qui dévorait toutes ses forces. . . . Enfin, ne pouvant bientôt plus former de sons, il mordit Pauline au sein" (p. 290).[19] It is the servant Jonathas who sums up for Porriquet, and for us, the real nature of the skin: "je lui demanderai comme ça; Faut-il le faire monter? Il répondra *oui* ou *non*. Jamais je ne lui dis: *Souhaitez-vous? voulez-vous? désirez-vous?* Ces mots-là sont rayés de la conversation" (p. 196). *Idée* depends upon the verbal translation of desire as a real force in the real world.

The reverse procedure confirms this interpretation of the magic skin's symbolism. Once an *Idée* has been thrust into the world by way of language, the skin reacts no further to reiteration. When Raphaël is besieged at Taillefer's orgy by potential borrowers, he remarks "J'ai presque envie de souhaiter votre mort à tous" (p. 191), and we note that although he clearly has the desire he merely refrains from expressing it. The skin remains unchanged. During an interview with Porriquet, Raphaël almost wishes the old man would leave; but now conscious of his danger, he closes his lips as he glances at the skin, which again remains unchanged (p. 199). During the same scene, having pro-

[19]True, he had already cried "Je veux être aimé de Pauline" (p. 210), but the formulation is passive, and in any case she had already expressed her love for him.

nounced a different "Je souhaite que . . . ," Raphaël's further elaborations on his intentions have no effect on the skin beyond its initial shrinkage, since the desire is already expressed (p. 202). And even when he spends a whole day with Pauline, the skin is only "légèrement rétrécie" (p. 219), because, as we are told, he has been dumbstruck most of the time.

The antiquarian explains why *Idée* can be so dangerous, and why misuse of the skin can lead to madness: "et qu'est-ce que la folie, sinon l'excès d'un vouloir ou d'un pouvoir?" (p. 40). *Idée* embodied in language exists in a kind of ontological no man's land, externalized but often, as in the case of Raphaël, failing to produce the world desired. Verbalized desire is only a Luciferian dream of total power,[20] which Raphaël cannot possibly fulfill. Foedora remains entirely beyond his grasp, as does Pauline. If Raphaël takes his verbalizing power literally, he must admit that it has gotten him nowhere; if he rejects the myth, he must also reject his own sense of selfhood. Either way, madness is his fate: "Je suis fou. . . . Je sens la folie rugir par moments dans mon cerveau. Mes idées sont comme des fantômes, elles dansent devant moi sans que je puisse les saisir. Je préfère la mort à cette vie" (p. 167).[21]

Raphaël consequently becomes his own torturer (p. 87), although it is clear that a properly conducted social life would have been one way of solving his original financial problem. He later observes that all millionaires are their own executioners (p. 190), and ultimately cries to the skin, the image of his own mind, "tu es mon bourreau" (p. 223).[22]

---

[20] In the words of Seylaz, "le rêve ou la jouissance d'un pouvoir surhumain appellent, chez la créature comme chez le créateur, une parole éloquente." See Jean-Luc Seylaz, "Reflexions sur Gobseck," *Etudes de lettres,* 1 (1968), 303.

[21] The ultimate dead end of naive realism is well symbolized by the distorting spectacles that Raphaël wears to the opera, "dont le verre microscopique artistement disposé, détruisait l'harmonie des plus beaux traits, en leur donnant un hideux aspect" (pp. 208–209).

[22] The immolated poet was a common romantic figure; but Raphaël represents the *self*-immolated thinker. Was it this aspect of the novel that

Everywhere he turns, Raphaël's intellectual bias betrays him. His theory of the will, based upon material *Idées* ("des êtres organisés, complets qui vivaient dans un monde invisible et influaient sur nos destinées" [p. 116]), is the most absurd failure. He cannot make Foedora love him, since she forbids him to speak to her of love; he cannot approach Pauline, since he will not speak of love to her. Nor is his theory of any help with finances. Only once does Raphaël come near to understanding his problem. Returning from a last stormy conversation with Foedora, walking on the slippery surface of sleet laid down by the cold winter, he remarks that he is reduced to doubting "la valeur nominale des paroles et des idées" (p. 128).

Clearly, then, naive realism provides the hero of *La Peau de chagrin* with no simple solutions. The failure is a failure of that "mécanisme" with which Balzac had originally begun. And the most interesting aspect of the novel is that in composing it Balzac wrote himself into a new understanding of this critical philosophical problem. Raphaël's failure, to the extent that it is talismanic of Balzac's failure, constitutes the necessary ash from which the *Comédie humaine* could arise. For in writing the novel, Balzac had an experience oddly similar to the one he describes in Raphaël. He, too, began with a certain amount of data, formalized verbalizations, "des êtres organisés, complets," as Raphaël puts it. These are the aphoristic fragments from the *Album,* the chief of which is the comment on "mécanisme" itself. In calling the *Album* the "grand parc de mes idées," Balzac was stressing the autonomy, maneuverability, and completeness of its components. The fragments exhibit many of the qualities the Balzacian narrator attributes to *Idée:* they claim objectivity; they claim totality; they are self-contained, concise, and purport to picture the real world. According to the theory of naive realism—that is, if *La Peau de chagrin* is a "picture" of some reality beyond itself—these fragments should remain as more or less fixed centers of

---

attracted Baudelaire's attention? It is interesting to speculate on what "L'Héautontimoroumenos" might owe to *La Peau de chagrin.*

development in the novel of which they became part. Such an eventuality would not be very surprising in view of the narrator's taste for aphorisms,[23] whose optimistic assumption of ability to make assertions about the world appeals to him. But if we examine the integration of these fragments into the novel, we discover a striking incompatibility between the theoretical absolutism of *Idée* and the necessities of creativity.

Aside from the remark on "mécanisme" itself, there are four significant fragments in the *Album* that appear in the final text. The first is: "L'homme qui aime voit en lui plus que lui-même" which becomes in the text "L'amour nous donne une sorte de religion pour nous-mêmes, nous respectons en nous une autre vie; il devient alors le plus horrible des malheurs, le malheur avec une espérance, une espérance qui nous fait accepter des tortures" (p. 133); the second is "Il y a la misère en bas de soie et la misère qui mendie," which becomes "Il y a deux misères, madame: celle qui va par les rues effrontément en haillons, qui, sans le savoir, recommence Diogène, se nourrissant de peu, réduisant la vie au simple. . . . Puis la misère du luxe, une misère espagnole, qui cache la mendicité sous un titre; fière, emplumée, cette misère en gilet blanc, en gants jaunes, a des carrosses, et perd une fortune faute d'un centime" (p. 162); the third is "Un grand crime, c'est quelquefois un poème," which becomes "Ah! quelquefois un crime doit être tout un poème, je l'ai compris" (p. 165); the fourth and perhaps most important is "Quelle pitié de voir l'opium, agent matériel, dominer ou déterminer le jeu d'une âme censée immatérielle," which becomes "Grâce à la puissance matérielle exercée par l'opium sur notre âme immatérielle, cet homme d'imagination si puissement ac-

[23] I do not mean to imply any overweening taste for the classical maxim on Balzac's part. That style died abruptly at the turn of the century, and there is no discernible ambition in Balzac to return to it. Nevertheless, the style of *Idée* does show obvious affinities with the style of the preceding intellectual era in which it was grounded. On aphorisms and maxims, see Gerhard Pfohl, ed., *Das Epigramm: Zur Geschichte einer inschriftlichen und Literarischen Gattung* (Darmstadt, 1969).

tive s'abaissa jusqu'à la hauteur de ces animaux paresseux qui croupissent au sein des forêts, sous la forme d'une dépouille végétale" (p. 286). In each case, except the third, the final version is much longer than the original fragment, and this gives us a clue to what happens. Integrated into the compositional process, the fragments are placed in unforeseen contexts; as a result, none of them can ultimately sustain claims to objectivity. What in the *Album* may have seemed to Balzac, the author, perfectly verifiable truisms about the real world, now become to the fictional narrator unmanageable lumps of language. An analysis of the important fourth fragment concerning the materiality of the soul will illuminate the nature of the process.

The statement as it stands in the *Album* strikes to the heart of Raphaël's theory of the will. The word "censée," with its implied sarcasm, indicates that the soul is indeed material; there would then be nothing strange in the symbol of the magic skin, and one could truly say that in a certain sense "la pensée tue," that is, a physical organ deteriorates through use. It might then be a pity that chemicals can affect the soul, but hardly surprising. But the whole novel shows that Raphaël is wrong; his confidence that a few drops of opium will end his problems is a chimera. So it comes as no surprise that when the fragment appears in the text as a narrator's statement, it loses the key word "censée"—which marks a shift away from the materialist point of view—as well as the word "pitié"—which eliminates the value judgement—while at the same time acquiring the word "grâce"—which seems like a last-ditch attempt to cling to materialism. In the end, the passage is confused and self-contradictory, mingling as it does the views of an author and the views of a narrator. The logicality, or lack of it, is not at issue here, but the impossibility of maintaining the integrity of the fragment when it moves from the "real" world into that of the novel.

The same process can be shown in the other fragments. The first one appears in the context of Foedora, but it is clear that it can only make sense in the context of Pauline, whom Raphaël truly loves. The second fragment about two kinds of love breaks down totally in the novel, since Raphaël is victim of neither kind of poverty ("Je ne suis ni peuple, ni roi, ni escroc . . . je suis une exception," he tells Foedora [p. 162]), but of a third kind: an intellectual poverty that eventually drives him to his death. The third fragment about crime appears when Foedora is afraid Raphaël will murder her in a "crime passionnel"—of which he is precisely incapable because he is a creature of comprehension ("je l'ai compris," he cries [p. 165]), rather than of passion.

These are not mere stylistic revisions; on the contrary, the changes involve real shifts in attitude and sometimes downright contradictions. It was not a case of rearranging words in order to say something better, but a case of words having to be rearranged in order to say something different. The structured, concretized organization of *Idée* turns out to be a very problematical thing. The encounter of the mind with the world is not a stable one; the "truth" of an author is not necessarily the "truth" of a narrator. Just as Raphaël's skin disappears to symbolize the betrayal of language, so Balzac's fragments tend to dissolve and be transformed in the process of redaction. Truly, as he himself once remarked, "A l'exécution tout a changé," and we can well understand that he liked to view this work not as a novel, but as a myth.

Yet, it should not be thought that the failure of naive realism signals the defeat of the creative artist. Quite the contrary. In *La Peau de chagrin,* a certain use of language is radically called into question. It was a step of immense importance, and one to which the Balzacian narrator repeatedly returns. All of his creative characters—writers, musicians, painters, sculptors—are subtypes of Raphaël. Those who fail are almost always trapped in the same difficulties, insisting on following out the logic of their thought, and arriving at what they take to be pictorial statements about the world. For most of them, such as Frenhofer, Gambara, and Balthasar Claës, that correspondence is mere fantasy, and they end as victims of their prior conceptions.

As for those who asked why Raphaël did not merely wish the skin to stretch, the real answer now seems obvious. At the moment of making the bargain, Raphaël enunciates the wish that englobes all the rest: "Je veux vivre avec excès." And since he regards enunciated wishes as reality, this statement precludes any further ones that contradict it. He does at times wish the skin would stop shrinking, but is prevented by his a priori assumption from verbalizing that wish. Here we must recognize some authorial intervention. The pronouncement of contradictory desires by Raphaël would raise problems insoluble on the level of *Idée*. Conveniently, then, he holds his tongue. But the problem was not thereby solved for the narrator who, if he were not to be accused of arbitrary manipulation, had to build other possibilities into his text. As one might expect, he did indeed do this, and created a whole series of parallel myths, to which we now turn.

The dilemma of *Idée* was one of the major consequences of regarding the world in terms of naive realism. If language had a one-to-one relationship with the world, so to speak, how could one make contradictory statements about a noncontradictory "real" world? If desire made the world, how were contradictory desires possible? The mechanistics that originally lay behind *La Peau de chagrin* led Raphaël to assume that if the word is possible the thing exists; conversely, if the thing exists the word is possible.

To find the theoretical description of this fallacy, one need go no further back than to that same John Locke whose influence had pervaded the *Dissertation*. In Locke's view one of the chief sins was the habit of taking words for things,[24] and Raphaël's experience can be seen as nothing more than a fictional interpretation of this fallacy. But Balzac had yet another source, which he openly and even

[24]On this problem see the commentaries of Alexander Campbell Fraser in his edition of the *Essay Concerning Human Understanding*, II, 132.

proudly declared: Laurence Sterne's *Tristram Shandy*. The typographical squiggle at the beginning of *La Peau de chagrin*, said by the narrator to represent Corporal Trim's eloquent gesture, has caused a great deal of confusion, starting with contemporary editions in which the squiggle was gradually converted by over-literal compositors from an apparently meaningless doodle into a snake. Snakes, needless to say, have nothing to do with the story.[25] And although there has been considerable puzzlement over the presence of the symbol, there has been no explanation of why Balzac deemed it to be an appropriate liminary sign.

It comes from Book IX, chapter 4 of *Tristram Shandy*, where Uncle Toby and Corporal Trim are discussing marriage and celibacy. They are approaching Widow Wadman's house—Uncle Toby rather reluctantly—as Corporal Trim tells of his brother Tom, a prisoner of the Inquisition for having married a Jewish widow. "Nothing," says Trim, "can be so sad as confinement for life—or so sweet, an' please your honour, as liberty."[26] Having said this, Trim gives "a flourish with his stick thus—" and the squiggle follows. Tristram's comment on Trim's gesture, however, gives the key: "A thousand of my father's most subtle syllogisms could not have said more for celibacy. My uncle *Toby* look'd earnestly towards his cottage and his bowling green. The corporal had unwarily conjured up the Spirit of Calculation with his wand; and he had nothing to do, but to conjure it down again with his story, and in this form of Exorcism, most un-ecclesiastically did the Corporal do it."[27]

The allusion to Walter's "most subtle syllogisms" puts the finger on one of Sterne's major themes: the satire of the same Lockian transgression we have been calling naive realism, or, in Balzac's literary transposition, *Idée*. Walter's

[25] The typographic history of the squiggle is set out in Maurice Allem's notes to the Garnier edition (pp. 303–304). Charles Spoelberch de Lovenjoul has given the bibliographical history of the text in his *Histoire des oeuvres d'Honoré de Balzac,* 3d ed. (Paris, 1888), pp. 163–77.

[26] Laurence Sterne, *Tristram Shandy,* edited by Ian Watt (New York, 1965), p. 464.

[27] *Ibid.,* p. 465.

view is that the world *is* words; words have more reality for him even than the objects they designate. Indeed, until it is put into language, the world doesn't exist in his eyes. The novel is filled with incidents in which Walter bypasses reality in favor of his syllogisms and hypotheses;[28] he is properly punished for his errors by the ultimate failure of all his major plans for his son Tristram.[29] On the other hand, Toby represents the opposite madness: inability or unwillingness to grant language any referential reliability at all. He is the champion of gestures and things. Tristram remarks at one point that Toby's life is "put in jeopardy by words"; consequently Toby would rather do than say, and if pushed hard enough he resorts to whistling. It is not without significance for Balzac that Trim's wordless communication with his stick has more effect on Toby than a thousand words. There is something about language that constricts the open spontaneity of Uncle Toby.

Balzac's liminary use of Trim's gesture, then, alludes directly to the Lockian problem of language, which is the central theme of *La Peau de chagrin.* At that point, however, the parallel ends. Sterne's bawdy comedy can hardly be thought of as a "source" for Balzac's tragic fantasy, although it did undoubtedly suggest that the Lockian dilemma could be used in narrative development. Balzac's tale, for all its fantastic qualities, is deeply rooted in social realities. He was less interested in "conjuring down the spirit of calculation" as an abstract principle, then he was in criticizing a *certain mode of calculation,* a typical way of confronting the world, which the narrator of *La Peau de chagrin* obviously considers to be the dominant mode of thought of the July Monarchy. His position is far more striking than that of Tristram: he proposes that it may be possible to

[28]As, for example, when Toby accidentally gives him a painful blow on the shinbone. Walter immediately launches into a peroration on chance and accident, relieving his physical pain by sheer garrulity.

[29]I am indebted for much of this interpretation to the important study by Juliet McMaster, "Experience to Expression: Thematic Character Contrasts in *Tristram Shandy,*" *Modern Language Quarterly,* XXXII, no. 1 (1971), 42–57.

employ words not only in the service of *Idée*, but as an expression of *Pensée* as well. His text becomes in part the search for a new language of imagination and intuition, embodying all those subtle processes that result in the construct we generally agree to call "literature."[30] Around this concept of language as the key to the treasure of mental life gather two groups of metaphors: dancing and staining.

Dancing has been, since the Renaissance, one of the most frequent images of creativity.[31] It is, significantly, located just at the point of transition between *Pensée* and *Idée*. In the presumably "objective" world of Raphaël de Valentin, phenomena of the mind must always be approached first through *Idée*. And so we first encounter the curious concept of the "dance of ideas." Raphaël first experiences it at the ball given by the duc de Navarreins, where his father unexpectedly gives him a purse of money: "Evoquées par cette somme, les joies de mon escapade apparurent devant moi, dansant comme les sorcières de Macbeth autour de leur chaudière, mais alléchantes, frémissantes, délicieuses" (p. 83). Again during his tormented affair with Foedora, the *Idées* that Raphaël had thought were so clear and well ordered (a good marriage, wealth, the rescue of the family fortunes) once again "dansent devant [lui] sans qu'[il] puisse les saisir" (p. 16), and the affair turns out quite differently from his expectations. But the dance of *Idée* is most

---

[30]Barbéris observes that in order to achieve plenitude of knowledge, Raphael should not speak at all. Through the various editions of the novel, as a matter of fact, bits of his dialogue are progressively transferred to other characters. But while this may prolong Raphael's life, it is hardly a solution for the narrator (*Balzac et le mal du siècle*, II, 1483).

[31]For a brief discussion see George Steiner, *Tolstoi or Dostoievsky* (London, 1959), p. 232. One inevitably thinks, of course, of Valéry's *Eupalinos ou la danse*. It is interesting to observe that Valéry speaks of the word as a plank thrown across an abyss; that is, as the connection between a concept and the expression it makes for itself. But Valéry put primary stress on the extension through time and space. For him, the poet must constantly move on: "surtout qu'il ne s'amuse pas à danser sur la mince plance pour éprouver sa résistance!" Paul Valéry, "Poésie et pensée abstraite," *Variété V* (Paris, 1945), p. 133. Mallarmé also played with the idea of the dance of word and thought. See Haskell Block, *Mallarmé and the Symbolist Drama* (Detroit, 1963), pp. 93–96.

dramatically expressed in the theme of debt. Debt is described in *La Peau de chagrin* as a creation of the imagination (p. 178) as well as a legal obligation. It is Raphaël himself who converts the latter into the former, who turns his debts into sheriff's agents, "à deux pattes, habillés de drap vert, portant des lunettes bleues ou des parapluies multicolores" (p. 177). Eventually he sees his debts not written on his furniture, as a note in the *Album* puts it, but fully engaged in a mad dance: "mes dettes jaillirent partout, comme des sauterelles; elles étaient dans ma pendule, sur mes fauteuils ou incrustées dans les meubles desquels je me servais avec le plus de plaisir" (p. 178). Raphaël views such dancing as a threat to his very existence. As long as he can prevent *Idée* from dancing, he feels safe. After concluding his pact, he explains to his obtuse servant, Jonathas, that all the joys of life dance before him like beautiful women: "si je les appelle, je meurs" (p. 202). Jonathas is charged chiefly with seeing that the dance does not begin. Indeed, dance music without dance, played by a blind clarinetist during an interrupted village fair, is described as the fantastic image of Raphaël's state of mind (p. 284). Rigidly committed to *Idée,* and to the externalization of desire through language in precise and verifiable ways, he cannot tolerate the incorporeality of the dance. Its transience points to a form of consciousness he must resist. Yet the dance is equivalent to what Frenhofer will call "méditer les brosses à la main"; what Balzac, with his maddening habit of confused vocabulary, later meant when he spoke of the need to "bien matérialiser ses idees."[32]

The dance of *Idée* suggests that even the naive realist must occasionally see that his projections of the world are not as solid or as dependable as he would have them be. From the dance spreads the subtle dynamism of "staining," an image even further removed from the criteria of specific shape and form. Through the metaphor of "staining," the most imperative of desires—love—escapes the monadic

[32]The phrase occurs in the preface to *Le Lys dans la vallée.*

structure of *Idée* almost completely: "L'amour passe par des transformations infinies avant de se mêler pour toujours à notre vie et de la teindre à jamais de sa couleur de flamme. Le secret de cette infusion imperceptible échappe à l'analyse de l'artiste" (p. 120). The artist here is potentially Raphaël. He knows what a poet he might have been, had he not surrendered to *Idée*. "Comment oser décrire ces teintes transitoires du sentiment," he asks, "ces riens qui ont tant de prix, ces mots dont l'accent épuise les trésors du langage, ces regards plus féconds que les plus riches poèmes?" (p. 121) These "teintes" exhaust language, but only if one regards language as limited to the domain of *Idée,* only if one approaches language with the prejudices of naive realism. With "staining" we enter the heartland of *Pensée,* and we broach the possibility that the hero's failure contains the possibilities of the novel's artistic success as a text. The main question is: can there be a language of *Pensée?* Can language do anything other than mime the objective world?

The antiquarian suggests, at one point, that the secret of *Pensée* lies in an alternative mode of thought which, in a celebrated passage, he calls *Savoir,* and whose main process is "jouir intuitivement" (p. 38). He stands in opposition to Raphaël, rejecting the equation of word and object, rejecting *Idée,* rejecting sensualism, materialism, and naive realism. His system of *Pensée* values thought for its own sake. The thinker achieves the fullness of his destiny by thinking; through self-awareness the creative man defines himself. As Jean-Luc Seylaz has observed, the antiquarian fulfills the dream of knowledge and gratification compatible with longevity.[33] Far from being destroyed, he finds his very being in thought, and incidentally maintains the skin at its full size. The conclusion seems inescapable that, contrary to the widely accepted view, Balzac saw intellectual activity as being varied in nature, and not necessarily fatal.[34]

[33] Seylaz, "Reflexions sur Gobseck," p. 297.

[34] There is, of course, still another alternative to Raphaël's naive realism,

Furthermore, it is clear that no human consciousness lies entirely in the domain of either *Idée* or *Pensée*. In the midst of his greatest cynicism, Raphaël can refer to himself as "un poète" (p. 168); he describes his life with Rastignac as "ce poème vivant" (p. 175); after concluding his pact, he retains enough traces of *Pensée* to envy the courtesans at Taillefer's orgy: "Sont-elles heureuses de pouvoir abdiquer ainsi leur raison" (p. 75). But such is the force of *Idée* in this poor and deformed spirit that he abandons imagination as "le malheur des poètes" (p. 93), and laughs off that lost, alter-Raphaël, "peut-être saint et sublime, qui n'existe plus" (p. 97).

What, then, in contrast to *Idée*, are the qualities of *Pensée*? It is, first, calm and tranquil. "Savoir," says the antiquarian, "laisse notre faible organisation dans un perpétuel état de calme" (p. 38), and he himself has the "tranquillité lucide" of a god (p. 30). This tranquility is the pleasure of thought itself; the delight in intellection that scorns to measure itself against its effects in the real world. The antiquarian has managed to live the greatest myth of mankind: the myth of observation freed from desire, and of desire freed from consummation: "Mes débauches étaient la contemplation des mers, des peuples, des forêts, des montagnes! J'ai tout vu, mais tranquillement, sans fatigue" (p. 39). Even Raphaël experiences certain forms of *Pensée*. He is fascinated by the "pensées confuses du premier sommeil" (p. 150), and later, watching Foedora sleep, senses "une sorte de langage auquel j'attachais des pensées et des sentiments" (p. 159). He also recognizes the validity of dreams, both in himself ("je me rêvais bien mis, en voiture, ayant une belle femme à mes côtés" [p. 83]), as well as in others ("Ah! je ne voudrais point pour ami d'un jeune homme qui dans ses

---

and that is the metaphysics of Louis Lambert. But although Lambert provides the basic terminology, his system ultimately fails because it falls into silence. There is thus no possibility of fitting it into a system of expression. This is precisely what vitiates so many attempts to describe the "visionary" aspects of the *Comédie humaine:* they lie beyond the boundaries of the system of language that constitutes Balzac's work. The antiquarian suggests no such avoidance of the issues of the mind-world problem.

rêves ne se serait pas tressé des couronnes, construit quelque piédestal ou donné de complaisantes maîtresses. Moi, j'ai souvent été général, empereur; j'ai été Byron, puis rien" [p. 94]). Raphaël has even had reflexive experiences like the antiquarian's: "L'abandon auquel j'étais condamné, l'habitude de refouler mes sentiments et de vivre dans mon coeur ne m'ont-ils pas investi du pouvoir de comparer, de méditer" (p. 93). During his campaign for Foedora's favors he experiences moments that are directly comparable to the antiquarian's *Savior.* He dreams of her, conjures her up in ecstatic visions, moves through time and space to join her in a mysterious world of "apparitions." And he admits that these effects of his "nature intérieure" are as natural as his "vision extérieure" (p. 122). This is a remarkable position for a committed empiricist to adopt, and not nearly as simple as he thinks it is. For all his poetic phraseology, he does not in the least understand *Pensée,* and in the ludicrous scene in Foedora's bedroom, he tries to do no less than "dream with her," "[s]'initier à ses secrets en pénétrant dans son sommeil" (p. 159). And if for a moment it seems as if he might understand the antiquarian's ideal of intuitive possession, he quickly rejects it as a "beau rêve auquel nous ne croyons pas longtemps" (p. 162). All of Raphaël's tragedy is bound up in that final remark, which underscores his commitment to *Idée* and to what he himself had earlier called "la chronologie, l'histoire des sots" (p. 92).

Being closely associated with sleep, revery, visions, and intuition, *Pensée* is naturally described in terms of fluidity. In the antiquarian's shop, the jumble of objects boils, cascades, and flows (p. 16); portraits radiate effluvia (p. 31); and when Raphaël later tries to reconstruct the experience for Emile, he instinctively describes the memory of it as bits of flotsam riding on the surf (pp. 140–41).[35] This liquidity

[35]At one point, Raphaël smokes a houka "dont les spirales émaillées gisaient comme un serpent dans sa chambre" (p. 197). Could this passage have helped in the transformation of Corporal Trim's squiggle into the coiled liminary serpent? For a detailed study of the *positive* nature of symbols of fluidity in the *Comédie humaine,* see Jean-Pierre Richard, *Etudes sur le romantisme* (Paris, 1970), pp. 57–65.

in no way contradicts the essential calm of *Pensée,* which consists chiefly of "ces rêveries matérielles, indolents et occupées, *sans but et conduisant néanmoins à quelque pensée*" (p. 278, my italics).[36] So subtle and mysterious are the processes of *Pensée* that very little within the range of human expression can cope with it. Words, paints, marble, and sounds will hardly do, for "qui dit art, dit mensonge" (p. 120).

So *Pensée* is ultimately linked to art, and paradoxically to all that which, in art, defies analysis. In this way, *Pensée* avoids the pitfalls of metaphysics and circularity. The narrator does not claim that *Pensée* is an ineffable, inexpressible phenomenon. Despite its reflexivity, it does lead to real manifestations in the real world, but *not to those of naive realism.* It leads to art, in its widest sense. It is not by chance that the word "mensonge" is linked to art. For art is a lie in the world of rationality; any attempt to describe its possibilities in everyday language is a false translation: "Eh! Comment pourrions-nous reproduire par des gloses les vives et mystérieuses agitations de l'âme, quand les paroles nous manquent pour peindre les mystères visibles de la beauté" (p. 121).

This, insofar as the novelist is concerned, is the vital rôle of *Pensée.* The creative mind must keep itself open to the possibilities that language itself offers: possibilities of complexity, echo, parallel, repetition, imagery, metaphor. The mind wanders, almost like a sleepwalker, among the words, motifs, and idioms of language, resisting the temptation of a "natural order" and preferring to imitate the painter who follows the suggestions of his own brush-strokes. But the apparent aimlessness of *Pensée* is nothing more than the preservation of that liberty to which Corporal Trim had pointed; it is the refusal to tie language to mimeticism; it is the husbanding of creative potential and the avoidance of commitment until the desired issue is found. The refusal to

[36]Here again, we need not be concerned with the precise words Balzac used; it is clear that what he calls "quelque pensée could not have the precision and structure of *Idée.*

engage himself is at times the only move the artist can make. It was something that Balzac himself recognized in *La Théorie de la démarche* as part of the mysterious "second stage" of creativity.

La Peau de chagrin proposes *Pensée* as a way of talking about aesthetic aspects of mind and language of which naive realism could give no account. It involved nothing less than the discovery of value and meaning in the newness of forms. Not all psychologists accept the validity of concepts such as *Pensée*, but at least one, Merleau-Ponty, echoes the Balzacian notion when he writes that the poet speaks as if no one had ever spoken before. Artistic expression can therefore never be merely the translation of an already-clear thought: "seule l'oeuvre faite et comprise prouvera qu'on devait trouver là *quelque chose* plutôt que rien."[37]

One must, however, recognize the difficulties such principles pose for the fictional narrator. *Idée* has an external component; it is possible to talk about the effects of thought in the objective world, and the image of the skin is perfectly adapted to the purpose. But *Pensée* is something else again, reflexive rather than mimetic. The traditional images used to talk about the functioning of the mind (the tabula rasa, the waxen tablet, the reflecting mirror, the flickering lamp, the awakening shepherd) were of little use to the Balzacian narrator because they remained in the realm of *Idée*, or because they tended to collapse into circularity. The difficulty was still Rousseau's vicious circle. The narrator of *La Peau de chagrin* refers to "le cerveau qui ne s'use pas et qui survit à tout" (p. 38), and he even maintains that "la pensée est la clef de tous les trésors" (p. 38), but he cannot open for us the realm of *Pensée* by persuasion or argumentation.

How then can the presence of *Pensée* in the text be rendered? Its very nature makes it difficult to isolate, and no modification of previously-existing fragments—as with *Idée*—can make it visible. Nevertheless, *La Peau de chagrin*

[37]Maurice Merleau-Ponty, *Sens et non-sens*, 5th ed. (Paris, 1966), p. 32.

can be viewed as a single enormous metaphor, suggesting the complexity of the relationship between *Pensée* and *Idée,* proposing the higher value of the former insofar as art is concerned, and making that value felt through the very arrangement of the language in which it is embodied. As tenuous as the approach might seem, an examination of *La Peau de chagrin* as a vast and complex image, rather than a mimetic discourse decorated with images, yields some interesting results. In the first place, the story is quite obviously not built around the fragments first recorded in the *Album.* One of the most striking conclusions one comes to, in examining the fragments, is that although they touch on subjects discussed in the novel—and often on very important ones—they by no means constitute its emotional centers. Rather, the novel proceeds by "abîmes, précipices, saillies, excroissances, hautes montagnes, profondeurs sans fond," to quote a review preserved in the Lovenjoul collection, quite possibly composed by Balzac himself.[38] We are invited to see the centers of force of *La Peau de chagrin* in a series of scenes where word evokes word and image evokes image, where fantasy and intuition are given full play at the expense of the secretary's craft. What emerges is the discovery that naive realism cannot "make" the work. Combined with elements of relatively straightforward description, we find the traces of the story's chancey emergence as a work of verbal art. Long, flowing, involved sentences run on in contradiction to what logic and naive realism would demand. Retrospectively describing his experience with Pauline, for example, Raphaël is so upset and frustrated that his words carry him far beyond an accurate picture of their relationship: "Combien de fois n'ai-je pas vêtu de satin les pieds mignons de Pauline, emprisonné sa taille svelte comme un jeune peuplier dans une robe de gaze, jeté sur son sein une légère écharpe en lui faisant fouler les tapis de son hôtel et la conduisant à une voiture élégante: je l'eusse adorée ainsi, je lui donnais une fierté qu'elle n'avait pas, je la dépouillais de toutes ses ver-

[38]Chantilly manuscript A–179, folio 9.

tus, de ses grâces naives, de son délicieux naturel, de son sourire ingénu pour la plonger dans le Styx de nos vices et lui rendre le coeur invulnérable, pour la farder de nos crimes, pour en faire la poupée fantasque de nos salons, une femme fluette qui se couche au matin pour renaître le soir, à l'aurore des bougies" (p. 109). This is all clearly contrary to what Pauline actually is: a virtuous young woman. It is also clearly contrary to every emotion Raphaël harbors toward her. But the sentence arrives quite naturally in terms of his current narrative position, as the culmination of the schizophrenic split between his overwhelming desire for Pauline and the suspicion—even before the demonic pact—that the expression of his desire would result in his own death. Only by reducing Pauline to a woman of easy virtue, whom he could possess without desiring, does Raphaël see a way out of his dilemma. But it is no way out at all in terms of the story, for neither she nor he would then be themselves. From a consideration of clothing, to the denial of virtue, to the plunge into vice, the sentence substitutes fantasy for logic, and myth for reality. It operates on the level of *Pensée,* expressing potentiality rather than actuality, and by its rhythms communicates the violence of frustrated, self-contradictory desire.

Pensée can be seen operating again in a sentence relating to the Mont-Dor, where Raphaël has gone to seek a cure. The narrator describes the landscape as tranquil, calm, and poetic. Raphaël establishes some kind of intuitive relationship with his surroundings and inexplicably begins to improve in health. If analyzed for what it actually says, the sentence seems to claim that Raphaël becomes one with the rocks, plants, and animals; that he enters into their existence in a way that has nothing to do with any kind of objective, discursive understanding of nature. There is no attempt to explain why his stay in the country helps him; there is only the suggestion that peace descends on the agitated mind when it abandons the attempt to explain. That suggestion arises not from what the sentence literally says (unacceptable in terms of *Idée,* for Raphaël could never "become" a rock or a plant), but from the flow and rhythm of its expression which, as before, holds to potential and "abeyance" rather than to definition and logic. And in this case we note that it is not Raphaël who verbalizes, for he has by now become convinced of the dangers of language; rather, it is the narrator, for whom *Pensée* remains—and must remain—the bedrock of narration: "Il réussit à devenir partie intégrante de cette large et puissante fructification; il avait épousé les intempéries de l'air, habité tous les creux des rochers, appris les moeurs et les habitudes de toutes les plantes, étudié le régime des eaux, leurs gisements, et fait connaissance avec les animaux; enfin, il s'était si parfaitement uni à cette terre animée, qu'il en avait en quelque sorte saisi l'âme et pénétré les secrets. Pour lui, les formes infinies de tous les règnes étaient les développements d'une même substance, les combinaisons d'un même mouvement, vaste respiration d'un être immense qui agissait, pensait, marchait, grandissait, et avec lequel il voulait grandir, marcher, penser, agir" (pp. 278–79). But the possibility of such a unity with nature exists for the narrator alone; it takes only a few words between the peasant hostess and his servant to destroy all the benefits that have accrued to Raphaël and send him rushing desperately back to Paris.

Pensée is not, however, limited to such very local manifestations. It can be seen in a series of set scenes, including the opening gambling scene, the ball of the duke of Navarreins, Taillefer's orgy, the spa at Aix, the village fair, and the antiquarian's shop. These episodes are the true aesthetic centers of the novel—the scenes that touch us most directly and strike us as possessing some meaning and significance other than purely descriptive, even if they are difficult to pin down.

Without any doubt, the most brilliant of these scenes is Raphaël's visit to the antiquarian's shop. It is an episode that contains all the themes and techniques we have discussed so far, and is no less than an excursion into the antiquarian's mind: "Les moeurs de toutes les nations du

globe et leurs sagesses se réunissaient sur sa face froide,
comme les productions du monde entier se trouvaient ac-
cumulées dans ses magasins poudreux" (p. 28).[39] During
their discussions, the antiquarian refers specifically to the
equivalency of his mind and his shop: "cette tête est encore
mieux meublée que ne le sont mes magasins. Là, dit-il, en
se frappant le front, là sont les vrais millions" (p. 39). The
contents of the shop—and of his mind—are the fruits of
the renunciation of empiricism, but not the renunciation of
all thought. The antiquarian is calm, but he is not a vegetable. The description of the shop uses, of course, the data of
reality; everything in it is identified in space and time. But
the observing mind composes, creates, imposes patterns.
By the same token, the text grows from within: everywhere
we find the marks of that burgeoning, fluid, rhythmic, yet
tranquil dynamism that Balzac called *Pensée*. In the words
of André Pieyre de Mandiargues, "la description du maga-
sin de l'Antiquaire . . . surpasse de très loin tout ce que pût
jamais offrir la réalité, . . . les trésors, les oeuvres d'art et les
bizarreries de l'univers entier y sont entassés moins comme
dans un musée composé par les hommes que dans la
mémoire d'un être surhumain."[40]

Raphaël, not yet having made his fatal choice, enters the
shop and by his severe countenance intimidates an atten-
dant, and gains the "right to be silent" (p. 17). The aban-
donment of language is significant and portends much for
the future. Raphaël has, in effect, entered the domain of
Pensée, where everything is vague, potential, and fluid:
"L'oreille croyait entendre des cris interrompus, l'esprit
saisir des drames inachevés, l'oeil apercevoir des lueurs mal
étouffees. Enfin une poussière obstinée avait jeté son léger
voile sur tous ces objets, dont les angles multipliés et les
sinuosités nombreuses produisaient les effets les plus pittoresques" (p. 19). Raphaël, when he first entered the shop,
had intended to pick and choose objects to study; that is, to

[39]Pléaide, ix, 32, reads "se résumaient sur sa face froide. . . ."
[40]André Pieyre de Mandiargues, "Le Supplice de la peau," *Nouvelle
Revue française,* iv (April–June 1966), 935.

exercise reason. But that is now impossible: "à force de regarder, de penser, de rêver, il tomba sous la puissance d'une fièvre . . . il sortit de la vie réelle, monta par degrés vers un monde idéal, arriva dans les palais enchantés de l'Extase où l'univers lui apparut par bribes et en traits de feu, comme l'avenir passa jadis flamboyant aux yeux de Saint-Jean dans Patmos" (p. 18).

Although Raphaël perceives the contents of the shop in roughly chronological order, in his fever he certainly does not examine the objects "logically." A vast amount of factual data is involved, it is true: we are dealing with a heteroclite collection of objects ranging from stuffed crocodiles, monkeys, and boas, down to sculpture, portraits, Renaissance silver work, and modern inventions. None of these objects is ever examined in itself; rather, they melt away into a general flow of impressions: "Cet océan de meubles, d'inventions, de modes, d'oeuvres, de ruines, lui composait un poème sans fin" (p. 21). But the point about all this, as Balzac had discovered years earlier in the work on the *Dissertation,* is that the mere collection of objects (or of words) is incomplete. The juxtaposition of discrete *Idées* constitutes a series, not a new entity; it is up to the observing mind to keep the flexibility necessary to find fundamental connections and meanings: "Le poète devait achever les croquis du grand peintre qui avait fait cette immense palette où les innombrables accidents de la vie humaine étaient jetés à profusion, avec dédain" (p. 21). All minds are poetic, to the extent that they assign value and meaning rather than confine themselves to the labelling processes of naive realism.

One of the narrator's chief methods of breaking down the assumptions of logic and syllogistic thinking is the incongruous juxtaposition of wildly divergent objects. Everything is heaped up pell-mell. A Sèvres vase stands next to a sphinx; stuffed animals lean against stained glass windows; a portrait of Madame Dubarry contemplates a water pipe.[41] A shock effect is clearly being sought: "toutes les

[41]One might note in passing another instance of snake imagery that

oeuvres humaines et divines se heurtaient" (p. 18), and the dynamism is further intensified by verbs that anthropomorphize the objects in the gallery: "une statue de marbre . . . *lui parla* des mythes voluptueux de la Grèce . . . la tête de Cicéron *lui déroulait* les pages de Tite-Live . . . les licteurs . . . *défilaient* lentement devant lui comme les vaporeuses figures d'un rêve" (p. 20, my italics). The dynamism rapidly communicates itself to Raphaël's mind. Abandoning his attempts to observe, understand, and analyze, he finds himself caught up in the magic of *Pensée:* "son âme s'élançait dans la chaude et fauve Italie; il assistait aux orgies des Borgia, courait dans les Abruzzes, aspirait aux amours italiennes, se passionnait pour les blancs visages aux longs yeux noirs. Il frémissait aux dénoûments nocturnes interrompus par la froide épée d'un mari" (p. 20). Soon Raphaël's consciousness is completely submerged in that of the antiquarian, and he finds himself participating in that calm yet dynamic "jouissance": "il devenait corsaire, et revêtait la terrible poésie empreinte dans le rôle de Lara . . . il épousait de nouveau l'étude . . . se couchait au fond d'une cellule, en contemplant par sa fenêtre en ogive les prairies . . . il endossait le casque d'un soldat . . . il caressait un tomhawk [*sic*] d'Illinois, et sentait le scalpel d'un Chérokée qui lui enlevait la peau du crâne" (p. 22). Ultimately Raphaël leaves the world of *Idée* far behind: "le bruit de ses pas retentissait dans son âme comme le son lointain d'un autre monde, comme la rumeur de Paris arrive sur les tours de Notre Dame" (p. 22).

Clearly, this scene is related to some fairly common romantic fantasies, as well as to techniques of narrative enumeration used both before and after Balzac's time. More importantly, the shop is an absurd collection of the leftovers of civilization whose crazy arrangement *makes any single view of reality impossible to maintain.* Logical unity is nowhere to be found; all that remains is the fact of Ra-

---

might have contributed to the transformation of the opening squiggle. Madame Du Barry's portrait faces a Chibouk, "en cherchant à deviner l'utilité des spirales qui serpentaient vers elle" (p. 18).

phaël's perception of this phenomenological chaos. He is led not to a classical sense of Self and World, but to paradox and contradiction, which can be resolved only by whatever significance he himself chooses to draw out of the collection in the shop. The ultimate stage arrives when Raphaël is no longer sure whether he is dead or alive; when the text trembles on the verge of losing all contact with the objective reality from which it began: "Poursuivi par les forces les plus étranges, par des créations merveilleuses assises sur les confins de la mort et de la vie, il marchait dans les enchantements d'un songe. Enfin, doutant de son existence, il était comme ces objets curieux, ni tout à fait mort, ni tout à fait vivant" (p. 22). In this state, he arrives at the third and highest gallery of all—the gallery of art. There, the mind is fatigued with the eternal fight with reality; the young man is "las de Raphaël" (a play on names not to be underestimated); he does not even glance at a Corréggio; he is stifled and oppressed by this gallery "qui . . . lui livraient un combat sans fin" (p. 24). And when his mind has arrived at this stage of renunciation and of availability, the symbol of the supreme choice appears before it: the magic skin, the link between *Pensée* and *Idée;* the symbol of the dialectic of that which is said and the manner of its saying; the representation (now pliable, now hard, now fixed, now shrinking) of the alternative possibilities of the mind. "Retournez-vous, dit le marchand . . . et regardez cette PEAU DE CHAGRIN" (p. 34).

All the elements of this scene have one quality in common: they involve Raphaël in adventures beyond the limits of logical thought. At their lowest common denominator they are episodes of fever and excitement in which Raphaël has more or less taken leave of his senses. On the other hand, they are manifestations of *Savoir* in the antiquarian's sense: that is, of the contemplative survey of all the possibilities offered by a chaotic reality, rather than the exhausting effort at labelling and arranging. The disorder of the antiquarian's shop reflects the coming disorder of the *Comédie humaine* itself, which, despite its drive towards unity and logic, and despite its obsessive categorizing, remains randomly and arbitrarily organized. The antiquarian's gallery is not a logical museum; the *Comédie humaine* is not a stenograph of nineteenth-century France. In both cases, values must be sought elsewhere.

Consequently, the myth of *La Peau de chagrin* is the myth of creativity rather than of mimesis, and every creative mind must, at every moment, face Raphaël's choice. Will the poet remain devoted to the criteria of reason and discursive intelligence? Will he use his words only to "label" the world, and at the uttermost extreme of naive realism, to reduce himself to silence? Or will he have the courage to withdraw into himself, to let thinking "become itself" in Merleau-Ponty's striking phrase? Of course he must use the data of objective reality, but that does not mean that his texts must be measurable against the objective world. Language can, on the other hand, be used to extend the world, not through the exhaustion of psychic energy, but through its generation. At some point, the real world might well become consonant with the world of art, and the mode of *Pensée* counterbalance that of *Idée*.[42] But the poet must have the courage to wait, to renounce when renunciation is necessary, to abandon prior plans when they reach dead ends, even to abandon the stenography of reality when language presents its own rich possibilities. Otherwise his fate will be Raphaël's. Equally, he must not lose himself entirely in the vast fields of abstract contemplation, or his fate will be that of Louis Lambert.[43]

The novel, then, appears as a kind of test case designed to discover how—or if—discourse can be patterned to

[42] Barbéris observes *(Balzac et le mal du siècle,* II, 1172), that for many Balzacian artists, "le monde merveilleux de la pensée . . . c'est le monde où tout serait logique, c'est le monde non-défiguré par l'argent." But this logic is the logic of freedom and self-realization.

[43] The critical place of *La Peau de chagrin* in Balzac's maturation is underscored by his interest, prior to 1830, in both documentary realism and in illuminist theories. They have been studied closely by Bernard Guyon, "Balzac et le mystère de la création littéraire," *Revue d'histoire littéraire de la France,* L, no. 2 (April–June 1950), 168–91.

move beyond its referential significance into the artistic significance of *Pensée.* Herein lies all the distinction between this novel and the preceding potboilers that resorted to hyperbole, prettification, and a posteriori rhetoric in order to achieve effects beyond those of mere reportage. It is a banal yet subtle problem, which every artist faces anew at every moment. In *La Peau de chagrin,* the problem is confronted as starkly as possible: with the "facts" of nineteenth-century Paris, the narrator fashions a Mephistophelian fantasy, and links the two through the symbol of the magic skin.

From this link grow the themes of monomania, of destructive thought, and of tragic creativity that characterize so many episodes of the *Comédie humaine.* But these themes are only the elements of *Idée,* without artistic significance unless held in the free flow of *Pensée* as the work emerges and fulfills its inherent possibilities. Neither can exist without the other; the work of art cannot exist unless both are in delicate balance. The poet must talk of *something,* but the demands of naive realism must always be tempered by the demands of the text as text. The narrator obviously begins with the desire to describe something, but he must attenuate the naive realism of *Idée* in favor of the intrinsic aesthetic interest of *Pensée.* There are even some who argue that this gradual elimination of initial a priori conceptions is in some way an essential element of the creative process generally, or at least of that creativity we call "literary."[44]

This situation places the Balzacian narrator in a dilemma. Rejecting, despite all, the mere description of effects, he bills himself as a seeker of "causes," and yet when the chips are down, causes and first principles turn out to be practically inexpressible: the fate of Raphaël de Valentin, as well as of Louis Lambert, is the loss of language. Unmediated desire and direct vision are precisely that: immediate, coincidental, and solipsistic. The alternative open

[44]Jean Grenier, "L'Aspect négatif de la création," *Nouvelle Revue française,* XIII (June 1965), 1004–15.

to these seekers of the absolute is to accomodate themselves to the existence of the "veil"—and that, of course, is what they will not do.[45]

But the Balzacian narrator takes up a common-sense position somewhere between the extremes represented by Raphaël and Louis Lambert. The paradox of *Pensée* and *Idée* is the very heart of the *Comédie humaine.* Baudelaire saw this clearly, when he recognized that the "realistic" Balzac was doubled by a "visionary." In this sense, the discovery of mere themes does not necessarily launch the creative process. Much more profound than theme or subject is the obsessive attention which the Balzacian narrator pays to the terrible problem of words and *his* struggle with the veil of language. From *La Peau de chagrin* grew one of the profound principles of the *Comédie humaine:* the realization that the pure "secretary of society" is not a creator of fiction, and that the only reality that realism can achieve is the filling of "le vide papier que la blancheur défend."

[45] Paul de Man has put it succinctly: "The simplest of wishes cannot express itself without hiding behind a screen of language that constitutes a world of intricate intersubjective relationships, all of them potentially inauthentic." Paul de Man, "The Crisis of Contemporary Criticism," *Arion,* VI (1967), 48. The attitude of the Balzacian narrator is, of course much more positive: while he may distrust language, he has nothing else to work with. A hint of this glimmers through one of Louis Lambert's "pensées," when he remarks that words engender substance. Among Balzac critics, only Jean-Pierre Richard has noticed this cautious optimism about words and thought. See Richard, *Etudes sur le romantisme,* p. 24.

CHAPTER IV

The Thought-Word Problem in the
Comédie humaine

> En me voyant amasser tant de faits et les peindre
> comme ils sont, avec la passion pour élément, quel-
> ques personnes ont imaginé, bien à tort, que j'appar-
> tenais à l'école sensualiste et matérialiste . . .
> *Avant-Propos*, i, 34

After *La Peau de chagrin,* Balzac continued exploring his
philosophical interests, but nowhere did he give a comprehensive treatment of the problems of thought and language that had been occupying him as far back as the *Dissertation sur l'homme.* His further remarks on problems of
language are scattered throughout the *Comédie humaine* and
the ancillary writings, from which they must be extracted
and grouped. After *La Peau de chagrin,* Balzac's view of
language did not change very much, but continued to fluc-
tuate between *Idée* and *Pensée.* There are therefore echoes
between works written as much as ten years apart, and
something like a body of characteristic statements—one
hesitates to call it a comprehensive theory—will emerge
from the totality of his writings.

One qualification must be made at the outset, that Balzac
had a singular weakness for the romantic tendency to use
the word "parole" as a synonym for "divinity," "creative
principle," and other such abstractions. This usage has little to do with problems of human language and psychology, and in texts such as *Louis Lambert* and *Séraphîta* it intro-
duces an element of inexactitude into a vocabulary already
vague and uncertain. "Parole" in this sense is not at issue
here; the divine word does not concern us, and the "Et
verbum caro factum est" about which Louis Lambert

speculates (pp. 107 and 169) is part of theology rather than psycholinguistics.[1]

As in the *Dissertation sur l'homme,* there lies under much of Balzac's later writings a distinctly eighteenth-century view of language. It is clearly discernible in the *Catéchisme social,* where the question of origins is discussed at length, leading to the conclusion that language is not of divine origin, but is the result of "acquisitions lentes" (CS, 694). The problem, of course, was to explain how these acquisitions were made. His evident perplexity on the subject led the novelist to adopt Rousseau's enigma about the symbiotic relationship of language and mind: whenever man is found, Balzac writes, he is "déjà penseur profond," and even in the most recently formed cultures a sufficient language always exists (CS, 693–94). As in the Cartesian doctrine, the Balzacian approach sees in language the keystone—indeed the proof—of the existence of mind.[2] Even in a work as heavily shot through with mysticism as *Séraphîta,* the narrator attempts to show that once the idea of the "divine word" is separated from human language, the latter remains as the fundamental evidence for the existence of mind. All human accomplishments, he claims, spring from our use of language, without which man would be merely a savage (Sér, 289).

The question of origins had two sides, moreover—the origin of language as a human phenomenon, and the acquisition of language by individuals—whose interplay attracted Balzac's attention. Years before, Maupertuis had suggest-

[1]An example from *Les Proscrits,* characteristically quoted by Maurice Bardèche, will suffice to illustrate the kind of usage I am excluding from this discussion: "Selon lui, la parole divine nourrissait la parole spirituelle, la parole spirituelle nourrissait la parole animée, la parole animée nourrissait la parole animale, la parole animale nourrissait la parole végétale, et la parole végétale exprimait la vie de la parole stérile" (quoted in Bardèche, *Une Lecture de Balzac,* p. 53). Such obscurities occur mainly in the *Etudes philosophiques* which, although they were intended to be the underpinning of the *Comédie humaine,* nevertheless remained the least developed section of the total work, and the part most minimally connected to the rest by such devices as reappearing characters.

[2]Noam Chomsky, *Cartesian Linguistics* (New York, 1966), p. 6.

ed that individual acquisition of language was dominated by social conventionality. The child, he maintained, is immediately surrounded by established words that reflect the prejudices of the group and obscure what might have been his own pristine vision.[3] Just this sort of linguistic dominance lies behind the drama of such novels as *Pierrette* and *Louis Lambert*. Pierrette accepts words such as "virtue," "obedience," and "duty" as meaning precisely what her cruel cousins tell her they mean; and this accounts for her inability to establish any real autonomy of self with which to fight off enemies who manipulate words and concepts to their own advantage. One wonders, otherwise, why she does not throw herself under the protection of the several sympathetic characters who would surely have helped her, or why she remains so strangely passive. Of course the narrator is deliberately playing on our sympathies, and is knowingly extracting all possible pathos from the situation. Nevertheless, Pierrette's virtue amounts to nothing but her acceptance of a group of social and conventional definitions; she is, in a word, a victim of language without any alternatives.

Lambert, far more sophisticated, preserves a Maupertuisian "original" intelligence that permits him to distance himself from the language of society. But by the same token, he finds himself caught in semantic isolation and subjective idealism. No one can communicate with him except on rare occasions and disjointedly. Ultimately no one can communicate with him at all. Can he be said to possess language within his walls? From what the reader can gather of Lambert's inner existence, it seems to be the final form of *Pensée:* a total refusal of language to measure itself against the world. Like Raphaël de Valentin and others possessed of extremely powerful mentalities, Lambert perceives all of reality at a glance, and understands all existence in a split second. His perception is global, undifferentiated, and ultimately coextensive with his own mind. The

[3]Maupertuis, "Réflexions philosophiques," quoted in Grimsley, *Maupertuis*, p. 32.

world as a vast predicate leads him only to himself. We are miles from Turgot's assignment of signs to objects by a priori self-conscious "subjects."[4]

Pierrette and Lambert present us with two extreme positions: that of the individual so totally dominated by semantic heritage that all sense of self is destroyed; and that of the individual so completely outside that heritage that only an amorphous, undefinable sense of self remains. The two novels pose in the starkest possible way the question of language as a function of ideology, but without providing precise answers. In *Illusions perdues,* the narrator makes some attempt to answer the question by comparing the acquisition of language to the groping progress of typography and paper-making (XI, 290–91). The comparison suggests that language is primarily an interpersonal phenomenon, and that the Lambertian ideal of an entirely private, hence totally free, language is one of the illusions we must lose. Even though language potential can be assumed as a given quality of mind, only social intercourse permits it actually to arise. As a result it is largely through language that Balzacian social species manifest themselves. *La Maison Nucingen* contains a long and highly amusing tirade on the "grande loi de l'*improper* qui régit l'Angleterre!" (p. 362), which is given as an example of the linguistic determinants of "Englishness."[5] Thus formalized and conventionalized, language in its wider sense becomes the very

[4]See Grimsley, *Maupertuis,* p. 4. Lambert may be reflecting Rousseau who, in the *Discours sur l'origine de l'inégalité,* also opted for the priority of predicates, claiming that man first spoke in whole propositions and only then became aware of the "parts" of speech. Biran sided with Turgot in claiming that such propositions were impossible, but he agreed with Maupertuis and Rousseau that the distinction of the predicate had to precede self-consciousness about language: "Avant le langage, il n'y avait point de proposition exprimée, mais il devait y avoir dans l'esprit de tout homme doué de *pensée* et capable de parler, quelque distinction établie entre le sujet et l'attribut . . . et d'abord entre le moi permanent et les sensations variables" (quoted in Grimsley, *Maupertuis,* p. 70). The debate has arisen again in contemporary theory, with Mikel Dufrenne being one of the principal defenders of the priority of predicates.

[5]The passage is much too long to be quoted here in its entirety, but a section of it will illustrate the point: "En Angleterre, Finot, tu te lies

basis of the human community, preserving the "best thoughts" by which that community asserts its existence and its history: "L'Italie, messieurs les faiseurs de lois, doit à ses beaux génies de recevoir les deux tiers des guinées qui sortent de l'Angleterre. Protégez donc les arts et la langue; car, quand vos intérêts matériels n'existeront plus, vous vivrez par vos pensées qui seront debout, et qui, si le pays pouvait disparaître, diraient: *Là fut la France*" (LA, 655).[6] This view was already implicit in the Port-Royal doctrine, as well as in Condillac; it has survived to our day in the work of epistemologists like Foucault, who holds that "de façon plus générale, chaque peuple dépose en son langage les progrès de son savoir."[7]

Such a concept clearly derives from ideology: if society prevents the individual from possessing his thoughts "sui generis," it obviously places something in their stead. No French thinker went quite so far as did Humboldt in Germany, who simply and purely equated "culture" and "language community." But everyone sensed, as did the Balzacian narrator, that the relationship of the individual to the group or, as a Saussurian might put it, of "langue" to "parole," was difficult and troublesome. At the same time,

---

extrêmmement avec une femme, pendant la nuit, au bal ou ailleurs; tu la rencontres le lendemain dans la rue, et tu as l'air de la reconnaître: improper! . . . vous vous échauffez, vous discutez, vous riez, vous répandez votre coeur, votre âme, votre esprit dans votre conversation; vous y exprimez des sentiments; vous jouez quand vous êtes au jeu, vous causez en causant et vous mangez en mangeant: *improper! improper! improper!*" (MN, 362–63).

[6]Although Balzac's statements are too diffuse to permit the identification of sources—if indeed specific sources do exist—one might take note of a highly suggestive passage in an author he is known to have read and admired: Bonald. According to Bonald, language has "des règles générales, communes à la syntaxe de tous les peuples, et des règles spéciales, particulières à la grammaire de chaque peuple; et il y a aussi dans chaque société une langue courante commune à tous les citoyens, et une langue *technique* particulière à chaque profession: car la langue du jurisconsulte n'est pas celle du guerrier" (Bonald, *Législation primitive*, I, 297–98). The passage bears directly on the point that so interested Balzac: the meeting between general and particular languages.

[7]Quoted in J. C. Chevalier, "La Grammaire générale de Port-Royal et la critique moderne," *Langages*, VII (1967), 18.

the question of what the individual "might have been," had the culture not imposed its words on him, is in many ways a nonquestion. For without socially induced responses, the individual might well remain without language at all; that is, he might meet the fate of Louis Lambert.[8] In our terms, if the potential of language is a defining quality of mind, an achieved language is the mark of a society. The relationship is a necessary one: Humboldt had already seen that only society, only the Other, can make the individual aware of his linguistic potential by, so to speak, drawing words out of him. It was, in a manner of speaking, a reply to Rousseau's paradox.[9]

One basis on which the connection between individual and society could be maintained was the sensualist notion of language as a "copy" of thought. Despite his basic mysticism, Louis Lambert has some oddly sensualist views of language. Who, he asks, will ever be able to explain the transitions from sensation to thought, and then to speech, to written signs, to the alphabet, and finally to narration (LL, 48)? In the same way, the *Avant-Propos* of the *Comédie humaine* retains certain sensualist undertones in the way it conceives of the word as one form of the "représentation matérielle," that man gives to his thoughts (p. xxvii). Language takes its place beside dress, dwellings, and social customs, and thought itself appears to be little more than a way station in the great sensualist chain from object to word.

[8]This appears to have been Saussure's own view: "La nature nous donne l'homme organisé pour le langage articulé, mais sans langage articulé. La langue est un fait social. L'individu, organisé pour parler, ne pourra arriver à utiliser son appareil que par la communauté qui l'environne," quoted in Rudolf Engler, "Théorie et critique d'un principe saussurien: l'arbitraire du signe," *Cahiers Ferdinand de Saussure,* XIX (1962), 5.

[9]Long before Rousseau, Vico had established philology as the queen of the sciences, and precisely on the same grounds that Balzac used to salute the importance of language: that is, that "each phase of the human mind, as it develops by stages in history, is reflected in the form of language, in the vocabulary, and in the type of word formation which is typical of that phase." Stuart Hampshire, "Vico and the Contemporary Philosophy of History," in Tagliacozzo and White, *Giambattista Vico,* p. 478.

One could, of course, point to genius as the optimum instance of the object-thought-word sequence. Here again, Humboldt anticipated much that Balzac and later French thinkers were to maintain, by defining genius as the transformation of potentialities of language into real structures that might well have been unexpected and unsuspected up to that point.[10] It is directly related to Balzac's sense that the superior mind enjoys a mysterious ability to articulate the qualities inherent in the language he uses.[11] One of the things that a genius can do is to reveal language as a repository of wisdom; not an a priori wisdom granted somehow from outside the collective consciousness, but wisdom inherent in language itself and potentially available: "Les *atomes crochus,* expression proverbiale dont chacun se sert, sont un de ces faits qui restent dans les langages pour démentir les niaiseries philosophiques dont s'occupent ceux qui aiment à vanner les épluchures des mots primitifs. On se sent aimé" (PG, 341).

But if the genius can give expression to his own ideas and thus perfect the language, it is because we naturally assume that words exactly fit ideas. The Balzacian narrator frequently offers this kind of guarantee as justification for situations in the novels. True, the simple correspondence of word and thought holds little dramatic interest; there are few things a narrator can do about it except point to it. In the *Théorie de la démarche* he speaks of man's language as "la traduction de ses pensées" or as "des transformations de la pensée dans la voix" (p. 621). Yet as undramatic as it is, the assumption of such a fit is a necessary premise for

[10]See Gipper, "Wilhelm von Humboldt," p. 14: "Das Gedankeninstrument steht bereit, aber es bedarf des Spielers, um alle seine Saiten zum Klingen zu bringen, und dieser Spieler ist überdies, wenn ihm Genialität beschieden ist, in der Lage, die Klaviatur zu erweitern und Niegehörtes, Ungeahntes zum Ausdruck zu bringen." ("The instrument of thought stands ready, but the player is needed before its strings can resonate; and this player, if he has been granted genius, is also in a position to broaden the keyboard and to express that which has never been heard and never been suspected.") Who, reading these lines, can fail to think of Rimbaud's pity for the wood "qui se réveille violon?"
[11]Barbéris, *Balzac et le mal du siècle,* ii, 1151.

metaphors of mind. Upon it depends whatever veracity can be ascribed to characters, or to a narrator, when they tell us what they think. Action, if not high drama, consequently becomes possible, as in *La Muse du département,* when Bianchon and Lousteau plan to tease Madame de la Baudraye and Monsieur de Clagny to find out if they are having an affair. "Pas mal," Bianchon observes, "il est difficile que l'un ou l'autre ne se trahissent pas par un geste ou par une réflexion" (p. 111). This is the fundamental narrative stance; not to admit it would introduce staggering complexities. It is the unspoken basis of the friendship between David Séchard and Lucien Chardon, for example; and it is significant that the narrator relies on it specifically when he feels that his story may be called into question: "cette phrase est la formule nette et précise des idées qui tenaillèrent le coeur de Lucien" (IP, xi, 295).

Yet to assume the "fit" of word to thought is not to claim that disjunctures are impossible. On the contrary, the obviousness of the assumption makes its opposite richly dramatic. Although in practice words and ideas could hardly be separated from each other, the possibility of *talking about* such a distinction held great fictional potential. As early as *Sténie* we encounter examples of this disjuncture in what the narrator calls "mots extraordinaires."[12] Indeed, one of the most important developments from the early parodic novels through the works of the late 1820s, and on to the *Comédie humaine* itself, is the narrator's increasing awareness of a phenomenon he several times called "varnish."[13] Linguistic varnish is the main subject of the essay *Des Mots à la mode:* "le mot vole de bouche en bouche; il fait fortune; il sert de cachet à l'esprit, à la toilette; c'est le vernis qui

[12]*Sténie,* p. 145.

[13]The term is not very satisfactory, for Balzac clearly uses it in a pejorative way. Whereas varnish on a painting is designed to enhance its lustre and bring out its true qualities, Balzac's varnish is meant as a glittering cover hiding much potential mediocrity. It is the only painterly term he uses in connection with expressivity which has negative overtones. See, on this point, Bernard Vannier, *L'Inscription du corps. Pour une sémiotique du portrait balzacien* (Paris, 1972), pp. 50–52 and 60–64.

donne au tableau toute sa beauté" (p. 36). The theory behind varnish was simple enough: words can be used to
create apparent profundity where there is none at all (p.
34). The "varnish" effect was more than a passing
metaphor to the narrator. Three years after *Des Mots à la
mode*, the narrator recorded an anecdote about John Locke
himself, who was said to have surreptitiously noted down a
drawing room conversation in order to demonstrate its inanity. From this the narrator concludes that all levels of
society are prone to using varnish—the only difference being the thickness of the layer (DL, 286–87). "Varnish" is not
necessarily all bad, of course. *De la propriété littéraire* praises
"le positif" of language, which is described as "un vernis
étendu sur la pensée" (p. 425). Indeed, "varnish" comes
close to an eighteenth-century concept of style: if words are
an inaccurate reflection of thought, the inaccuracy can express itself as ornamentation, as something added to an
assumed kernel of meaning. Dr. Sigier envelops his ideas in
mystical terms and in the bizarre Latin of the Renaissance
without compromising his ability to communicate (Pro, 25);
Séraphîta appears to human observers as a kind of
superior actress using oratorical techniques to put thoughts
and emotions into sentences that are actually quite vulgar
(Sér, 304–305), and Raoul Nathan writes impassioned love
letters consisting of "la pensée revêtue de ses fleurs" (FE,
159). More comically, but using the same technique, César
Birotteau constructs a whole language of clichés and
sonorously empty bombast (CB, 41), while his opponent
Molineux deliberately uses linguistic "varnish" as a business
façade (CB, 89–90).

But the "varnish" metaphor raised the possibility that if
language were a "varnish" it would not be derived from
thought. The "varnish," after all, must come from somewhere other than from the move of consciousness to meet
the world;[14] otherwise it could not be perceived as being

[14]Jacques Derrida has pointed out the uncertain position of "style" or
"form" in his article "La Forme et le vouloir-dire," *Revue internationale de
philosophie*, xxi (1967), 277–99. He quotes a phrase from Husserl that has

separate from the basic expressivity of language. The link
of intention to expression is immediately placed in doubt
by the concept of "varnish." From this it was but a short
step to the possibility that language might be so unfaithful
to thought and intention that the relationship would become random. That is, the possibility of inaccurate correspondence might be pushed to the point where a state of
linguistic freewheeling is reached, in which language exists
without reference to supportive thought. From a sensualist
point of view, such freewheeling could only be viewed as a
malfunction, indeed a quasi impossibility. In contemplating such a situation, the Balzacian narrator is distinctly
stepping beyond the theoretical possibilities contained in
the linguistic speculation of his age. But he is writing fiction, not linguistic theory, and what might have seemed
foolish as a scientific proposition worked eminently well as
a narrative technique. The suggestion of malfunction
nevertheless tends to color his use of the device with implications of wrongdoing, if not evil. Lousteau's successful
attempt to seduce Dinah de la Baudraye is based upon his
ability "singer la passion par des phrases" (MD, 175); he is
one of that species whom the narrator of *La Peau de chagrin*
had called "intriguants riches de mots et dépourvus
d'idées" (97). Certain Balzacian types are particularly
prone to this sort of thing. The man of money, the man of
contracts, the man of law, all replace ideas with words and
emotions with sentences: "leur âme devient un larynx"
(FYO, 331). In these cases there is not even a layer of
"varnish" left; there is only lack of meaning and emptiness.
Félicie, listening to the maudlin compliments of an admirer, "prit le vide pour de la profondeur" (RA, 285);
César Birotteau plays with various names for his useless
hair oil and mistakes this "activité dans le vide" for real

---

extraordinarily Balzacian overtones: "En effet, il ne faut pas trop
présumer de l'image de la stratification; l'expression n'est pas une sorte de
vernis plaqué ou de vêtement surajouté; c'est une formation spirituelle
qui exerce de nouvelles fonctions intentionnelles à l'egard de la couche
intentionnelle sousjacente" (p. 281).

talent in himself (CB, 100–101). Men about town are warned of the "parole vide" of society ladies (FF, 196); and at the farcical extreme we find the incredible salesman Gaudissart explaining that his techniques are based on the same phenomenon. Speculation, he says, lives on words, just as birds live on grains of millet (IG, 9). Like that of Gaudissart, the portrait of the abbé Birotteau is based to a large extent upon the inanity of his freewheeling speech: "doué d'une loquacité vide et sonore comme le retentisse-ment d'un ballon, il prétendait, sans avoir jamais pu don-ner aux médecins une seule raison de son opinion, que les paroles favorisaient la digestion. Mademoiselle, qui par-tageait cette doctrine hygiénique, n'avait pas encore man-qué, malgré leur mésintelligence, à causer pendant les re-pas" (CT, 197).[15] The stupid abbé, for all his being a carica-ture, illustrates the sensualist implication that a disjuncture between word and thought is a mental malfunction of some sort. Although a parody, he exemplifies those dan-gers of language of which both Locke and Condillac had warned. And it was because he was so painfully aware of the potential emptiness and falsity of language that Balzac could observe that "en littérature ou en morale, un homme adroit formule un système, une idée, un fait, par un mot qui sert de science et de raison suprême aux masses" (DAr, 142). It was, once again, the lesson of *La Peau de chagrin.*

The disparity between words and thoughts carries over, obviously, into the self-consciousness of characters. Al-though one may know one's words to be false, one hardly considers them empty. Sometimes, indeed, the disparity can make a character aware of levels of meaning different from those actually expressed. This rather subtle point is made in *La Bourse,* when the painter Schinner sees the poverty of Adelaïde Leseigneur but refrains from making any comment. The difference between his words and his

[15]One wonders if Balzac had noticed a remark by Destutt de Tracy to the effect that "sans nous en apercevoir, nous sommes conduits par les mots comme par les caractères algébraïques." *Elemens d'idéologie* (Paris, 1827), I, 230.

thoughts reveals to him, in a surge of discomfort, a depth of attachment he had hardly been conscious of before (p. 404). Areas of awareness are thus opened up that are difficult to reach in other ways, even though that awareness derives not from expressive embodiment in language but precisely from the absence of such an embodiment.[16]

This is no longer malfunction; rather, the whole sensualist theory of language is being turned inside out. To suggest that words might generate meanings other than those of which the speaker is consciously aware and which he wishes to express literally, is already to suggest that language might function in a significant manner other than that of being the reflection of thoughts or objects. If Hector Hulot can betray to Valérie Marneffe the secret of his daughter's impending marriage to Steinbock, it is because "la parole trahit souvent la pensée" (Be, 121). This is the direction in which *La Peau de chagrin* had been moving; the "betrayal" of language becomes, by its very failure as mimesis, a dramatic narrative device. In the end, language can take over entirely. Men can come to believe in what they say simply because they hear themselves speaking (IP, xii, 406). A person like Raoul Nathan becomes so fascinated with his own eloquence that he eventually believes in, and becomes, what he represents himself as being (FE, 150). Somehow, the sentences of human speech can thus contain "plus d'idées que les mots n'en pouvaient exprimer" (FE, 71). This curious conception of sentences adding up to more than the "sum" of their words points clearly to a freer and more creative concept of language than sensualist theories could have allowed.

[16]At times, the narrator will use freewheeling language as a basis for sarcasm that can amount to downright cruelty. Rose Cormon really longs for a lover, although she would hardly admit this to herself, and the narrator finds irony all too easy: "Sans qu'elle s'en doutât, les pensées de mademoiselle Cormon sur le trop sage chevalier pouvaient se traduire par ce mot: "Quel dommage qu'il ne soit un peu libertin'" (VF, 336). Often, however, freewheeling holds potential for tragedy. Both Véronique Graslin (CV, 140) and Sabine de Grandlieu (B, 294) find themselves in situations where extreme emotion causes involuntary and uncontrolled speech. Sabine's tormented words "mon Dieu" in a moment of crisis "tenaient lieu de toutes ses idées."

Although the hero of *Louis Lambert* has surprisingly, as we have seen, a foot in the sensualist camp, he is also fully aware of alternate possibilities. He recognizes that language is not merely a copy of thought, or sensation, or objects, but also implies some "ideal" of perfect expression: "Après avoir passé des choses à leur expression pure, des mots à leur substance idéale, de cette substance à des principes; après avoir tout abstrait, il aspirait pour vivre, à d'autres créations intellectuelles" (LL, 112). The passage is vague enough, but it seems to say that there is a set of linguistic meanings and values independent of sensation and perception. In a closely related passage, the narrator proposes the possibility that this kind of thought might be the object rather than the cause of language: "Pour lui [Lambert], la Pensée était lente ou prompte, lourde ou agile, claire ou obscure . . . il en surprenait la vie en en spécifiant tous les actes par *les bizarreries de notre langage*" (LL, 197; my italics).[17] Clearly, the word *bizarreries* implies that the relationship of language to thought is not necessarily a logical one, and that language might, in certain circumstances, be far from a "picture" of thought. Lambert sees language as the link between *Pensée* and *Idée,* but in order to act instrumentally it cannot be the product of either. Moreover, if language is "bizarre" (that is, random) its usefulness as an analytical instrument is nil, and the whole question of its correct or incorrect reflection of thought becomes meaningless. This is the view that Lambert ultimately accepts, and we can understand how he is driven to reject sensualism and try to find, like the young Balzac of the *Dissertation,* a "substance idéale" in language that would not constitute a veil between mind and world, but would rather generate both word and world.

Lambert's rather naive discussion of the words "vrai" and "vol" indicates that this "substance ideale" is the musi-

[17] In the *Catéchisme social,* Balzac speculates on the possibility that language might be anterior to thought rather than a consequence of it: "Beaucoup de peuplades ont été trouvées sans la faculté de penser. La pensée a ses lois, et ses lois sont dues à la société, car penser a été la conséquence du langage et le langage est une conquête de la société" (CS, 698).

cality of language, and that the value system it refers to is an aesthetic one. "N'existe-t-il pas dans le mot VRAI une sorte de rectitude fantastique?" he observes. "Ne se trouve-t-il pas dans le son bref qu'il exige une vague image de la chaste nudité, de la simplicité du vrai en toute chose? Cette syllabe respire je ne sais quelle fraîcheur. J'ai pris pour exemple la formule d'une idée abstraite, ne voulant pas expliquer le problème par un mot qui le rendît trop facile à comprendre, comme celui de VOL, où tout parle aux sens" (LL, 49). Comprehension, we must conclude from this passage, tends to mask musicality because an appeal to sense hides the sound of the word. We can see through words with a high sensory content and focus on their referents; whereas we are more aware of abstractions because they lack objective correlatives in the real world.

The idea of the musicality of language as a component of meaning in *Louis Lambert* has been ridiculed as a hopeless naïveté by some critics.[18] Yet it is far from naive if seen less as a seriously proposed principle of linguistics (although it is not entirely to be ignored on that account either), and more as an expression of the narrator's most pressing obsessions. He uses it often, and especially in *La Duchesse de Langeais, Massimilla Doni, Ursule Mirouet, Une Fille d'Eve,* and *Béatrix.* In these works we encounter with fair frequency the insistence that music *is* the ultimate form of language, capable of conveying aesthetic sensations and meanings for which words provide no vehicle. The feelings of General Montriveau as he listens to Antoinette de Langeais playing the organ are, like concepts such as Death, God, or Eternity, beyond words, and achieve only through musicality "le léger point de contact qu'elles ont avec les hommes" (DL, 158).[19] It is significant that the narrator does not talk about music as a divine afflatus, but rather points to its "léger point de contact" with man. Mus-

[18]See especially Hunt, *Balzac's Comedie humaine,* pp. 142–43.
[19]Haskell Block has pointed out something of the same conception in Flaubert, in his "Theory of Language in Flaubert and Joyce," *Revue de littérature comparée,* xxxv, no. 2 (1961), 199.

icality is not the same as the "parole" of the mystic tradition; it has only the significance that man attaches to it, and
it functions at times like a transcendental abstraction only
because man has chosen to regulate things that way. Even
when the narrator makes the claim, as in *Ursule Mirouet,*
that music is a "céleste langage développé par le
catholicisme," the adjective is more a general superlative
than a literal judgement. His statement is based on the fact
that the seven notes of the scale get their names from the
initial syllables of seven verses of a hymn to Saint John
(UM, 64), and he seems moreover to be talking about litur-
gical music specifically. Nowhere, even in this novel of the
spiritual and the supernatural, does he claim that music is
an ineffable or divine language.[20] Even Minna, in love with
the male form of the androgynous angel Séraphîta-
Séraphîtus, claims only that "sa parole . . . est la musique
de la pensée,"—again linking musicality to meaning and
human consciousness rather than to any conception of
divinity (Sér, 223). In the very down-to-earth novel *Le
Cousin Pons,* the hero and his friend Schmucke think of
music as a "heavenly" phenomenon; but it is again clear
that their description is merely a search for superlatives,
since these simple men see in the musicality of language
the link between the physical form of words and their most
cherished aesthetic values (CP, 21).

Musicality in language and music as language are therefore vehicles of human expression, capable of conveying
meaning that does not duplicate the meaning embodied in
the referentiality of words. In this perspective, it seems
quite reasonable, when Antoinette de Langeais realizes in

[20] It should be obvious, then, that I reject Bertault's argument that Balzac's interest in music either springs from, or proves his attachment to, the
church. Here, as in so many other passages, Balzac is writing in a series of
standard expressions, even clichés. See Philippe Bertault, *Balzac et la
musique religieuse* (Paris, 1929), pp. 72–76. The tradition in which Balzac
seems to be situating himself is less Roman than Rousseauesque: Rousseau
considered that melody and words found their simultaneous origin in the
passions. For a penetrating discussion of this point see Jacques Derrida,
De La Grammatologie (Paris, 1967), pp. 280–81 and 306–307.

her organ-loft that General Montriveau is in the convent chapel, that her soul should fly to him on the wings of music, and move with the movement of the sound (DL, 161). The naturalness of this occurence is underscored by the probability that such incidents derive not only from Balzac's theories of thought and language, but also from the nineteenth-century French habit of improvisation, which was, in his lifetime, an important and much admired component of virtuosity. Improvisation was intended specifically to demonstrate the individuality and creativity of the performer. The latter, in a sense, conveyed his own meanings to the audience, not merely those he could express through the interpretation of someone else's composition. This is precisely what occurs in *L'Envers de l'histoire contemporaine,* where Vanda, bedridden and paralyzed except for her face and arms, is reduced to expressing herself through a lap organ: "la malade, dont les doigts avaient retrouvé momentanément de la force et de l'agilité, répéta des variations sur la *Prière de Moïse* que son fils était allé lui acheter et qu'elle avait composées dans quelques heures. Godefroid reconnut un talent identique avec celui de Chopin. C'était une âme qui se manifestait par des sons divins où dominait une douceur mélancolique" (EHC, 425). Similarly, Camille improvises on a cavatina from *Robert-le-diable* (B, 90), touching the heart of Calyste du Guénic; and Ursule Mirouet exercises no small part of her seductive powers over Savinien de Portenduère through her gifts of improvisation and interpretation (UM, 151–52). The narrator's description of Ursule's experience is instructive: he not only makes the stock observation that music communicates "sans le secours de la parole" (UM, 152), but maintains that a performer "peut donner du sens et de la poésie à des phrases sans grande valeur" (UM, 151). The notion that performance could endow a feeble piece of music with meaning parallels the idea that somehow the words of a sentence could add up to more than the sum of their meanings. This "additional" meaning is clearly only potential in the nature of language or music, and could not exist apart from the individuals speaking or performing.[21]

Inevitably, the reach back to some referent not in the world but in language and consciousness came to be couched in familiar antiempirical terms: "Les hommes de science ou de poésie qui peuvent à la fois comprendre et jouir sans que la réflexion nuise à leurs plaisirs, sentent que l'alphabet et la phraséologie musicale sont des instruments intimes du musicien, comme le bois ou le cuivre sont ceux de l'exécutant" (DL, 236). The "musicality" of the poet— taken in its widest sense—is clearly a means of access to those levels of thought we have called *Pensée*, and which are here unequivocally associated with aesthetic valuation. The Balzacian narrator understands that in the improvisational situation the performer becomes a creator, expressing his most intimate thoughts in "quelque sublime mélodie, espèce de poème perdu" (DL, 237). Such a view of language takes us far beyond the possibilities of sensualism, and suggests a way in which language can preserve elements of *Pensée* despite the structuring of *Idée* necessitated by the encounter of mind and world.[22]

The theme of language and music comes to a head in *Massimilla Doni*, where Balzac examines opera and the issue of whether it belongs to the verbal or musical arts. Capraja

[21] The habit of improvisation lived on longer in France than anywhere else. It was particularly deep-rooted in the organ tradition of the Gallican church. Even today it forms an important part of the French organist's training. It is not mere chance that both Vanda and Antoinette are organists. One must also note that it was extremely difficult for the Balzacian narrator to verbalize about such rather elusive concepts. On more than one occasion he falls back on terminology that is still colored by sensualist theories. In *La Duchesse de Langeais* he maintains that music is an art that sensitive souls "développent au gré de leurs souvenirs" (DL, 164); in *Massimilla Doni* he argues that the art of music is to "réveiller par des sons certains souvenirs dans notre intelligence" (Do, 456).

[22] Balzac had touched on the question of musicality as early as *Sténie*, where he observed the power of music to "make listeners think." But as Barbéris had noted (*Balzac et le mal du siècle*, I, 456–57), in *Sténie* each auditor finds his own meaning in Job's improvisations, and each remains essentially isolated. In *La Duchesse de Langeais*, the problem is one of communication and dialogue.

argues in favor of the latter, maintaining that the uniqueness of opera resides in the trill or "roulade." He regrets
the necessary presence of words, which he calls "des intérêts factices"—a merely deforming and interfering element in an art form whose value resides in the exploitation
of its inherent complexities. Capraja's position might easily
be applied to language itself, where "musicality" represents
aesthetic potential. Indeed, the metaphor of music was
simply a way of talking about all those dimensions of verbal
expression that were apart from mimeticism. In the view
of the narrator, music objectifies thought without altering
it. All other arts impose on thought their own specific
forms—"des créations définies"—whereas music leaves
thought pure and unchanged (Do, 431). The lesson of *La
Peau de chagrin* is still with us: art is great to the extent that
it remains in the domain of *Pensée*.

From the concept of the "roulade" it was easy enough to
move to the notion of language as a combinatory function.
Laromiguière had already pointed out the way in which
language permitted man to arrange his thoughts in aesthetically pleasing patterns,[23] and in so doing he was merely
developing an insight already expressed by Locke. If language is thus the vehicle through which thoughts are arranged, then it becomes at the same time the framework
through which reality is perceived. For better or for worse,
man's world becomes a world of words: "La grande question de notre époque," writes Balzac of a political issue, "et
qui l'arrête dans son chemin de progrès, est donc une question de mots" (DG, 550). Indeed, in the essay on artists,
Balzac was prepared to go well beyond contemporary
theory and to dissociate words from ideas as well as from
objects: "Comment faire comprendre à une masse ig-
norante qu'il y a une poésie indépendente d'une idée, et
qui ne gît que dans les mots, dans une musique verbale,
dans une succession de consonnes et de voyelles; puis, qu'il

[23]Pierre Laromiguière, *Leçons de philosophie,* 2d ed. (Paris, 1820), I, 21—
22. This is the published form of the highly popular lecture series given at
the University of Paris in 1811.

y a aussi une poésie d'idées qui peut se passer de ce qui constitue la poésie des mots" (DAr, 142).[24]

The whole proposition that language can be viewed as an autonomous system of signs and not solely as a mimetic device leads to the possibility that language can generate meaning, thus in effect bypassing the classical sensualist process. At a moment of crisis, when Antoinette de Langeais' whole consciousness is reduced to the three words "laissez-vous posséder" (DL, 242)—a phrase which the narrator describes as "horriblement égoiste"—the force of the phrase is not attributable to the mimetic functioning of language, but on the contrary to the fact that the words arouse no recollection nor even any image in the duchess' mind. That is, the phrase itself leads her to discoveries about herself that have nothing to do with memory and experience. Had they, her life might well have evolved in quite other ways than it did. Indeed, in *Le Cousin Pons* we learn that the successive transformations of the meanings of words are largely random, thus undercutting consistent and stable value. The narrator even uses Louis Lambert's term "bizarrerie" to describe the changes (CP, 187). What he calls in the same passage "la vie et la mort des mots" is simply an arbitrary fact; no one can explain the status of a given word at a given moment in time: "Le mépris qui frappe les mots *homme de lettres,* et *homme de loi* s'arrête au pluriel. On dit très bien sans blesser personne *les gens de lettres, les gens de loi*" (CP, 188). There being no logic discernible in the derivation of language from experience, nor anything to be said about the evolution of meaning through time other than its arbitrariness (which does not, of course, contradict the notion that language may produce the wisdom of a nation), the Balzacian narrator as systematic thinker retains very little positive theory about the evolution of language. The only possibility that appears to re-

[24]The same distinction appears in the essay on Stendhal, where Balzac opposes "littérature des Idées" to "littérature des Images"; and in *Illusions perdues* during Lucien's introduction to the practice of journalism (IP, xii, 230).

main is to examine the operation of language simply as a phenomenon in the here and now as against questions of origins, history, and causality.

Meanings might, in this perspective, arise simply from the combinatory nature of language systems; that is, from contexts and use. In *Des Artistes,* right alongside speculations of a distinctly sensualist tone, Balzac identifies what one might call the "contextual system" of language. He describes the actor Talma's ability to endow a simple speech with intense meaning simply by placing it in a particular relationship to gesture and other words. His speech can become "poétique par *juxtà*-position" (DAr, 143). Talma's success in communicating meaning results from the whole performance, not from any a priori categories, sensualist or otherwise. This is the ultimate development of that side of Balzac's theorizing according to which language was neither empirically grounded nor a reflexion of thought. But such a position had some rather grave consequences for a secretary of society. How, one wonders, can a novelist who recognizes autonomous structures in language be certain that his description of society is anything other than the pattern of his own words? Pure contextuality would seem to deny all possibility of verification. But like Molière and Montaigne, two of his intellectual heroes, Balzac opts for a wise and moderate middle ground between the extremes of naive realism and "pure" language. The narrator's description of Calyste du Guénic's declaration to Béatrix provides an excellent view of the compromise he intermittently reached. Rather than record Calyste's passionately inarticulate letter, the narrator devises a series of his own words that convey Calyste's meaning by describing how rather than what he writes: "il y procédait par phrases exclamatives; il y avait beaucoup de ces points prodigués par la littérature moderne dans les passages dangereux, comme des planches offertes à l'imagination du lecteur pour lui faire franchir les abîmes" (B, 183). By so doing, the narrator can claim the security of truth as well as the freedom of imagination. He is released from the chain that links his words to the empirical world except where he chooses to assert that link, and he maneuvers himself into an ideal position from which to induce us to accept what he presents as true on the same basis as what we know to be true.

This is most apparent in the *Etudes philosophiques,* where the narrator is faced with reducing to words a series of largely inexpressible doctrines. The narrator of *Louis Lambert* confesses to such problems as he tries to describe Lambert's system, for a good deal of it is contained in the suggestive qualities of mystical language. Lambert uses a "diction obscure, pleine d'abstractions" which produces "des fantaisies aussi multiformes que peuvent l'être les rêves produits par l'opium" (LL, 81). This raises the whole problem of the status to be accorded to the text. The narrator is attempting to reduce to communicable language a doctrine largely composed of nonverbal perceptions, which nevertheless depends upon verbal expression to exist at all outside Lambert's mind.[25] In a sense, all texts fall short of their ideal of referentiality; but what makes the narrator's attempt even remotely reasonable is the possibility that even if he cannot set forth his hero's doctrine explicitly, he can hope to convey its sense by the contextual arrangement of his own words. While there is no verification or proof of correspondence, the reader in the real world may find some sense of Lambert's doctrines in the reality of the text. It is this elusive concept that the novel suggests in a key passage: "Mais il est en l'homme un phénomène primitif et dominateur qui ne souffre acune analyse. On décomposera l'homme en entier, l'on trouvera peut-être les éléments de la Pensée et de la Volonté; mais on rencontrera toujours, sans pouvoir le résoudre, cet x contre lequel je me suis autrefois heurté. Cet x est la Parole, dont la communcation brûle et dévore ceux qui ne sont pas préparés à la recevoir.

[25]"Et qu'est-ce d'ailleurs qu'une pensée inexprimée?" plaintively asks the narrator of *La Fausse Maîtresse* (p. 33).

Elle engendre incessamment la SUBSTANCE" (LL, 165).[26]
The substance to which the narrator refers is not the empirical world, but the aesthetic qualities of *this text*. At one
stroke, then, he can free himself from the quandary of
verifiable expression, lead us to accept his contextual structure as Lambert's thought, and eliminate the "veil" between
world and word by telescoping the two into one.

Such techniques are not limited to the *Etudes*
philosophiques. The sensitive hunchback Butscha remarks
that "Un poète . . . n'est pas plus la poèsie que la graine
n'est la fleur" (MM, 136), thus locating beauty in the poetry
itself rather than in any external relationships it might
have. In his best moments, Lucien de Rubempré also
reaches this ideal, "cette manière neuve et originale où la
pensée résultait du choc des mots" (IP XII, 234). Even Pons
and Schmucke speculate on the systems of relationships
within music that operate independently of empirical reality. In *Séraphîta* the point is explicitly made that thought is a
kind of language because it is made up of "faisceaux,"
bundles of relationships (Sér, 285).

It would be too much to expect the Balzacian narrator to
have anticipated, much less reached, modern concepts of
contextuality and the assimilation of meaning to use. But
when in *Séraphîta* we read of "la pensée dans la parole" (p.
248), or when Louis Lambert maintains that "[les verbes]
sont empreints d'un vivant pouvoir qu'ils tiennent de l'âme,
et qu'ils restituent par les mystères d'une action et d'une
réaction merveilleuse entre la parole et la pensée" (LL, 49),
it does seem that the Balzacian narrator takes his stand at a
turning point in theories of language and of human
psychology. One would very much like to know more about
the "réaction merveilleuse" of which Lambert speaks, but
the best the narrator can do is to suggest that "Par leur
seule physionomie, les mots raniment dans notre cerveau

---

[26]The similarity in phraseology to that of *La Peau de chagrin* supports my
view that we are dealing here with questions of language and psychology,
not with mystical theology to which, as a matter of fact, Louis Lambert
could not subscribe.

les créatures auxquelles ils servent de vêtements" (LL, 48), which is a neat, if rather unsatisfactory, attempt to cover all possibilities in a single statement.

Unsatisfactory indeed. And yet Balzac returned again and again to the crucial idea of the centrality of language in the human experience, especially in the creation of aesthetic value, which he considered the highest operation of the mind. In *Séraphîta* he identifies language as the locus of the scholar's work: as a "torche jetée dans un souterrain" (Sér, 271). This passage is closely allied to the celebrated text in which Balzac attempted to describe the artist's moment of creative conception, in which, again, language plays a central role: "Un soir, au milieu de la rue, un matin en se levant, ou au sein d'une joyeuse orgie, il arrive qu'un charbon ardent touche ce crâne, ces mains, cette langue; tout à coup, un mot réveille les idées; elles naissent, grandissent, fermentent" (DAr, 137). Language, so difficult, so irritating, so provocative, is nevertheless the radiant center of creativity. Balzac had indeed gone well beyond the romantic cliché that the mind is the lamp that lights up reality; for him, the magic lamp was simply language itself: "L'or et le plaisir. Prenez ces deux mots comme une lumière et parcourez cette grande cage de plâtre, cette ruche à ruisseaux noirs, et suivez-y les serpenteaux de cette pensée qui l'agite, la soulève, la travaille" (FYO, 323). Language is consequently the "propre" of man, and in ways more compelling than sensualism could account for. The narrator of *Louis Lambert* sees the essential human role as the governance of the world "par la Parole ou par l'Action" (LL, 114), the only alternative being a vegetable-like renunciation. Language *is* life; when it must be treated as anything other than the luminous center of our existence, then existence itself becomes impossible (IP, xii, 480). Curiously, we have come back full circle to the Cartesian principle that language alone testifies to the existence of mind. Now, however, it is not merely a means of ascertaining mind in others, but the very stuff of the narrator's own presence in the world. The liminary remark of the *Comédie humaine* might very well have been *dico ergo sum*.

Clearly, then, the dilemmas and contradictions in Balzac's view of language were more than interesting, abstract problems. The inability to reach a "solution" to problems of the word-thought-object relationship risked compromising the narrator's whole undertaking and led to a solution of desperation: both the inadequate mechanistics of empiricism and the insoluble enigmas of contextuality give way before the simple presence of language. Whatever theories may have been evolved on the matter, the overriding fact to Balzac, and to his narrator, is that language *is there*—unavoidable, indispensable, both an obstacle and a plank on the vertiginous route toward the ideal of aesthetic value. The marvelous and satisfying thing about Balzac's theorizing is that despite its vagaries and inconsistencies, it always results from, or ends in, the production of language. There is a kind of "justification par le récit" in operation here; the theories are imbedded in the narration and are, indeed, an important part of it. Theories are therefore not "proven"; they simply constitute language about language, speculation on what is going on in the narrative. Theory becomes part of contextuality, deriving from and leading to narrative events. The latter find their grounding less in allusions to the empirical reality of the July Monarchy than in internal relationships between theorizing and storytelling. Lisbeth Fischer is described, at the beginning of *La Cousine Bette,* as a "paysanne des Vosges, dans toute l'extension du mot" (Be, 42). The "extension" of which the narrator speaks is really the entirety of the following novel, as constituted by the succeeding sequence of words and meanings. The full import of this early statement is clear only in terms of everything that follows; conversely, the body of the novel, insofar as it is an extended description of Bette, must be understood as an internally consistent development of the initial definition. Whether or not *La Cousine Bette* has anything to do with actual peasants from the Vosges is undoubtedly a legitimate question, but quite different from the one to which we are addressing ourselves. The point about *La Cousine Bette* is that although some knowledge of the Vosgian peasantry might give us helpful hints at the outset, no one *need* know anything about such peasants in order to understand the novel as a novel.[27]

In quite explicit ways, the Balzacian narrator is fully aware of the curious position in which he finds himself. One encounters such odd statements as "Le jour où le récit de ce drame recommence . . ." (Be, 190), which seems to indicate how interest can inhere not in the story itself —"drame"—but in the method of telling—"récit." "Récit" is more than just the technique of telling considered separately from events; it is the "drame" *plus* all those techniques of narration which in their turn become part of the "drame." And so to mix "drame" with "récit" is not a simplistic error on the narrator's part; it is the acknowledgement that the two are one. There simply was no other way; spinning true tales about an imaginary world and imaginary tales about a true world leaves one, finally, alone with one's words: "le récit des événements auxquels sont dus de si terribles bouleversements de physiognomie est la seule ressource qui reste au poète pour les faire comprendre" (FT, 208).

"La seule ressource"—perhaps we ought to be thankful for the complexities that enmeshed Balzac and his narrator on the level of theory. His fluctuation between various approaches to theory of language drove him back to the simple—and complicated—act of production. Where Raphaël de Valentin and Louis Lambert had lost themselves in the labyrinths of theory and abstract speculation, Daniel

[27]Once again, curious parallels with German speculation can be pointed out. Humboldt observed, in the introduction to the *Kawi Grammar*, that "the highest and most delicate [picture of language] is not apparent in. . . isolated elements, and can only be observed and felt in continuous discourse, which is so much more proof that language is essentially to be found in the act of its real production. In all investigations which are supposed to penetrate into the real nature of language, only continuous discourse must be thought of as real and primary." Quoted in Hugo Mueller, "On Re-reading Humboldt," *Problems in Semantics,* edited by F. P. Dineen (Washington, D.C., 1966), p. 100.

d'Arthez—the only truly great writer of the *Comédie humaine,* and another alter ego for Balzac himself—does something far different: "D'Arthez avait une oeuvre d'imagination, entreprise uniquement pour étudier les ressources de la langue. . . . C'était une oeuvre psychologique et de haute portée sous la forme du roman" (IP, xii, 74). Here all our themes come together: language, psychology, and narration, underscored by the explicit reference to the novel, which Balzac was inclined in lesser contexts to downgrade in favor of the more mimetically oriented "histoires."[28] Like Balzac, d'Arthez was driven by the perplexities of language theory back to the simple act of writing. For the narrator of the *Comédie humaine* as well, the result of contradiction was not silence, but speech: words spinning out after words in an orgiastic indulgence of freedom, which alone carried any possibility of moving beyond paradox into a language that might—vain dream!—be utterly consonant with a world-become-art. If Balzac recognized that "il y a une grande différence entre les mots et les choses signifiées par eux" (SS, 314), he also recognized that writing was the never-ending attempt to reduce that difference and tear down the veil. Ultimately, theory and practice met in the enigmatic existence of the work of art.

[28] N. Benachevitch, "Le Mot 'roman' dans les romans de Balzac," *Le Français moderne,* xxxi, no. 2 (1963), pp. 81–93. Derrida expresses the same approach in modern terms: "il n'y a pas de signe linguistique avant l'écriture" *(De la Grammatologie,* p. 26).

Problems of Narration

CHAPTER V

Language and Characterization in the
Comédie humaine

Matters of theory, as we have seen, were never "resolved" by the Balzacian narrator. At worst they were simply ignored; at best they were transcended by the assimilation of contradictory attitudes into the act of narration as the needs of the moment directed. But the very telling of a story is the effectuation of a theory. We must, then, examine the practical results of the narrator's interest in themes of language, and first of all in matters of characterization.

Balzac's characterization is based upon his familiar distinction between "types" and "individuals." His interest in this duality may well have arisen from the fact that he was the child of a particularly unsettled period, when linguistic and literary canons were disintegrating and group norms on which "types" could be based were difficult to define. For the Balzacian narrator, there was much less certainty about correctness and acceptability than there had been, for example, for Madame de Lafayette. The Empire and July Monarchy were periods of particularly active social—hence linguistic—mixing.[1] It was symptomatic of the times that there was considerable theorizing about the nature of neologisms, and arguments over whether they represented the movement of people (and lexical items) upwards from below, or downward from on high.[2] There were few periods when standards were so questioned, or people so self-aware.

---

[1]Dagneaud, *Elements populaires,* p. 15.
[2]*Ibid.,* p. 20. Balzac himself relished neologisms; some of these have been studied by Marisol Amar, "Le Néologisme de type hapax: quelques exemples et leur usage chez Balzac," *L'Année balzacienne* (1972), pp. 339–45.

For the modern critic, the question of norms is a tricky one ideed. One might compare a sampling of Balzac's prose with some other sampling of nineteenth-century French, in the hope of discovering some of the "licences and restrictions" that mark the *Comédie humaine*.[3] But aside from the staggering logistics of the operation, it is questionable whether one would end with anything more than a wealth of trivial detail. "Notre chimie," exclaimed Balzac in the *Lettre à Charles Nodier*, "a déjà dévoré tant de nomenclatures. . . ."

Yet it remains one of the commonplaces of both literary criticism and linguistic analysis that the functioning of metaphor is dependent in some degree and in some way upon the principle of deviation from a norm.[4] The Balzacian narrator, interestingly, adopts the *concept* of norms and draws it into his own prose, quite apart from any connection to real norms drawn from the objective world. As elsewhere, the narrator is not trying to be a scholar (although he would be pleased to impress us with his erudition) but a novelist; his norms are those he needs aesthetically rather than those he finds in the real world around him.

To put the matter in another way: the Balzacian narrator is concerned to establish a universe of discourse—a body of language with identifiable, internal standards. In *La Maison Nucingen,* for example, Bixiou tells the story of Godefroid's travels around Europe, during which he frequents all the fashionable spas and resorts. Everywhere he turns, Godefroid encounters "le suprême de volaille, l'aspic et les vins de France" (MN, 366–67). But more than the products of France, what he encounters everywhere is a common life style and a common world view, of which the French lan-

---

[3]The terms are used by William Baker, "Literary Criticism and Linguistics," *Style,* ii (1968), 1.

[4]For a detailed discussion of literary norms, see F. Bar, "La Notion de langue littéraire," *Revue des sciences humaines,* no. 106 (1962), p. 281. The logical problems involved in the notion of stylistic norms have been well set out by Rebecca Posner, "Linguistique et littérature," *Marche romane,* xiii (1963), 50–51.

guage is the most profound expression: "Il entendit parler français à tout le monde, [et] ne sut pas sortir de Paris" (MN, 366–67). The "Paris" from which he cannot escape has actually only minimal connections with the capital of France. Like most of his social coevals, Godefroid carries around with him a certain linguistic—and consequently psychological—framework, given that "la langue sera toujours la plus infaillible formule d'une nation" (DL, 179–80). Such ideas were fairly common in the early nineteenth century. Both the rationalist French tradition represented by Condillac and the German tradition seen in Humboldt envisioned language as the symptom as well as the chief component of cultural unity.[5]

But how does a narrator of fiction establish a unity that is more internal and aesthetic than scientific or referentially descriptive? One way is to isolate the nature of the present from the nature of the past. Neither past nor present may be susceptible to scientific description, but the narrator can play off his conception of the one against his conception of the other. Here the political and linguistic conservatism of the Balzacian narrator meet, as they so often do. He objects to the old use of the word "privilège" because he thinks the rights so designated were real distinctions, not granted favors (Pay, 178); elsewhere he launches into a long discussion of "domesticité," which he claims is now almost invariably misunderstood, and to which he undertakes to restore the original meaning (CA, 166). He has caustic things to say about the new "liberté"—which he says is ill-defined, little understood, and too often equated to revolt and vengeance (VF, 340). Behind the word "égalité" he finds only social insubordination (IP, XII, 485); and he is especially indig-

---

[5] Even Maupertuis had admitted that at the beginning of time all men had the same perceptions, but that in the course of cultural development they attached different signs to different perceptions and thus established the arbitrary differences that exist presently among languages, See Grimsley, *Maupertuis, Turgot et Maine de Biran,* p. 40, for Maupertuis' most characteristic statement. The German version of the same idea has been conveniently set out and analyzed by Gipper, "Wilhelm von Humboldt als Begründer moderner Sprachforschung," *Wirkendes Wort,* XV (1965), 14.

nant that the word "artiste" should lately cover what ought to be called merely "exagéré" (PrB, 391). The Balzacian narrator engages very heavily in this kind of comparative maneuver. In his view, as one can see, semantic changes are often for the worse.

Unquestionably, some of the narrator's most engaging allusions to the past are his evocations of "old-style" conversation. Remnants of the best in "old style" French are found in Evelina's family, where conversation was never frivolous and jokes never cruel (MC, 216). The nostalgia here is two-fold: not merely reaching back to some undefined period of the past, but also to less complex *forms* of society.[6] The narrator regrets the "old" conversation "qui mitonne, comme un potage bien soigné, lorsqu'il ne reste devant la cheminée que trois ou quatre amis de qui l'on est sûr et qui ne répètent rien de ce qui se dit, que chez eux, quand ils se trouvent avec trois ou quatre autres amis bien sûrs" (DA, 285). Despite the touch of sarcasm in the phrase, the narrator does not see in old-style talk the destructive edge he perceives in contemporary speech. A distinction is also implied between city and country talk; quite possibly because of the real or supposed lag in the evolution of country manners.[7] When Victurnien d'Esgrignon comes to Paris he no longer finds the "douce familiarité, l'abandon spirituel des anciennes causeries françaises" he had known at home (CA, 68). In the city fashionable people are too concerned with horses, taxes, income, and politics for "conversation française" to remain what it had been (FM, 8). Not surprisingly, the narrator attributes the

---

[6]Some of this nostalgia may owe something to Balzac's unceasing interest in Rabelais and the Renaissance. This conceptual link between Rabelais and Balzac has been all but ignored. Even the major study of Maurice Lecuyer, *Balzac et Rabelais* (Paris, 1956) passes over it in silence.

[7]Pierre Barbéris has pointed out that nostalgia is not necessarily retrogressive: faced with an inadmissible present and no obvious path to the future, a fictional narrator may have no choice but to revalorize the past as a means of holding himself "in abeyance" until new possibilities become clear. *(Balzac et le mal du siècle,* II, 861). This may be the underlying reason for the narrator's preference for the "good old talk," faced as he is with the corruption of language in a venal society.

decline in conversational quality to modern principles of equality, which eliminate nuances and reduce verbal interchange to a dreary, monotonous process.[8] The younger Hulot is a typical example of the youthful man about town of the 1830s, "lâchant des phrases au lieu de ces mots incisifs, les diamants de la conversation française" (Be, 63).[9]

For better or worse, changes had taken place: quiet, sparkling elegance had given way either to cruelty or empty bombast, and a novelist concerned with change had to take cognizance of the fact. This, perhaps as much as the model of Sir Walter Scott, is what lies behind d'Arthez' advice to Lucien de Rubempré concerning the latter's novel. D'Arthez judges its dialogue to be "diffuse . . . sans couleur," and he suggests that it be replaced by "des descriptions auxquelles se prête si bien notre langue" (IP, XII, 72).[10] D'Arthez has his finger on the mood of the times. The old conversation, which perks by the fire like a good soup, is gone, and Scott is of no help. Even an historical novel must be written in the idiom of the present, and the novelist must change his proportions: "Que chez vous le dialogue soit la conséquence attendue qui couronne vos préparatifs" (IP, XII, 72).

Chief among the qualities of modern speech to which the narrator points is wit of a special and particular nature. Wit, in the Balzacian world, depends upon clarity, logic, and order. Thanks to its clarity, French is "la trompette du monde" (UM, 66); but the tunes the trumpet plays are

[8]Stendhal made similar observations in his descriptions of the receptions at the Hôtel de la Môle, although he was less directly concerned than Balzac with the question of language as such.

[9]To a certain extent the change is attributed by the narrator to the press, for which Balzac had a well-known dislike: "Les conversations françaises se font en iroquois révolutionnaire d'un bout à l'autre de la France par de longues colonnes imprimées dans des hôtels où grince une presse à la place des cercles élégants qui y brillaient jadis" (FF, 200).

[10]One might well wonder whether the dialogues of Scott, as they came through Defauconpret's insipid translations, could have struck Balzac very forcibly. Prioult suggested, many years ago, that Balzac's dialogue owes much more to French romantic drama than to Scott's novels, and his argument seems convincing to me. (*Balzac avant la Comédie humaine,* p. 402.)

often as nasty as they are clever. Mlle de Verneuil sees in society talk both finesse and witty disdain for truth (Ch, 299). She is observing the society of the Revolution, and in her view—which is the narrator's—wit enables men to paint human sentiments with precision because distance and mockery lead to disinterested accuracy, and because enigmatic language puts "toute une aventure dans un mot" (Ch, 298).[11] Innumerable times we hear of the "ton exquis" of Parisian talk (DL, 285), or of its sparkle and brilliance. But in describing a later period, the narrator is rather more prepared to distrust wit than to admire it. Doctor Benassis observes that in France, "l'horreur d'un crime disparaît toujours dans la finesse d'un bon mot" (MC, 208); Antoinette de Langeais discerns among her acquaintances a speech "armée de précautions . . . sèche . . . vide . . ." (DL, 285), and she has good reason to know that the conversation of the salons can quickly turn into cruelty and impertinence (DL, 285). In a world whose laissez-faire is not merely economic, wit is important for survival. Charles Grandet boasts to his country cousin that he is spared the usual Parisian mockery because he is an excellent shot (EG, 351); and that other country girl, Modeste Mignon, is astonished at the sharpness of the "esprit parisien" of her suitor (MM, 218). It is Bixiou who quite naturally sums it all up in a remark to Léon de Lora: "le langage parisien . . . n'a jamais que deux rhythmes: l'intérêt ou la vanité" (CSS, 351).

Was talk in the salons of the "real" Paris quite as destructive as this? One may doubt it. The narrator is trying to convey some feeling for a national consciousness in a quite Humboldtian sense: "the urge by means of which a nation creates validity in language for its thoughts and feelings."[12]

---

[11]The narrator curiously links. wit to the classics, speaking of "cet atticisme si familier à Paris" (H, 311). In high society, atticism becomes "la finesse de l'esprit" whereas in lower classes it turns into "une expression grotesque" (Pay, 60). If one can see how Parisian elegance might be related in the narrator's mind to atticism, it is difficult to see how it is connected to the grotesquerie of the peasantry.

[12]Quoted in Mueller, "On Re-reading Humboldt," p. 103.

But the nation involved here is that of the *Comédie humaine* much more than that of the real France. The narrator regrets the transformation of wit for reasons he presents as historical: but he is primarily interested in exploiting it as a device for describing his present, fictional world. Despite his advertised distrust of wit, he finds in it an inexhaustible source of drama. For the same reason he is prepared to salute the new school—romanticism—for its broadening of the literary possibilities of French: "La langue française lui doit d'avoir reçu une forte dose de poésie qui lui était nécessaire, car elle a développé le sentiment poétique auquel a longtemps résisté le positivisme, pardonnez-moi ce mot, de notre langue, et la sécheresse à elle imprimée par les écrivains du xviiie siècle" (EB, 372). Many characters observe that the dry analytic mode alone does not suffice. Not everyone is a "positivist," and poetry was a way of correcting the corrosive effects of "wit."

There are ample signs of the new "poetic" discourse in the *Comédie humaine,* although it is accompanied by the same ambivalences that characterize the treatment of wit. When the Marquis de Ronquerolles refers to a stylish woman as "un cheval pur sang," the narrator takes the opportunity of welcoming the modern imagery: *"Cheval de pur sang, femme de race,* ces locutions commençaient à remplacer les anges du ciel, les figures ossianiques, toute l'ancienne mythologie amoureuse repoussée par le dandysme" (PG, 245). On the other hand, he ascribes to Bixiou an opinion of modern "poetry" that is harsh, to say the least: "Ces deux amants s'écrivaient les plus stupides lettres du monde, en se renvoyant sur du papier parfumé des mots à la mode: *ange! harpe éolienne! avec toi je serai complet! il y a un coeur dans ma poitrine d'homme! faible femme! pauvre moi!* toute la friperie du coeur moderne" (MN, 387). Despite these uncertainties, however, the narrator quite willingly pictures certain characters—particularly virtuous women—as taking easy refuge in fashionable, "poetic" platitudes. "Que faites-vous, ma mère?" queries a young protagonist in *Une Ténébreuse Affaire.* "Je prie," is the maternal answer (p. 54), "et pour eux, et pour vous." Question and answer are trite enough, but one is really taken aback by the narrator's comment: "mot sublime!" When another mother reveals herself to a long-lost daughter, the intervention of the narrator is positively maudlin: "l'accent avec lequel madame d'Aiglemont prononça ces paroles peignit une effusion de coeur et une émotion intime dont il serait difficile de donner une idée sans employer le mot de sainteté" (FT, 213). How, one wonders, could a narrator sensitive to the "friperie du coeur moderne" come to this? Undoubtedly he comes to it because of what he perceives as the need for something to counterbalance the corrosiveness of modern wit. But poetic discourse is not his strong point, especially when he strains for sentimental effects. True "poetry" comes to him when he is paying attention to something else, as in *Le Lys dans la vallée,* or, as we shall see, in the Vautrin novels.

But wit and poetry were in themselves too abstract to convey adequately the narrator's sense of the governing standards of his language. The process of story-telling involves him in a long series of expressions which he labels as normative by pointing out that they are things "one" says. We learn, for example, that "ce qu'on nomme enfin *une connaissance*" is something between a total stranger and a friend (EHC, 277); that a certain piece of furniture is "[ce] qu'on nomme aujourd'hui un canapé" (V, 7); that an artificial smile is something for which "on a créé le mot *poupin*" (DA, 295); that a self-satisfied smile is something "que l'on nomme familièrement *faire la bouche en coeur*" (Lys, 62). The *Comédie humaine* is filled with terms that depend on "on," and which range from the now-familiar "paix armée" (TA, 41) to the more exotic "mirobolant" (CP, 8).

But who is represented by this "on"? Terms such as "le je ne sais quoi" (B, 279), or "une position" (MR, 320), or "perdu," referring to a woman's reputation (IP, xi, 310), point toward the middle and upper-middle classes. At the same time the vagueness of the "on" suggests that the narrator is trying to avoid any overly-precise identification of a reference group. He is, perhaps, caught in the dilemma of rejecting the values of the social class that gives him his basic language.[13] Yet because he is writing at such a critical juncture in the French intellectual tradition, the absence of strong norms is matched by the idea of "recapturing" his words. Again and again, the nature of language and description is pinpointed as a central issue in his narration. If the attenuation of norms leaves the narrator floating, it also leaves him free; and he uses that freedom to explore language in a way that makes a common linguistic usage the source rather than the result of the cohesive social groupings he called "types."[14] What binds together such disparate characters as Madame d'Espard and Lucien de Rubempré is, ultimately, their common tongue and their membership in a common linguistic world we might call, for want of a better term, "Balzacian prose." The linguistic range we can so name in the *Comédie humaine* includes all those characters whose language is not described as eccentric, and that portion of the narrator's own language which is the base to which eccentricities are compared. "Balzacian prose" therefore includes fictional speakers of all social levels and all geographical locations. The habitués of the *Cabinet des antiques,* distant from Paris and living in a world long since gone by, speak pretty much as do Antoinette de Langeais and her friends in the mainstream of Parisian society; Eugénie Grandet and her cousin Charles, coming

---

[13]Jean Blot has drawn an analogy between the "on" and the Freudian concept of superego: "Jamais visage d'autorité ou du Père n'aura été plus impérieux puisque, faute de lui obéir, je suis menacé d'être détruit. . . jamais plus arbitraire puisque le code auquel je dois me soumettre est le produit de la seul convention, ne se réfère à aucune donnée biologique et n'en refléte aucune. On me vole mon cri et mon désir. Dans le langage, ce n'est pas moi qui parle: c'est eux, c'est *On!"* Jean Blot, "Le Roman et son langage," *Nouvelle Revue française,* no. 198 (1 June 1969), 1159.

[14]Dagneaud has described the "fausse élite" of 1820–1840 in terms that graphically suggest why the Balzacian narrator feels so little security in external norms: "Ce monde voyant et remuant où se mêlent commerçants enrichis, aventuriers de la finance, aristocrates encanaillés, filles de luxe, et ceux qui vivent de la publicité qu'ils donnent à ses goûts où à ses manies: journalistes, chroniqueurs, romanciers, auteurs de comédies ou de vaude- villes" (Dagneaud, *Eléments populaires,* p. 142).

from utterly different social worlds, have more in common linguistically than do Eugénie and her father. It is significant that although the narrator alludes to the "education" in the speech of the capital of Lucien de Rubempré, of Eugène de Rastignac, of Félix de Vandenesse, and of many other social climbers, he never gives the reader direct examples of these transformations. They must all "apprendre la langue," as it is put in *Le Père Goriot,* but we hear nothing specific about this process, nor indeed, is there any observable difference between their original, provincial speech and the presumably sparkling brilliance of their talk after a few months or years in Paris. We are given to understand that their provincialisms have disappeared, that they have polished their wit, or acquired a poetic diction; that they have learned the art of repartee, that they have acquired the latest fashions in jargon. But we never witness these changes, because fundamentally such characters are all insiders from the outset.[15]

Not even in the Parisian adventures of Louise de Bargeton and Lucien de Rubempré is the linguistic transformation explicitly recorded. We are told of no progressive transformation, of no gradual learning process such as was common among provincial "arrivistes" when they first arrived in the capital. Louise immediately recognizes, understands, and responds to the language she hears, and is instantaneously and magically mistress of an idiom she had been capable of using all the time (IP, xII, 30). On his side, Lucien is momentarily dumb-struck "comme un étranger qui ne savait pas la langue" (IP, xII, 30); but like Louise, he recognizes and adopts his true idiom quickly and efficiently. Indeed his very adeptness turns out to be his eventual undoing. In truth, neither of them has emigrated in coming to Paris. Conversely, when the evil Philippe Brideau comes back to Issoudun, his speech is said to reflect "ses

---

[15]Obviously, being an "insider" in this sense has nothing to do with the character's eventual social success or failure. The sharks of the world of the *Comédie humaine* eat each other as well as interlopers.

liaisons à Paris"; but it is hard to see wherein it is particularly Parisian except, perhaps, for an occasional colorful adverb: "Mon cher oncle, vous aimez cette fille, et vous avez diablement raison, elle est sucrement belle! Au lieu de vous *chouchouter,* elle vous a fait aller comme un valet, c'est encore tout simple; elle voudrait vous voir à six pieds sous terre, afin d'épouser Maxence, qu'elle adore" (R, 514).

Clearly, a reference group that ranges from the aristocracy to the vicious adventurer Philippe Brideau cannot be very useful as a standard of usage. It is characteristic of "Balzacian prose" that although it seems centered on the middle class, it is not limited to rendering the middle class language of the objective world. Quite the contrary: "Balzacian prose" is a fictional concept, a normative standard internal to the *Comédie humaine,* worked out as the act of writing took place. One can sympathize, then, with the difficulties the narrator experiences as he attempts to locate and attach value to words. For to have described his own language from within would have involved him in complexities of which fictional narrators became aware only a century later. Faced with these perplexities, he often resorts to the device of trying to describe his norms by pointing to what he excludes from them. The narrator of *Les Chouans* confesses to editing the speech of his military characters as a concession to taste (p. 41); and in a similar way the excessive frankness of medical terminology is largely proscribed, so as not to compromise "la pudibonde phraséologie" of the text (PG, 478). The general trend is to avoid verbal violence and unpleasantness even at the cost of losing some effectiveness, as the narrator of *Un Prince de la Bohème* tells us: "voici ce qu'il me dit, si toutefois les phrases que souffre la typographie parmi les plus violentes injures peuvent représenter les atroces paroles, les vénimeuses pensées qui ruisselèrent de sa bouche" (p. 390). These proscriptions may seem a bit odd in works obsessed with human ruthlessness; but they have point and purpose. The façade of manners and gentility is very thin, and there will be dramatic moments when the narrator's own "varnish" will crack.[16]

More frequently, however, norms are suggested by the overt and identified borrowing of terms from distant semantic fields. The narrator is characteristically frank about the effect he seeks: the *fact* of borrowing is as important as the borrowed item itself, because it permits him to emphasize the sense of norms he is trying to convey.[17] Thus he will borrow the slang word "gars," even though it and its derivatives are "proscrits du discours comme mal séants" (Ch, 18). Actually, the status of the word is irrelevant to the story except insofar as it helps establish the narrator as being at once the guardian of a norm and the honest recorder of a deviation from it. The opening of *La Dernière Incarnation de Vautrin* is probably the most celebrated passage of this sort, with its elaborate justification of the use of thieves" jargon, "dont l'affreuse poésie est indispensable dans cette partie du récit" (p. 164).[18] Like "gars," it serves the purpose of suggesting to the reader what the normative discourse is *not*.[19]

[16]See chapter 6, "The Word-Event."

[17]Dagneaud refers, in this connection, to the "vocabulaire excentrique" spoken by certain of Balzac's characters. In our terms, these are the characters who are defined in part by their exclusion from the world of "Balzacian prose"; but since Dagneaud constantly measures the dialogue of the *Comédie humaine* against what he supposes to have been the real speech of the July Monarchy, he is led to call their speech simply "l'art de mal parler" (Dagneaud, *Eléments populaires*, p. 114).

[18]It is interesting to note that Balzac's dealings with jargons go back at least as far as *Jean-Louis*, where, as Prioult has pointed out, we find the same pseudo-German verbiage that was later assigned to Nucingen and Schmucke (Prioult, *Balzac avant la Comédie humaine*, pp. 130–33). There is also the sailors' jargon in *Annette et le criminel*.

[19]The movement back and forth between these various ranges sometimes provides illuminating insights. One of Balzac's important terms, "probité," indicates in the "langage des filles" the fidelity of the prostitute to her man while the latter is in prison (SM, xvi, 172). An admirable quality indeed, shining through a situation of questionable morality. But who can fail to think of César Birotteau and his "probité": the dogged uprightness of a victim, clinging to a few shreds of honor after having unsuccessfully tried to play the pirate in a piratical society. The situation is basically the same in both cases, although César's behavior is covered by a more respectable veneer. Lest one be too tempted to sympathize with the

In view of Balzac's quantitative, nineteenth-century approach to matters of ratiocination, it is almost to be expected that the phenomenon of borrowing should suscitate metaphors of energy. To move from one semantic spectrum to another—especially from a "lower" one to a "higher" one—requires, in some sense, an expenditure of effort. A character such as Philippe Brideau is more evil than most villains of the *Comédie humaine;* as a result his total rascality can be conveyed only by a term stronger than is natural in "Balzacian prose": "Il était tout simplement devenu ce que le peuple nomme assez énergiquement un *chenapan"* (R, 289). In the same way, only the force of popular speech can properly describe police vehicles, "appelées par le peuple dans sa langue énergique des paniers à salade" (SM, xvi, 1). Not surprisingly, the discharge of "energy," with its implication of penetration and accuracy leads the Balzacian narrator to visual and painterly metaphors. Such images always imply heightened perception and highly adequate expression. The word "ensemble" is borrowed from studio talk in both *Ferragus* (p. 103) and *Les Paysans* (p. 217) to indicate the rightness of parts in a visual and conceptual whole. Efficient communication is thus associated with penetrating vision; below the rightness of surface arrangements, indicated by "ensemble," is the rightness of the underlying structure that the image evokes. The same sense of depth analysis is associated with "écorché," a word used to suggest buried significance as opposed to surface description: "Ici donc," we read in *La Femme de trente ans,* "s'arrête cette leçon ou plutôt cette étude faite sur *l'écorché,* s'il est permis d'emprunter à la peinture une de ses expressions les plus pittoresques; car cette histoire explique les dangers et le mécanisme de l'amour plus qu'elle ne le peint" (FT, 121).[20] In sum, borrowings, energetic lan-

---

perfume merchant, one should recall that he is perfectly well aware that his newly developed hair oil does nothing that any oily matter could not do. He justifies his prices on the grounds that he adds perfume to the oil and puts it in fancy bottles.

[20] Among the many other uses of painters' terms one might especially

guage, and the terminology of painting, all give us clues to what "Balzacian prose" is not. They enable the narrator to overcome the difficulty of rendering at least partially observable a norm that is not designed to portray objective reality, but which is felt to be above all appropriate to the fictional purposes of a text.

Norms, however, do function positively to define social groupings and determine the angle of vision from which these groups are seen. Many of Balzac's early *Monographies* depended upon the identification and interpretive presentation of social groups in terms of their language. One of the most amusing is the grocer:

> Vous allez par une voiture publique à Meaux, Melun, Orléans; vous trouvez en face de vous un homme bien couvert qui jette sur vous un regard défiant; vous vous épuisez en conjectures sur ce particulier d'abord taciturne. Est-ce un avoué? est-ce un nouveau pair de France? est-ce un bureaucrate? Une femme souffrante dit qu'elle n'est pas encore remise du choléra. La conversation s'engage. L'inconnu prend la parole.
>
> 'Môsieu. . . .'
>
> Tout est dit, l'épicier se déclare. Un épicier ne prononce ni *monsieur,* ce qui est affecté, ni *m'sieur,* ce qui semble infiniment méprisant; il a trouvé son triomphant *môsieu,* qui est entre le respect et la protection, exprime sa considération et donne à sa personne une saveur merveilleuse (EP, 19).

That "môsieu" will reappear in the *Comédie humaine* to become the hallmark of a certain kind of vulgarity shared by various small entrepreneurs, office workers, and petty

---

note the use of "repoussoir" to indicate a striking contrast in both *Les Chouans* (p. 74) and in *La Cousine Bette* (p. 258). Picturesque terms are not borrowed exclusively from the language of painting itself; the narrator seeks out such words wherever he can find them. When Canalis finds himself at the end of his creative powers, he is described as having "selon la pittoresque expression des journalistes, vidé son sac" (MM, 60). The association of energy, painting, and crime may have been suggested by a similar juxtaposition in Diderot's *Salon de 1765*. See Donald Fanger, *Dostoievsky and Romantic Realism* (Cambridge, Mass., 1965), pp. 37–38 and 282.

bourgeois. Such linguistic typings are extensive. If the grocer will only say "mon épouse" and never "ma femme" (EP, 19), the peasant for his part will speak only of "sa dame" (Pay, 286). The distinction is not necessarily meant to be referentially exact, but rather to underscore the narrative points of the two texts: the delicate social position of the grocer, and the bluff, hearty ways of the peasant. Not all grocers and not all peasants, needless to say, can be so described. When, therefore, the narrator of *Madame Firmiani* exclaims that there are within the French language as many languages as varieties of Frenchmen (p. 356), he is putting things in reverse order: as a matter of fact, as many linguistically-based types and groups exist as Balzac could create.

There are consequently an astonishing number and variety of generalizations about what groups of people say. Aristocrats such as Madame de Lenoncourt speak the cold, formal language of the old court: "elle prononçait les *oit* en *ait* et disait *frait* pour *froid, porteux* au lieu de *porteurs*" (Lys, 97). The bourgeoisie is also defined to a great extent by its homely, materialistic aphorisms: *"Chacun pour soi, chacun chez soi,* ces deux terribles phrases formeront avec le *Qu'est-ce que cela me fait?* la sagesse trinitaire du bourgeois et du petit propriétaire" (CV, 214). Student talk, artists' jargon, thieves' argot, as well as the talk of small shopkeepers, minor bureaucrats, and peasants, stud the texts. The purpose is not to provide philological history but fiction, and if it is artistically necessary to stress the hermeticism of certain worlds, the narrator is even quite willing to sacrifice comprehensibility. "Portez à trois A tout J-J, tout M-P, et le reste de V-D-O," we read in *La Maison du chat-qui-pelote* (p. 28), a small shop whose problematical survival is at least partially compromised by its owner's conservative jargon.

The difficulty was particularly acute in the Vautrin novels, where the narrator conveys a sense of the uniqueness of the thieves' world by emphasizing the privateness of their language. At times he must resort to translation in order to make himself understood at all: "Vous verrez une terrible danse au préau, pour peu qu'il y ait des *chevaux de retour* (anciens forçats, en argot)" (SM, xvi, 46). At times he simply gives us the translation alone: "Que veux-tu? Que dois-je faire? dit madame de Saint-Esteban dans l'argot convenu entre la tante et le neveu" (SM, xvi, 208). Eventually, we become sufficiently accustomed to a small vocabulary to be able to follow brief passages of dialogue, such as a conversation between La Pouraille, Le Biffon, and Fil-de-soie (SM, xvi, 179), or one between Jacques Collin and a policeman (SM, xvi, 204).

Because norms are not meant primarily to portray groups of persons in the real world, they frequently operate in ways that have nothing to do with referential realism. The word "gobichonner . . . mot populaire mais expressif," for example, explains not only Sylvain Pons' love of good food in a certain dinner scene, but also opens up the whole contrast between his harmless, self-indulgent consumption and the gluttony of his relatives (CP, 14). As in many similar cases, the word itself is not repeated, although there are myriad allusions to the themes of eating, collecting, and possessing.[21] A major theme of *La Cousine Bette* is summed up in the word "excentricités," which is defined as a "mot trouvé par les Anglais pour les folies non pas des petites mais des grandes maisons" (Be, 42). In a complex way, this sentence points to all the varieties of madness with which the novel is concerned. Bette, Baron Hulot, and even Adélaïde, are no ordinary cases to be confined to an asylum (that is, to the *petites maisons*); at the same time, the family's obsession with wealth and with social appearances (that is, with the prerogatives of a *grande maison*), is ultimately the cause of most of the drama and

---

[21]Another group of expressions refers to the hunting necessary to satisfy gluttony. When his wealthy cousin begins to suspect that Pons might indeed possess treasures, we get a typical instance: "Ah! ca, pourquoi ne le voit-on plus? demanda le président de l'air d'un homme qui ressent une commotion produite par mille observations oubliées dont la réunion subite *fait balle,* pour employer une expression aux chasseurs (CP, 74–75).

tragedy of the story. None of these characters is insane, yet all have qualities that take them well out of the ordinary patterns of behavior; "excentricités" leads us into a network of expressions that keep this problem constantly in the forefront as the main concern of the text.[22]

The process of making norms can obviously be driven to unnecessary extremes. There is no need for the narrator to assert that all upper-class women torment their husbands with "des mots piquants" in order to assert that Madame Hulot does so (Be, 38); nor need he claim that "toutes les mères appellent leurs filles qui ont vingt-trois ans, des *fillettes*" (CB, 86), when only Madame Camusot does it. There seems to be, in such cases, an almost irresistible drive towards generalization and law-making; yet in truth these are not laws at all. Such statements merely mask under their authoritative tone the fact that they are formalized accentuations of specific points the narrator wishes to make at certain junctures in the text. If these needs are contradictory from one place to another, the "law" can adapt easily to changed requirements. We are told, in one place, that in the provinces "l'ennui est le fond de la langue" (FP, 225); and elsewhere that in Touraine, "la jalousie forme, comme dans la plupart des provinces, le fond de la langue (CT, 212). Neither ennui nor jealousy is an element of descriptive linguistics; but each is an important element of the text in which the generalization appears. All such statements, of course, contain their grain of truth; otherwise they would

---

[22]The statistical importance of such words must not be overestimated. Many of them occur only a few times, and some occur only once. What is important is the way their centrality to main themes is underscored. "Faire la cour" and "modestie" are singled out in *Modeste Mignon* (pp. 96 and 131); Rose Cormon has "la beauté de diable" (VF, 311), although in the Garnier edition (p. 89), she is said thus to be "improprement appellée;" M. Phellion is "épaissi . . . pour se servir du terme de la langue bourgeoise" (Bou, 90); la mère Cardinal is said to have "fait plus d'une journée la nuit" in the "langage à figures hardies" spoken in the market-place (Bou, 190); and the marital rights of husbands are summed up in certain provinces by the verb "jouir" (Pay, 285). The point in such cases is not linguistic description, but the location of the discourse with respect to "Balzacian prose" from which it deviates.

not be effective at all. But the purpose of appealing to a norm is merely to lend credence to the case at hand.

Such elaborate attention to typified language obviously points to more than a facile exploitation of "local color," as Roland Barthes has implied.[23] Especially in the case of the thieves' jargon, a particular language means a particular world view: "il n'y a rien de sacré pour la haute pègre. Ces sauvages ne respectent ni la loi, ni la religion, rien, pas même l'histoire naturelle, dont la sainte nomenclature est, comme on le voit, parodiée par eux" (SM, XVI, 164). If the thieves' language is brutal, terrible, and merciless in its sarcasm, it is because its speakers see life that way. We should not be led astray by the slightly eighteenth-century flavor of the narrator's allusion to "savages," or by a certain element of romanticizing in his descriptions. What he says of the language of criminals might be said equally well of their life and their world view: "Tout est farouche dans cet idiome. Les syllabes qui commencent ou qui finissent les mots sont âpres et étonnent singulièrement" (SM, XVI, 165). The savagery was contemporary, not historical; it was European, not Melanesian.[24] Between the wit of the Parisian salons and the jargon of criminals there was perhaps not very much distance.

But the jargon of the underworld also enables the narrator to find again his much-sought ideal of poetry. He is fascinated by *"douze plombes crossent,"* by *"une largue,"* by *"la plume de Beauce,"* by *"rincer une cabriole [sic],"* by *"se piausser,"* and other expressions.[25] Because of its adversary position, the counter-language of the underworld constantly grows and creates: "L'argot va toujours, d'ailleurs! Il suit la civilisation, il la talonne, il s'enrichit d'expressions nou-

---

[23]Roland Barthes, *Le Degré zéro de l'écriture* (Paris, 1965), p. 65.

[24]This metaphor of the savage must be distinguished from the metaphor of *evil* savages who, says the narrator of *La Cousine Bette,* "pensent beaucoup et parlent peu" (p. 46). Bette herself is such a savage, as are certain other individuals of the *Comédie humaine,* but this is quite a different matter from the eighteenth-century model of "primitive" man evoked in *Splendeurs et misères des courtisanes.*

[25]"Cabriole," which appears in the Conard edition, is an obvious misprint for "cambriole," which is correctly given in *Pléiade,* V, 1015.

velles à chaque nouvelle invention" (SM, xvi, 166). The real poetry of argot is grounded in hard experience: "Quand on songe que le bagne se nomme *le pré,* vraiment ceux qui s'occupent de linguistique doivent admirer la création de ces affreux vocables" (SM, xvi, 166). In his fascination, the narrator himself comes to share the poetry and energy of argot, and we find him carried away by the very qualities he tries to convey: "En argot on ne dort pas, *on pionce.* Remarquez avec quelle énergie ce verbe exprime le sommeil particulier à la bête traquée, fatiguée, défiante, appelée Voleur, et qui, dès qu'elle est en sûreté, tombe et roule dans les abîmes d'un sommeil profond et nécessaire sous les puissantes ailes du Soupçon planant toujours sur elle. Affreux sommeil, semblable à celui de l'animal sauvage qui dort, qui ronfle, et dont néanmoins les oreilles veillent doublées de prudence!" (SM, xvi, 165).

How appropriate that the Balzacian narrator, so acutely sensitive to the crimes and horrors of the July Monarchy, should find its most poetic tongue in the language of its criminals. No wonder that a priori norms should be so hard to define in a world where opposites are established in terms of each other, where the prison yard is connected to the aristocratic salon, where Vautrin is linked to his most distinguished opponents. "On voit," the narrator remarks somewhat wryly, "qu'à tous les étages de la société les usages se ressemblent, et ne diffèrent que par les manières, les façons, les nuances. Le grand monde a son argot. Mais cet argot s'appelle le *style*" (SM, xvi, 231).

But norms, we have said, imply deviations. In the case of such characters as old Grandet, Madame Olivier, Baron Nucingen, or Madame Cibot, the narrator's intentions seem to run counter to the basic drive towards generalization. Although Baron Nucingen's linguistic traits, for example, are said to be socially determined, there is much in them that pertains to the baron alone. There are other Germans in the *Comédie humaine;* yet despite the narrator's occasional remarks about the mess they make of French, they are all perfectly comprehensible. Nor does the narrator make any sustained effort to record the deviant French of Spaniards, Englishmen, or Italians. The baron's peculiar French, as well as the narrator's excruciating transcriptions of it, have nothing to do with the technicalities of jargons, dialects, or argots, but spring rather from narrative necessities. Part of this relates to the baron himself; a little-noticed passage indicates that he knows perfectly well what he is doing, and that he uses his bad French as a business technique: "Le fin baron, pour avoir des motifs de revenir sur des paroles bien données et mal entendues, avait gardé l'horrible prononciation des juifs allemands qui se flattent de parler français" (CB, 244). At the same time, the baron's speech is part of a narrative strategy that makes of him the most ruthless yet most helpless, the most naive yet most despicable, victim in the *Comédie humaine*. Even though the Alsatian accent is described as "la glu la plus adhérente de toutes les matières collantes" (MN, 385), it is the baron who falls into Vautrin's trap, not vice versa. We are not asked to believe that all German bankers speak an atrocious gibberish, or that all miserly peasants stutter, or that all lady door-keepers ride their manias on waves of logorrhea; but we are told that Nucingen, Goriot, and Madame Cibot do these things. Their individuality is an artistic, not a scientific, phenomenon. Within the "types" we must distinguish "individuals."

We thus find ourselves at the intersection of two concepts: what one might call the *animal loquens,* a type possessing generalized language ability; as against the *homo parlans,* the individual finding his particular speech within the general human capacity. If groups could have their collective "thought worlds," there was no reason why individuals could not have theirs, objectified in both cases by patterns of speech.[26]

[26]On this aspect of romantic theory, see Chomsky, *Cartesian Linguistics,* p. 21. Balzac was almost surely unaware of German debates on the question of universal as against individual languages; but enough was being said in France to color his own speculations on the subject. Bardèche has some penetrating pages on the various techniques of dialogue used by Balzac, and the way in which excessively elliptical dialogue, entirely in-

One of the troublesome aspects of this approach, from the point of view of the practicing novelist, was "fitting" the speech of a character into the narrator's general prose. Both as a presence within the story and as an outsider determining it, the narrator has his own language which includes that of other characters. How does he deal with the difficulties that arise when their language is far removed from his own "Balzacian prose"? The perplexity is most clearly set out in *Béatrix: "Tirer une carotte!* . . . Ce mot est devenu si populaire qu'il faut bien lui permettre de salir cette page. D'ailleurs, en pénétrant dans le treizième arrondissement, il faut bien en accepter le patois pittoresque" (p. 323). The contradiction between "salir" and "pittoresque" pinpoints the narrator's unease: his sensitivity to standards of respectability conflicts with his need to fit the colloquial expression into his language in an aesthetically satisfying way. By pointing out his own dilemma, he attempts to establish both his characters' linguistic autonomy, and his own normative preferences. Where characteristic traits of speech are technical, there are no stylistic dilemmas;[27] equally, as long as characters belong to the middle and upper classes, there was little apparent conflict between their dialogue and the general language of "Balzacian prose." They spoke conventionally, and conventions of their speech were generally the same as the conventions of literary discourse. But alongside those characters whose speech is unexceptionable, we encounter many characters who speak "their own language." The four servants of Rose Cormon see their position deteriorating as the elderly lady grows ever more nervous and difficult: "Mais, comme ils disaient dans leur langage, ils avaient mangé leur pain

---

terior to individual thought-worlds, is explained and enlarged upon by the narrator through successive editions of certain novels. Bardèche, *Balzac romancier*, pp. 579–83.

[27] Thus, "la tête du pays" indicates the best vinyard in a given region (EG, 281); "part à goinfre" indicates a secret profit (MN, 405); du Tillet uses an "homme de paille," which necessitates a brief explanation (CB, 68); "exécuter" is explained as a financial term meaning to ruin (FE, 201); etc.

blanc en premier" (VF, 323). If old Sauviat redoubles business activities, it is because he wants to make up for "ce que, dans son langage, il appelait les déchets de sa fille" (CV, 12). Such traits illuminate the character in a far more effective way than would many a lengthy description. One should observe, moreover, that the narrator tends to reduce lower-class speech to caricature. When he is dealing with shopkeepers, minor bureaucrats, and employees, the social separation he feels from them is indicated by the clear distance of their language from "Balzacian prose." The narrator even overcomes his dislike of cruel wit to emphasize this chasm at the characters' expense: "il est à remarquer, dans l'intérêt de cette histoire, que l'avocat se tenait au plus près de ces esprits vulgaires; il naviguait dans leurs eaux, il leur parlait leur langage. . . . Parmentier, *l'auteur de la pomme de terre,* valait trente Raphaëls; l'homme au petit manteau bleu lui paraissait *une soeur de charité.* Ces expressions de Thuillier, il les rappelait parfois" (Bou, 63). Language used as a descriptive trait could hardly be more judgemental. Minard, in the same novel, is treated quite savagely; he is a "ballon bouffi" largely because of his language: "Ces mots, qui ne disent rien et répondent à tout: progrès, vapeur, bitume, garde nationale, ordre, élément démocratique, esprit d'association, légalité, mouvement et résistance, intimidation, semblaient à chaque phase politique inventés pour Minard, qui paraphrasait alors les idées de son journal" (Bou, 38). Equally dull and equally parodied in his language is M. Phellion, who hopes that "le Roi (Roâ) daignerait récompenser ses services" (Bou, 89), who intones the telltale "môsieu" while modestly asserting that "j'ai fait mon devoir (devouar) et voilà tout (toute)" (Bou, 92). Interestingly enough, his friend La Peyrade also uses the "môsieu" of ill repute, in the course of a long, irrational, and nearly incomprehensible compliment to Phellion (Bou, 95). And their collective and typically French preoccupation with language is parodied shortly thereafter at a gathering: "j'ai mis un mot à Phellion, dont la femme est liée avec madame Pron, la successeur . . . La successrice, dit Madame Minard. Eh! non, redit Thuillier, ce serait la successeresse, comme on dit la mairesse" (Bou, 101).[28]

This kind of loquacious stupidity eventually results in individual languages clearly distinguished from "Balzacian prose." To such an extent do Jérôme Rogron and his sister carry on their mindless babble that it eventually forms a "vocabulaire Rogron," of which we are treated to several specimens.[29] The Rogron lexicon is matched by the "Dictionnaire Vermichel et Fourchon" (Pay, 68 and 217), by the "vocabulaire Saillard" (E, 61), by the "style Phellion" (E, 93), and other individual "languages." Such language is more than a standard technique of dialogue: its items have a significance beyond conventional and accepted usage. They become emblematic symbols of the unique qualities of the character—"thermometers," as the narrator once aptly says, of the inner temperature of the mind (Bou, 154). The most striking instance of emblematic language is surely the sly question of Baron Hulot who, after being forgiven and welcomed back by his family, asks his wife if he can bring his teenaged mistress with him (Be, 494).[30] These lexicons are profoundly rooted in the human psyche, and can amount to a veritable embodiment of the self. The child-hero of *L'Enfant maudit* hears such a "retentissement de l'âme" in certain words that those around him

[28]The same kind of folk-etymology is exploited in *Le Père Goriot* a propos the word "armoire," which becomes "ormoire" (PG, 238).

[29]"Il faut élever les enfants à la dure. . . . Vous feriez de Pierrette une *picheline* (P, 75); "Eh! bien, comment as-tu dormi? . . . Ne me trouves-tu pas le teint *mâchuré*" (P, 102). Rogron also habitually remarks, when there is fine weather and customers spend little time shopping and much time strolling, "Mauvais temps pour la vente!" (P, 20).

[30]In their emblematic function, it is not necessary that individual lexicons observe the general rules of language. Peyrade establishes for himself a "langage particulier," which consists of "des mots où la langue était souvent violée, mais, par cela même, énergiques et pittoresques" (SM, xv, 146). Nor need the lexicon even be vocalized. Marius, the master salesman, keeps up with the times by using the word "client" instead of the old "pratique"; but in his own mind he uses neither: "Pour lui vous êtes une *tête* plus ou moins susceptible de l'occuper. Pour Marius il n'y a plus d'hommes, il n'y a que des *têtes*" (CSS, 336).

must watch their language in order not to wound him (EM, 432). Louis Lambert must create new words or revise old ones in order to express his innermost self (LL, 90); and language assumes, between Félix de Vandenesse and Madame de Mortsauf, a series of "formes énigmatiques" which, through "de mystérieuses significations," enable these two to communicate with an intimacy and a perfection rarely achieved in human dialogue (Lys, 114–15).

As deeply seated as these lexicons may be, they are significant within the story only to the extent that they are used in communication. Indeed, it is externalized language alone that allows the selfhood of characters to become visible in the human context.[31] And it is precisely that externalization—its relative clarity or opacity, its relative honesty or falsity—that lies at the heart of so many Balzacian dramas. We have come quite a distance from the *Dissertation sur l'homme:* externalization involves not theorizing about abstract man or about groups, but rather the concrete acts of specific characters as they encounter other specific individuals. This is the heartland of the Balzacian jungle. At the same time, the weight of his eighteenth-century philosophical heritage leads the narrator to equate verbal externalization with rationality. We observe calculative forces at play between characters, and we may even glimpse the hidden motivations behind them when they are inadvertently revealed. But we never penetrate deeply into psychological interiors—nor do Balzacian creatures themselves.[32] The one direction in which desire and will

[31] Per Nykrog has observed that in the *Comédie humaine,* "l'expérience humaine subit l'action de la personnalité; elle ne peut sortir du sujet qui l'éprouve que transformée selon la constitution psychique de cette personnalité." See *La Pensée de Balzac dans la Comédie humaine* (Copenhagen, 1965), p. 31. He goes on to assert that *Les Proscrits,* interpreted this way, constitutes a veritable theory of communication. Aside from the difficulty of knowing what one can mean by "l'expérience humaine" divorced from the concreteness of individual existence, it seems obvious that all texts imply a theory of communication. The interest of *Les Proscrits* is that it is based not upon some abstract model of "human experience" but upon specific language: its chief incident is the sermon delivered by Sigier and its effects upon an assembled congregation.

[32] This is not to say that some characters may not be self-aware in the

never move in the *Comédie humaine* is that of self-discovery. There is consequently description, revelation, even some illumination of psychological motives, but there is little self-comprehension. That kind of development is too often incompatible with the dramatic externalization by which psychological drives are made explicit in the *Comédie humaine*. Things happen; they rarely evolve. This is the basis of the sparring and maneuvering in which so many Balzacian characters engage. Just as Baron Nucingen uses his bad French as a strategic device, old Séchard develops a kind of talk that constitutes a veritable "guêpier où il ne fallait pas mettre le pied" (IP, XII, 474). Yet even though this kind of characterization may not entirely satisfy modern taste, it has its own legitimacy: the legitimacy of an "interior theater," not in the round, but along the traditional line that moves from the world to the mind and, sometimes explosively, back to the world again.

And yet there is something more. Even in the case of the superior man, rational interaction with external reality is not always dominant. There is also the steady functioning of the mind on a level other than that of reason, a level that Balzac might have called the "preverbal" or the "prerational," if he had had those terms, but which he called *Pensée*. By the time the initial psychic energy of *Pensée* is transformed into *Idée* and encounters the world, it is true that rationality has shaped it, and we have little chance of knowing to what degree it has been transformed, or, even in what sense "word" or "intention" could be said to exist before being rendered explicit in the world. There are, however, suggestions in the *Comédie humaine* of mental ac-

---

middle of the social game; but the process of progressive self-understanding is not their primary concern. Even Madame de Mortsauf, that exquisitely sensitive creature, gives Vandenesse advice that might have come from one of the social climbers of *Illusions perdues:* "Cultivez donc ma mère . . . elle vous introduira dans les salons où vous acquerrez cette fatale science du monde, l'art d'écouter, de parler, de répondre, de vous présenter, de sortir; le langage précis, ce *je ne sais quoi* qui n'est pas plus la supériorité que l'habit ne constitue le génie, mais sans lequel le plus beau talent ne sera jamais admis" (Lys, 155).

tivity, of drives and desires that emerge independently—for better or for worse—of the thrusts and impressions of the world. This central core of spontaneity surfaces in a steady series of minute behavioral events that open startling momentary perspectives on the inner existence of Balzacian characters. Since the narrator's methodology substitutes the unravelling of mysteries for the classical, logical analysis of behavior, the devices he uses depend largely on the possibilities of disjuncture and contradiction between "inner" and "outer" man. The most common one first appeared in the novels of 1822: it is the mechanism of "laisser échapper," now enormously expanded and enriched.[33]

In its developed form, the "laisser échapper" device must be related to the long-standing eighteenth-century debates on gesture. The argument bore on the place of gesture, considered as the first link forged by man between the arbitrary sign and the object designated. Furthermore, the discussion of gestures—including verbal gestures—raised the much wider question of form versus movement. The full significance of Balzac's "laisser échapper" cannot be seen except in the context of this debate.

Balzac, to be sure, might have come across the question of gestural language in the works of his favorite illuminist writers—Madame Guyon and Saint-Martin had both taken up the matter in their own ways[34]—but he more probably encountered the notion in the course of his classical education.[35] In addition, Balzac discovered at some point an

[33] See chapter 2, p. 50.

[34] Saint-Martin wrote extensively on the "harmonious action" that links man to divinity in *De l'esprit des choses* (Paris, an 8; see especially Vol. 2, 75–76); Madame Guyon took the traditional mystic attitude that gesture is an interior phenomenon—the turning of the soul towards God—and that all physical acts are but degraded forms of the transcendental Act.

[35] Cicero had remarked on the correspondence of body and soul in an aphorism widely quoted in such contemporary compendia as the *Dictionnaire de grammaire et de littérature* (Liège, 1789), ii, 417: "Chaque mouvement de l'âme a son expression naturelle dans les traits du visage, dans le geste et dans la voix." This line of thought came into French philosophy through such men as Montaigne, La Chambre, Buffon, and Lebrun.

obscure seventeenth-century anatomist whose work seemed sufficiently impressive to merit enshrinement in *La Théorie de la démarche:* Giovanni Alfonso Borelli, author of a work called *De Motu animalium.*[36] To the modern eye, Borelli's book is chiefly impressive for its engravings; the intellectual level of his treatise is sufficiently demonstrated by his observations that animate creatures are able to move as long as they are alive, but lose the faculty of motion when they are dead. His work is chiefly concerned with the geometry and physics of muscular action, and is full of striking diagrams. But he did make two observations that must have caught Balzac's eye: he described motion as having its source somewhere other than in the physical body itself (he variously called this source "anima" or "virtu"),[37] and claimed that this quality manifested itself in the body through a spiritual humor whose existence is proven by the very effects it produces.[38] Circularity of reasoning to one side, Borelli's work tended to suggest that human motion—and thus human life—could not be explained on purely materialistic premises. His argument was conducted in the light of seventeenth-century theological debates, of course; but read in the context of post-sensualist dissatisfactions, it must have seemed very striking indeed.

Balzac could not have missed, moreover, the discussions of gestural language that filled the works of the sensualist and ideologist philosophers. Arnauld, Condillac, and Tur-

[36]Giovanni Alfonso Borelli, *De Motu animalium,* 2 vols. (Rome, 1680–1681).

[37]Borelli's curious and amusing Latin makes great play on words and word roots. His explanation of "anima" is typical: "Quod nempè principium, et causa effectiva motus animalium sit anima, nemo profecto ignorat, cum animantia per animam vivant, et durante vita motus in eis perseveret; Extincto vero animali, idest non amplius anima operante, machina animalis omninò iners, et immobilis relinquitur." (Given that the soul is the efficient cause and principle of animal motion, no one can be ignorant of the fact that animals live through the soul, and that during life, motion persists in them; on the other hand when the animal is dead, that is, when the soul is not operating, the animal machine is completely inert and is left motionless.) (I, 2).

[38]Evincitur ab effectibus ipsis, quos producit" (made evident by the very effects it produces) (II, 317).

|155|

got had all agreed that gestures were the most primitive, and consequently the most spontaneous, form of human expression. Condillac had asserted unequivocally that all states of the soul could be expressed by bodily motions, thus establishing the familiar sensualist link between "inner" and "outer" man. Destutt, on the other hand, appeared to see in gestural language something more than just another form of sensualism: he held that if gesture is the poorest and least developed of all systems of expression, it remains the most "energetic" and most vehement, and the only one we can use when excessive passion deprives us of rational, conventional language.[39] After all has been swept away, Destutt maintains, physical gesture remains as an immediate way of asserting oneself in the world.[40]

But it was Lavater who had the most direct influence upon Balzac; specifically, Lavater as presented in an edition containing an important introduction by Moreau de la Sarthe.[41] Moreau's essay dealt at great length with the theory of gesture as it relates to acting. He discerned two schools of acting: one held that gesture was the natural result of emotions, and should be allowed free, spontane-

[39]Destutt de Tracy, *Elémens d'idéologie* (Paris, 1827), i, 215–16.

[40]Balzac's interest in physical gesture as a means of communication might also have been fed by a knowledge of the work of the abbé de l'Epée, the celebrated developer of a sign language for the deaf and dumb. De l'Epée insisted that the deaf and dumb were capable of gestural language quite superior to the gestures of animals, to which the attempts of the handicapped to communicate had been assimilated. Underlying his efforts was the common 18th-century view that gesture was "more natural" than words, and consequently less dependent on conventions. As a consequence of his work, the deaf and dumb were gradually recognized as being normal people, rather than the victims of a species of idiocy. The work of de l'Epée and his followers (especially Roch-Ambroise Cucurron de Sicard) was disseminated far beyond the small group of deaf-mute specialists because, like Diderot's work before them, their books had considerable philosophical implications. For a succinct discussion of the subject, see James R. Knowleson, "The Idea of Gesture as a Universal Language in the xviith and xviiith Centuries," *Journal of the History of Ideas,* xxvi (1965), 495–508.

[41]The edition alluded to here is G. Lavater, *L'Art de connoitre les hommes par la phisionomie. Nouvelle édition augmentée d'une Exposition . . . par Moreau*

|156|

ous play; the other maintained that gesture was a voluntary movement, and should be consciously cultivated and perfected by the actor. Moreau associated himself with the latter view, citing Lessing as an authority. Moreau's essay argued for man's ability to imitate, mask, or conceal inner motivations; Lavater's own work, on the other hand, argued for the *impossibility* of doing these things.[42] Indeed, Lavater anticipated objections to his theory by asserting that the observer who thinks he discerns external features that do not reflect inner selfhood has simply not been subtle enough.[43] "Masks," in his view were not possible. As far

---

de la Sarthe, 5 vols. (Paris, 1820). This may have been the edition Balzac is known to have acquired in 1822. Furthermore, it is worth noting that the work is full of hommage to Raphael, and has many engraved reproductions of his portraits. One allusion to Raphael is so "Balzacian" in tone that one might be tempted to speak of a "source": "Albert Dürer mesura l'homme, Raphaël le mesura aussi; mais il le sentit et le pénétra: le premier copia la nature en artiste . . . l'autre traça l'idéal avec ses proportions, et ses dessins n'en furent pas moins l'expression de la nature. Le physionomiste purement savant mesure comme Dürer; le génie physiognomonique mesure et sent comme Raphaël" (I, 273). Lavater's influence on Balzac was established very early, and needs no further elaboration. Prioult goes so far as to claim that by 1824 Lavater had provided Balzac with the framework for his future novels *(Balzac avant la Comédie humaine,* pp. 207–208). The claim has been considered exaggerated, and justly so. Pierre Abraham has undoubtedly taken the Lavaterian interpretation farther than anyone else, but even he is cautious about the extent of Balzac's direct debt. See Pierre Abraham, *Créatures chez Balzac* (Paris, 1931). Much of this theory rests on the emphasis Lavater gave to the eyes as a key to character, but this was obviously merely a reformulation of the ancient doctrine of the eyes as windows on the soul. A much more modern interpretation of the role of the eyes can be found in Lucienne Frappier-Mazur, "Espace et regard dans la *Comédie humaine,*" *L'Année balzacienne* (1967), pp. 325–38. The face and body as general systems of signs coherently exploited by the Balzacian narrator have been exhaustively studied according to semiological methods in Tahsin Yücel, *Figures et messages dans "La Comédie humaine,"* Tours, 1972.

[42]Although Moreau does not mention Diderot, the philosopher's *Paradoxe sur le comedien* springs immediately to mind. Moreau does cite the work of J. J. Engel, director of the Berlin theater, who had published a celebrated treatise, *Ideen zur Mimik,* in 1788, of which a French translation, *Idées sur le geste et l'action théâtrale,* had appeared in 1795.

[43]Lavater, *L'Art de connoître,* I, 366–75. Lavater's own "subtlety" is staggering. His work consists chiefly of correlating emotions with various physical features; his lists of the attributes of noses, chins, foreheads, and so on are as amusing and vague as they are long.

as what it could suggest to Balzac in connection with characterization, then, the book was something of a paradox.

In pointing up the importance of gesture, Moreau was stressing a concept that Lavater himself distinctly minimized. Lavater was quite specific about the distinction between form and movement, and distinguished two corresponding sciences: physiognomonics and pathognomonics.[44] Though Lavater has some amusing passages on the interpretation of gesture,[45] it is quite clear that his main concern is with physiognomonics, not pathognomonics. He insists that the true basis for knowing "inner" man is not movement, but structure. In the shape of the human body, and especially in the face, the self is invariably manifested. Lavater repeatedly recommends that those interested in physiognomonics study silhouettes, cadavers, and plaster casts.[46] In a celebrated interview with Emperor Joseph I, Lavater remarked that "je me suis plus plus occupé de la physiognomonie en repos, que de la physiognomonie en mouvement."[47] This attitude culminates in his uncompromising statements that "il n'est aucune espèce de déguisement ou de dissimulation qui n'ait des caractères certains et sensibles,"[48] and that "de toutes les dissimulations, celle du langage, quelque raffinée qu'elle soit, est la plus aisée à découvrir."[49] From this point of view, the influence of Lavater on Balzac's characterization (as distinct from purely descriptive techniques) must be acknowledged to be slighter than that of Moreau. For had Balzac taken such assertions seriously, it would have

[44]*Ibid.*, I, 226.
[45]We are warned to beware of "ces gens qui glissent plutôt qu'ils ne marchent," and especially of "hommes qui, toujours occupés de leur lourd individu, vont toujours mâchant, crachant, se mouchant prenant du tabac, et confiant sans façon au plancher tout ce dont ils se débarrassent." The former types are said to be deceptive, the latter vain (*ibid.*, III, 115). We are also warned to beware of anyone who holds his head high and back (*ibid.*, p. 120).
[46]*Ibid.*, V, 24.
[47]Cited by Lavater himself, *ibid.*, I, 82.
[48]*Ibid.*, V, 273.
[49]*Ibid.*, III, 35.

rendered many of his characterizations impossible. In Lavaterian terms, successive "incarnations" of Vautrin could exist only as errors of observation on the part of other characters.[50]

The distinction between physiognomonics and pathognomonics is stated even more decisively in the work of Gall and Spurzheim.[51] Gall read Condillac as arguing that gesture was not only preverbal, but premental and operative on some obscure instinctual level; conversely, he interpreted Tracy as arguing that gesture followed thought. It was another version of the old thought-word quarrel, and in it Gall sided with Tracy.[52] Since what Gall calls "le langage d'action" is the product of mental activity, it would seem infinitely more important to analyze movement than structure. When Gall comes to make his own definitions of the two arts described by Lavater, therefore, he emphatically underscores the importance of pathognomonics by calling it an art "fondé dans la nature même."[53]

The language of gestures was rich in possibilities, of course, and the extensive contemporary speculation is clearly reflected in Balzac's works. The *Traité de la vie élégante* mentions a future chapter on the theory of deportment (p. 169), which possibly became the essay entitled *Théorie de la démarche*. And the catalogue of 1845 indicates that he still intended to group a whole set of essays, including the *Théorie*, into a *Pathologie de la vie sociale* to form part of the *Etudes analytiques*. There are no extant parallel plans to compose a physiognomonic essay. As whimsical as it might be, the *Traité* is infinitely more interesting than La-

[50]Maurice Bardèche has summed up the role of Lavater, but without making this essential distinction between movement and structure. *(Balzac romancier,* pp. 555–56).

[51]Balzac's knowledge of Gall and Spurzheim may have come through the family friend Dr. Jean-Baptiste Nacquart, who had published a *Traité sur la nouvelle physiologie du cerveau, ou exposition de la doctrine de Gall sur la structure et les fonctions de cet organe* (Paris, 1808).

[52]Franz-Joseph Gall and Johann Christoph Spurzheim, *Anatomie et physiologie du système nerveux en général et du cerveau en particulier* (Paris, 1810), IV, 317.

[53]*Ibid.,* IV, 288.

vater's simple-minded analysis of noses and chins, because it states with clarity the importance of action in descriptive techniques. It is also enlightening to read, in the *Mémoires de deux jeunes mariées* (p. 191), that the principal element in the conversion of a provincial girl into a "femme du monde" is the acquisition of the ability to read gestures (including verbal). Louise de Chaulieu, who voices this opinion, is uncompromising in her denigration of physiognomonics, which she condemns as "stupide"; but pathognomonics is a different matter altogether, and seems to her to form the basis of all social relations.[54]

"Laisser échapper" was an ideal device through which to exploit the complexities of gesture as primary evidence of acts of mind. In a world where everything depends upon correct strategy and good maneuvering, Carlos Herrera is well advised to warn Lucien of the importance of gesture: "Eh! bien, reçois cet homme . . . mais ne dis pas un seul mot compromettant, ne laisse pas échapper un geste d'étonnement, c'est l'ennemi" (SM, xv, 269). Esther Gobseck, for her part, needs no instructions. When she is first presented to Baron Nucingen, "[elle] regarda le banquier célèbre en laissant échapper un geste d'étonnement admirablement joué" (SM, xv, 186), In such cases, control is everything; and if Esther succeeds where Lucien fails, it is because she plays her role in Vautrin's game with an exactitude her lover cannot muster. Even Louise de Bargeton knows how to maneuvre gestures in critical situations: "Elle laissa échapper un superbe sourire, et se croisa les bras en regardant les rideaux de son boudoir" (IP, xi, 319); and the gentle Pillerault uses the technique to impress on César Birotteau his unshakeable faith in the honesty of the notary Roguin: "Après avoir laissé échapper un sourire d'in-

[54]In practice, of course, Balzac depended heavily on physiognomonics for descriptive effects. In *Le Cousin Pons,* he explicitly defines it as "l'expression totale du corps" (p. 130), and it appears to be the element of totality which distinguishes it from merely "le physique." But it remains tied exclusively to "outer" man, and Balzac never automatically commits himself to Lavater's rather elementary procedures.

crédulité, Pillerault alla dechirer d'un livret un petit paper, écrivit la somme, et signa" (CB, 108).[55]

Such incidents are powerful because they seem to imply spontaneity. On the other hand, when true spontaneity intervenes in human behavior to disrupt the smooth course of events, the result can be danger and risk to society, as well as to the individual who allows an inner emotion to be seen. When Baron Nucingen boasts, in Lucien's presence, of possessing Esther Gobseck, the young man smiles. It is a smile noticed by Horace Bianchon, who later comments on it: "Lucien a laissé échapper un sourire qui me ferait croire qu'elle est de sa connaissance" (SM, xv, 90). Horace doesn't realize the danger his remark carries for Lucien; but Lucien himself is immediately aware of having committed a grave error, for he later tells Esther that "j'ai laissé échapper un sourire involontaire, imprudent" (SM, xv, 112). How often could Lucien's word "imprudent" be used to describe the spontaneously escaping reaction! Not even Vautrin, past master of the art of dissimulation, can entirely dominate the forces erupting from within when certain sensitive spots are touched: "le masque aux formes athlétiques laissa échapper un mouvement qui, bien que concentré, fut surpris par Rastignac" (SM, xv 16).

The device of "laisser échapper" thus effectively connects the notion of rationality to the notion of spontaneity. In the free quality of the escaped gesture, we recognize echoes of the eighteenth-century supposition that gestures were a more "primitive" kind of expression than was rational discourse. And indeed the Balzacian device works best as a symbol of the irrisistible and unpredictable explo-

[55]This kind of voluntary gesturing is exploited to the fullest in such pairs of characters as the Cointet brothers, who divide between themselves two distinct types of negotiations: "Jean se chargeait des paroles dures, des exécutions qui répugnaient à la mansuétude de son frère. Jean avait le département des colères, il s'emportait, il laissait échapper des propositions inacceptables, qui rendaient celles de son frère plus douces; et ils arrivaient ainsi, tôt ou tard, à leurs fins" (IP, xii, 388). The Keller brothers of *César Birotteau* have precisely the same arrangement between them.

sion of inner energies.[56] When word or physical act arrive with too much force to enter smoothly into the flow of behavior, the escape mechanism characteristically moves us from a more conventional, rational, "advanced" verbal stage back to what was regarded as a more primitive, pre-rational, gestural stage. Typical incidents of this sort begin with words, and end in gestures. When Lucien de Rubem-pré cuts off the Marquise d'Espard, the lady "ne put réprimer un petit mouvement sec" (SM, xv, 7); when abbé Troubert observes that Birotteau rarely reads theological works, Mlle Gamard "laiss[a] échapper un sourire de dé-dain" (CT, 196). Such incidents can be cited on almost every page of the *Comédie humaine*. They are most frequent, obviously, at moments of great crisis, and can even be considered to function as a kind of narrative marker, indicating important turning points in the course of a novel. One of the most touching of such incidents occurs in *La Vendet-ta*. Ginevra di Piombo has been hiding from her parents a love affair with the son of her family's mortal enemy. Her conscience afflicts her more and more, until the breaking point is reached: "'Qu'as-tu donc, Ginevra? Tu pâlis,' lui dit sa mere. 'Non!' s'écria la jeune fille en laissant échapper un geste de résolution, 'non, il ne sera pas dit que Ginevra Piombo aura menti une fois dans sa vie' " (Ven, 182). Unable to continue her sham before the parents who have utmost faith in her and the greatest possible parental love, Ginevra drops her defenses for a moment, and the conflict that has been buried deep within her rises to the surface.

[56] In all orthodoxy, Balzac should not have taken this view. The Catholic Bonald, who considered language to be a divine gift, denied the position of gesture as a "primitive" means of expression. He insisted on a radical disjuncture between gesture and word, although he did concede that man possesses both systems of expression (*Législation primitive*, I, 316). But the one did not lead to the other in his view, and he insists that men without language would not really be men at all (I, 73). For a discussion of this point, see Moulinié, *De Bonald*, pp. 228, 243–44. Bonald did not see, of course, that the real distinction between word and gesture is that the former alone is based upon the principle of symbolism—that is, on the separation of the network of signs from the acts and objects of reality. See Michel Foucault, *Les Mots et les choses* (Paris, 1966), pp. 120–21.

For his part, her father finds himself torn between his love for his daughter and his undying hatred for his old enemy. He too, then, finds his innermost energies surfacing with uncontrollable violence: "'Jamais,' dit Piombo. 'J'aimerai mieux te voir dans ton cercueil, Ginevra.' Le vieux Corse se leva, se mit à parcourir à grands pas le salon et laissa échapper ces paroles après des pauses qui peignaient toute son agitation: 'Vous croyez peut-être faire plier ma volonté? Détrompez-vous: je ne veux pas qu'un Porta soit mon gendre. Telle est ma sentence. Qu'il ne soit plus question de ceci entre nous. Je suis Bartholoméo di Piombo, entendez-vous, Ginevra?' " (Ven, 193) As long as contradictions remain buried, family life can go on. But the moment Ginevra touches upon the spring that controls her father's—and her own—innermost passions, the escape mechanism comes into play, with unmanageable force and unforseeable results.[57]

Like all narrative techniques, the escape mechanism has its dangers and drawbacks. There are many gestures and exclamations of the "romanesque" type—traditional, literary, worn out. How many Balzacian heroines cast their eyes up to heaven in response to how many sentimental crises? It was too easy, too often, for the narrator to foreshorten his descriptions and shortcircuit his analyses, in favor of tired clichés of gesture. The vocabulary of gesture could easily become stereotyped and ossified; and if the Balzacian narrator is aware of the danger to the point of satirizing it, he is not immune to it.[58]

Although the escape mechanism springs from a predominantly sensualist notion of human psychology, its practical effect in narration was to imply an active "inner" life in characters who were not ordinarily aware of this dimension

[57]Examples are legion, but some of the most striking are: Charles de Vandenesse's encounter with Madame d'Aiglemont (FT, 123); Hélène d'Aiglemot's first encounter with her future husband (FT, 162–63); Peyrade's discovery of his daughter's abduction (SM, 293); Pierrette's inadvertent dropping of her guard vis-a-vis her cousins (P, 68).

[58]*Les Deux Amis* has an especially amusing passage on "toutes les cabrioles que les auteurs font subir à leurs créatures" (p. 237).

of their own existence. A few do have, nevertheless, a sensation of selfhood quite apart from their sense of overt presence in the objective world. "Je sens bien des moi en moi!" exclaims Madame de Mortsauf (Lys, 211), and her remark, a rarity in the *Comédie humaine,* underscores a lacuna in Balzac's psychological characterization which has been often criticized. Yet he did, in his fashion, try to convey an inner sense of self-consciousness—indeed a sense of *existence*—which his characters experience upon occasion. Perhaps he drew something from Maine de Biran's striking image of the "self-plucking harp" to describe these obscure, buried levels of mental life. Whatever the source, the images we find at moments of crisis are predominantly auditory.[59] Characters hear voices, ringing bells, and buzzing sounds, as premonitions and intuitions intervene from within to subvert all that reason says is proper. They hear the voice of remorse (Lys, 62), the voice of conscience (AS, 88 and F, 120), the voice of the heart (DL, 313), the voice of the demon (EG, 392), and many other "voices" that represent areas of self-consciousness they are not prepared to recognize willingly. These disembodied voices become metaphors for half-perceived, half-suppressed motives, desires, and instincts that surface into consciousness quite independently of rational volition. Undoubtedly the most beautiful expression of this phenomenon, and of its relationship to the standard romantic images of lamps and sparks, occurs in *La Vieille Fille,* when Suzanne, the future Madame du Val-Noble, first sees Athanase: "La grisette, qui certes a l'instinct de la misère et des souffrances du coeur, ressentit cette étincelle électrique, jaillie on ne sait d'où, qui ne s'explique point, que nient certains esprits forts. . . . C'est tout à la fois une lumière qui éclaire les ténèbres de l'avenir, un pressentiment des jouissances

[59]The reason Biran gives for the privileged nature of auditory images is that vocalization permits an organism both to generate sound and perceive it without any intervention from the outside world, thereby making self-consciousness independent of objective reality: the mind becomes "la harpe animée qui se pince elle-même." Quoted in Bémol, "La Représentation imagée," p. 146.

pures de l'amour partagé, la certitude de se comprendre l'un et l'autre. C'est surtout comme une touche habile et forte faite par une main de maître sur le clavier des sens. Le regard est fasciné par une irrésistible attraction, le coeur est ému, les mélodies du bonheur retentissent dans l'âme et aux oreilles, une voix crie: 'C'est lui' " (VF, 294). Reason is not merely different from this process of mind; it is destructive of it. The narrator of *La Vieille Fille* observes that if, as often happens, reason throws its cold water on such an experience, all is lost (VF, 294). And given the disjuncture between "voices" and the rational processes of mind, it is not in the least startling that Benassis should be haunted by the voice of conscience in his sleep, "un nom . . . qu'une voix me crie souvent pendant mon sommeil" (MC, 220); or that Lucien de Rubempré, "enhardi par la voix secrète qu'entendent parfois les joueurs" gambles on red and wins (IP, xii 313).[60] There is no logical explanation for these things: the voices represent a function of mind over which the character has no control, and which he is at a loss to explain. How much of the reasonable, ordered world is dependent upon such inexplicable events! Young Popinot experiences voices when he sees an oddly-shaped bottle in a glass-merchant's window: "Ah! il m'a crevé les yeux comme une lumière subite, une voix m'a crié: 'Voilà ton affaire' " (CB, 130). César's response is entirely appropriate: "Né commerçant, il aura ma fille" (CB, 130). The sudden revelation embodied in the voice is the basis for the success of Popinot and Company, for Popinot's marriage with Césarine, and for the eventual rescue of César's honor. As between César's calculated speculations and Popinot's inexplicable voice, who would not choose the latter?

Even more distantly removed from the process of verbalization is the ringing or tolling that some characters hear at critical junctures in their lives. Ringing fits exactly Biran's definition of vocalization as the effective source of a

[60] Immediately thereafter, and "malgré la voix," he switches to black—and loses.

sense of mind: it obliterates contact with the outer world. Caused quite simply by a sudden rise in blood pressure, it is a sensation produced and perceived entirely within, and independent of connections with the objective world. Modeste Mignon, at a difficult moment, hears "un bruit de cloches dans ses oreilles, elle vit tout sombre devant elle" (MM, 254); César Birotteau's ears "tintèrent" at the moment he concludes his fatal pact with the nefarious Roguin (CB, 71); Minoret thinks he hears "un carillon à chacune de ses oreilles" when he discovers thirty banknotes in a book (UM, 184). Although not always a harbinger of misfortune, this tolling is often "le glas du désastre" (Be, 94), the warnings of instinct against the deceptions and betrayals of rationality.

Not all Balzacian characters hear voices; still fewer experience ringing. Such retreats into the self are the exception rather than the rule in the Balzacian world. These characters are, for the most part, far too strategically minded, far too anxious to use verbalization for the purposes of aggression in and against the world. Words interest them less as a means of self-discovery than as a source of external power. It is a power they are not loath to use against each other, a power the narrator is not loath to use in his relationship with his putative reader. Once this power is recognized, the word becomes an event; even more seriously and dangerously, it can become a weapon.

CHAPTER VI

The Narrator and his Words:
The Word-Event

"A Paris, le mot et la chose sont comme le cheval et
le cavalier" *(Les Petits Bourgeois,* p. 42)

Part way through *La Dernière Incarnation de Vautrin,*
Madame d'Espard's maid rushes in to announce to her
mistress "Madame, madame Camusot pour une affaire très
pressante, et que sait madame!" (p. 221). The effect on
Madame d'Espard is electrical, and the narrator characteristically offers us a "théorie [qui] explique le pouvoir de
ces mots." The one he gives is the simple observation that
when influential people ask for an interview, their motives
must be compelling. But the incident is significant, and
offers a model of what we shall call "word-events": peculiar
nodes of significance to which the narrator calls special
attention in terms of words themselves. When, in another
instance, Gaston de Nueil returns to the provinces after the
excitements of Paris, the dullness and monotony of his
existence are described primarily through the absence of
such linguistic events: it is a life "sans une phrase qui
frappa son oreille et lui apporta soudain une émotion
semblable à celle que lui aurait causée quelque motif original parmi les accompagnements d'un opéra ennuyeux"
(FA, 263).

There are many ways in which words become word-
events in the *Comédie humaine.* A favorite technique is,
again, coining and identifying neologisms. If the narrator
uses "exclusivité" to describe the passion of Esther Gobseck
for Lucien de Rubempré, he claims that he must "faire un
mot pour rendre une idée si peu mise en pratique" (SM,
xv, 214). "Post-existence" is identified as "un mot nouveau
pour rendre un effet innommé" (LL, 101); "spectrale-

ment" is similarly tagged (CP, 132); so is "désangoulêmer" (IP, XII, 11), among many others. Balzac's narrator seems to have regarded such word-events as he regarded the fragments of bone from which, as he claimed elsewhere, Cuvier could reconstruct an entire extinct animal. They had force because they implied conceptual structures around them. By their very nature, neologisms are emphatic, and thus are possibly the simplest form of the word-event.

But they are thereby the least interesting. The word-event reveals its full richness when a perfectly ordinary word is charged with special meaning. These meanings characteristically arise through processes of condensation or of expansion. Some whist players in *Modeste Mignon* typify the word-event as condensation, for they communicate with each other in "phrases hiéroglyphiques" that summarize all their previous discussion and knowledge of the game (MM, 39). Elsewhere, Calyste du Guénic is told "Tu seras aimé!" and the words enable him to cope with his as yet unrequited love (B, 173). Such words are variously described as being "le résumé de toutes les affections vraies de l'homme" (SM, XVI, 181), as "toute l'histoire" of a person or institution, as "la formule breve" of a large conception, or as the simplification of a wide-ranging idea.[1]

As the product of the expansive process, on the other hand, the word-event is often said to "germinate"; that is, to stand at the beginning of a long psychological development. Germination is described theoretically in *Modeste Mignon:* "Combien de fois un mot n'a-t-il pas décidé de la vie d'un homme? L'ancien président de la République Cisalpine, le plus grand avocat du Piémont, Colla, s'entend dire, à quarante ans, par un ami, qu'il ne connaît rien à la botanique; il se pique, devient un Jussieu, cultive les fleurs, en invente, et publie la *Flore du Piémont,* en latin, l'ouvrage de dix ans" (p. 60). Lucien de Rubempré is one of many dozens of characters whose lives are affected by germinating words. In his case the word "jobard," carelessly dropped

---

[1]For other examples of this maneuver, see SM, XVI, 51 and XV, 98; FT, 76; B, 366; FE, 170; TA, 126. Instances elsewhere are legion.

by Coralie, contributes strongly to his estrangement from d'Arthez and his group. The same thing happens to Gaston de Nueil, as he pursues Madame de Beauséant (FA, 291); and in *La Recherche de l'absolu,* Pierquin doggedly courts Marguérite, thinking that the words "marriage," "liberty," and "fortune" will germinate in her mind (p. 244). Philippe Brideau plants the words "la femme du colonel Brideau" in Flore's mind, hoping to bring her around to the idea of vengeance (R, 459); and even Félix de Vandenesse observes the operation of this principle in himself as Madame de Mortsauf's remark "Aimez-moi comme m'aimait ma tante" acquires ever richer meaning (Lys, 101). Such germination of meaning can come close to summing up the whole subject of a novel.

Yet the word-event is not only an attribute of characters. As germination it concerns the narrator in the most direct way, since it is he who identifies it as such. The word-event can accomplish for him what the device of "laisser échapper" accomplishes for the characters themselves: it represents the bursting forth of conceptions from some subverbal level. And this transition, not from inner character to outer character, but from inner narrator to outer narrator, is one of the finest dramatic devices to be found in the *Comédie humaine.* It pinpoints the way in which a word-event pushes narration forward: "Sur le costume, un observateur se fût dit: 'Voilà un homme infâme, il boit, il joue, il a des vices, mais il ne se soûle pas, mais il ne triche pas, ce n'est ni un voleur, ni un assassin.' Et Contenson était vraiment indéfinissable jusqu'à ce que le mot espion se fût venu dans la pensée" (SM, xv 120–21).[2]

The *sine qua non* of the word-event is that the germinating force is out of proportion to the context. There is, for example, an extraordinary series of rapid-fire word-events in *Illusions perdues,* when Lousteau and Finot lay their plans to exploit Lucien. The text has already told us all we need to know about these two sharks of Parisian journalism, and

---

[2]This passage is exactly parallel to Balzac's well-known inability to visualize César Birotteau until the word "probité" popped into his mind.

we require very little help in understanding the quick exchange: "Ce fut un parti pris rapidemment et compris dans toute son étendue entre ces deux hommes par deux phrases dites d'oreille à oreille: 'Il a du talent,' 'Il sera exigeant,' 'Oh, bon' " (IP, XII, 181). This dialogue marks the point in the text at which the machinations of Lousteau and Finot focus directly and intently on Lucien—a point which we cannot help noticing because of the way in which the words spark forth and are tagged by the narrator. The extraordinary intensity of these verbal events springs from the fact that the words crystallize and give form to themes and motivations that were, until then, relatively inchoate. The word-event thus assumes the status of a real happening, a recognizable moment of the creative process recorded in the text itself, and it helps explain the narrator's difficulty in rejecting naive realism out of hand. In the world of the narrator, which is the world of the text, words are indeed real things, not to be lightly handled, for they can be explosive. In that quasibiographical novel, *Le Lys dans la vallée*, the narrator quite rightly observes that in the presence of the slightest personal weakness, a word or a gesture have the power of poison (p. 202). Death is precisely the fate of Madame Claës, who, after receiving so many verbal blows from her husband, spends the last of her life-energy in a final call to her daughter. "Cette dernière exclamation," observes the narrator, "fut tout un testament" (RA, 234).[3] As a matter of fact, the whole drama of *La Recherche de l'absolu* is based on the few words exchanged between a Polish soldier and Balthasar Claës, because of which the latter acquires his interest in alchemy. Of this, too, Madame Claës is aware: "Comment! . . . cet homme, en passant une nuit sous notre toit, nous a enlevé tes affections, a détruit, par une seule phrase, par un seul mot, le bonheur d'une famille" (RA, 188). Her suffering is such that there is no more agonizing way for it to be brought

---

[3] A more or less full statement of this aspect of word-events appears in *Les Martyrs ignorés*, where we find a discussion of the particular situations in which words can have fatal effects.

home to the reader than for the narrator to reveal—to her
and to us—the terrible power of words.

It was, perhaps, a very neat way of getting around the
old problem of the veil. If the world of the narrator is but
this fictional structure, and if its constituent parts are but
words, then words and things are one, and the veil has
disappeared. By the same token it is clear that word-events
are not primarily mimetic. They exist only as differentials
of emphasis, or as concentrations of themes and values
arising from within the text itself. It is not really an exaggeration, then, if the narrator treats certain words as if they
were "real" objects in his fictional world, having quite tangible effects. When Asie tells Peyrade that his daughter has
been kidnapped and will be forced into prostitution unless
he ceases to interfere in Vautrin's affairs, the results are
direly physical: "Asie laissa Peyrade dans un état à faire
pitié, chaque mot fut un coup de massue" (SM, xv, 294).
This kind of formulation can be found dozens of times,
and the very repetition tends to make the reader accept
words as something more than just mimetic signs. Sometimes such tropes are a real weakness in narrative
technique; they are in part an easy way out of descriptive
problems, and conform to the narrator's habit of substituting hyperbole for analysis. Allusions to word-events seem
inevitably to suggest exaggeration to Balzac, and the following little exchange between Lucien de Rubempré and
Esther Gobseck is not atypical: "A ce mot dit exprès par
Lucien, Esther se dressa comme une bête fauve, ses
cheveux dénoués entourèrent sa sublime figure comme
d'un feuillage. Elle regarda Lucien d'un oeil fixe" (SM, xv,
110). Even though Lucien has just intimated that his life is
in danger, the modern reader tends to smile rather than
shudder.

Yet it would be a mistake to accuse the Balzacian narrator of simply avoiding difficulties. The particular rhetorical device he was exploiting had a long career in the
eighteenth-century novel. Restif's *Le Paysan et la paysanne*

pervertis furnishes an excellent example, when the heroine Ursule tells her parents that her brother Edmond has been condemned to the galleys:

> Notre bonne mère lui a dit: "O ma pauvre fille, où est-il ton frère?"
>
> "Aux galères."
>
> A ce mot notre père a frémi. "Monsieur Loiseau . . ." Il n'a pas achevé. . . .

The father then expires under the stress of the words.[4] Hence when Balzac composes the death scene of Agathe Bridau, he is only partially inventing. Agathe is told frankly by her confessor, the abbé Loraux, that of her two children only Joseph has been a real son to her: "En entendant ce mot qu'elle comprit, Agathe eut une crise par laquelle commença son agonie. Elle mourut vingt heures après" (R, 570). The critical difference between Restif's scene and Balzac's is that abbé Loraux's words are not mere hyperbolic gesturing. They come as the culmination of a theme that has been carefully built up through the entire novel: Agathe's willful blindness to the relative virtues of her two sons. That blindness is a major thread in a complex plot, and accounts for many turns in events. The narrator has been creating considerable tension: Agathe cannot go on forever refusing to admit the perfidy of her son Philippe. The moment comes when the narrator must bring things to a head, when the strands of the plot he has woven must come together even at the risk of explosion. And so the abbé Loraux's word is one that "elle comprit"—for the first time, and at the cost of her life. In quite the same way, Baron Hulot's words to a servant-girl, "ma femme n'a pas longtemps à vivre, et si tu veux tu pourras être baronne" (Be, 500), overheard by his wife at the end of *La Cousine Bette,* are identified by the narrator as the cause of her death because she finally accepts them at their full value,

[4]Quoted by Vivienne Mylne, *The Eighteenth Century French Novel: Techniques of Illusion* (New York, 1965), p. 231.

and admits that he is a hopeless profligate. But nowhere is the technique used to better advantage, or more consistently, than in *Pierrette,* which is an excellent example of the intelligent and sensitive handling of what might have been merely caricature. Pierrette is described by the narrator as being literally the victim of her cousins' speech; she is constantly "maltraitée en paroles" (p. 74). As a result, she suffers a series of physical effects, including "une horrible contraction au coeur" (p. 102); "une contraction à l'estomac" and "un vomissement affreux" (p. 105). The net effect, based upon the explosive externalization of themes in the narrative voice, is powerful and moving.

Behind this technique there undoubtedly lay more than certain traditions of the eighteenth-century novel. One is tempted to see in the word-event the literary exploitation of the notion of naive realism most clearly enunciated by Turgot: the theory that words were designed to apply to objects and not to ideas, and thus could possess exchange value.[5] It was a theory calculated to delight a novelist such as Balzac, and tied in neatly with his obsession with the money orientation of the July Monarchy. In the *Comédie humaine,* money values invade all domains of human activity, including language. *Illusions perdues* has much to say on the buying and selling of words at the crude level of journalism. Vernou puts it as bluntly as possible: "Mais nous sommes des marchands de phrases et nous vivons de notre commerce . . . des articles lus aujourd'hui, oubliés demain, ça ne vaut à mes yeux que ce qu'on les paie" (IP, XII, 248). In this area, Turgot's theories could be extrapolated in a straight line: words are tags for objects, words *are* objects, and can be sold at so much per line. And as Turgot had pointed out, a value theory of words proposed, along with its linking of word and object, the disassociation of word from idea. By extending the notion, already broached by

[5]Turgot summed up the theory of "monetized" words in his article "Etymologie" in the *Encyclopédie.* See also Foucault, *Les Mots et les choses* pp. 90 and 202–21, where the role of words and money in the formation of value systems is analyzed.

some philosophers, that language could "generate" world-views, it was feasible to conceive of a possibility of startling richness: that through his use of words, the narrator *creates value.*[6]

The link between word and object, as difficult to sustain as it might be in the real world, was a perfectly viable literary device in a narrative world made up only of words. And it might well have been that Balzac found support for this notion in Bonald, at whatever date he read him; for Bonald enunciates a similar idea that is especially suggestive in a Balzacian context: "La parole est donc, dans le commerce des pensées, ce que l'argent est dans le commerce des marchandises, expression réelle de valeurs, parce qu'elle est valeur elle-même. Nos sophistes veulent en faire un signe de convention, à peu près comme le papier-monnaie."[7] Here, in two sentences, is the theoretical statement of the word-event, and the narrator's instrument for tearing aside the veil. The word-event is object and value, rather than the symbolization of objects and values.

At the same time, the value theory of words left entirely open the matter of *what* values words embody. Here mimesis plays a certain role. The revulsion from the journalistic and literary industries of the 1830s and 1840s springs from the narrator's conviction that the values usually attached to words were ignoble, and this contributes in no small measure to his distrust of language insofar as it was a tool of bourgeois social hegemony. It also accounts for the negative qualities the narrator generally attributes to the word-event when it functions as a counter for middle-class values. The monetization of language can be traced in great detail through *La Cousine Bette,* where Val-

[6]Balzac was not, as a matter of fact, the first to equate signs and money. Years before, Degérando had spoken of certain classes of signs which operated like paper money in that they did not designate precise objects but rather methods of discovering precise objects. These were largely abstractions, such as "nation" or "constitution," whose specific content is subject to change and negotiation. See Acton, "Philosophy of Language," p. 210.

[7]Bonald, *Législation primitive,* I, 96.

érie Marneffe is clever enough to understand that her attractions are worth considerable money to such a man as the retired merchant Crevel: "Ce mot: 'Je n'ai jamais eu de femme du monde!' dit par Crevel à Lisbeth, et rapporté par Lisbeth à sa chère Valérie, avait été largement escompté dans la transaction à laquelle elle dut ses six mille francs de rente en cinq pour-cent" (p. 180). It is not only Valérie who converts eight words into six thousand francs; Crevel himself exploits the convertibility of words into money as he tries to seduce Adéline Hulot by offering to save her from financial disaster: "Le monde," he says to her, "aime le succès! Voyons? Vient-il chercher votre sublime vertu dont le tarif est de deux cent mille francs?" (p. 349) The words in which the link is established prove disastrous to Adéline: "Ce mot fit frissonner madame Hulot, qui fut reprise de son tremblement nerveux" (p. 349). And once again, as the force of the words becomes too great, it spills over from the narrator's consciousness into that of his creatures: "Pour avoir seulement entendu ces quatre mots: *Deux cent mille francs,*" gloats Bette to Valérie, "la baronne est à la mort. Oh! tu les tiens tous par cette histoire" (p. 466).

The only way in which the dire results of the word-event could be avoided would seem to be the avoidance of language itself. In *L'Envers de l'histoire contemporaine* the tranquility of Madame de la Chanterie's household is explained as the absence of certain words (p. 299). But here, as in *La Peau de chagrin,* the need for language will overcome the fear, and the drama of Madame de la Chanterie will eventually be played out. Similarly, the failure of the old aristocracy to ask itself "sommes-nous assez forts pour porter le pouvoir" (DL, 184) accounts for the fact that they do indeed lose their grip on the society of the July Monarchy.

Word-events, then, stem from concerns with language that go back at least as far as the adventure of Raphaël de Valentin. But the "opacity" that the word-event confers on language brings the reader on to a level of experience that is quite complex: we perceive that what might be terribly destructive for the Balzacian creature is constructive for the narrator. It is he, the narrator, who charges these words with special meanings; it is his psychic energy that endows them with their heightened significance; it is he who tags them and turns them into narrative devices of unavoidable significance. That significance is always expressed in what one might call the word-event's "second stage." Often this development is overexplanatory or, in some cases, somewhat patronizing. The "second stage", nevertheless, almost always constitutes a step forward in the narrative. An incident in *Le Cabinet des antiques* illustrates this straightforward method to perfection. The old marquis remarks at one point to his half sister, "Vous êtes une d'Esgrignon, ma soeur!"—clearly a self-evident truth. The puzzle requires a "second stage" of narration, which explains the mystery and at the same time tells us succinctly much that we need to know about the d'Esgrignon family: "La noble fille tressaillit et pleura. Dans ses vieux jours, monsieur d'Esgrignon, père du marquis, avait épousé la petite-fille d'un traitant anobli sous Louis XIV. Ce mariage fut considéré comme une horrible mésalliance par la famille, mais sans importance, puisqu'il n'en était résulté qu'une fille. Armande savait cela. Quoique son frère fût excellent pour elle, il la regardait toujours comme une étrangère, *et ce mot la légitimait*" (p. 9, my italics). The "second stage" confers on the marquis' remark a force that could hardly be matched by any amount of hyperbole. It not only sums up a certain amount of past history, but also establishes one of the pivots on which the story turns: the question of legitimacy, what it is, how it is acquired, and how it is retained. It establishes those overtones of absolutism to which the old marquis clings, and which will be systematically devalorized by the succeeding events of the novel.

The word-event, then, not only allows the narrator to explore and explain what has been building up in him, but also to focus more sharply than he might otherwise have done on basic themes and motifs, and above all to pinpoint the moments when they enter explicitly into the narration.

We may be permitted to wonder whether Lucien's interest in Coralie would have become such an infatuation, had she not whispered to him, "Je t'aimerais laid et malade!" (IP, XII, 180); we can watch Madame Cibot's greed being unleashed by the "diabolical words" of her neighbor the ironmonger (CP, 122); or wonder if Diane de Maufrigneuse would have conquered d'Arthez had she not whispered to him "Une fille doit-elle jamais livrer sa mère?" (SPC, 347). Here we catch the Balzacian word-event at its sharpest: while he was not willing to accept at face value the simplistic view that sentiments were reducible to some kind of negotiable quantity, the narrator nevertheless knows that sentiments have meaning only insofar as he can embody them in words.

"Sachez-le bien: de toutes les blessures, celles que font la langue et l'oeil, la moquerie et le dédain sont incurables." So comments the narrator of *Le Cabinet des antiques* at the beginning of his novel, thus proposing the most extreme case of the word-event—that of the word as weapon (p. 21). Forces that explode in the word-event can be so overpowering that the narrator comes to regard words as literally the most dangerous of weapons. This requires a rather special attitude toward language: words are both the vehicle and object of the narrator's thought. Nowhere is this double view more decisive than when the narrator extends the Turgotian analogy to its uttermost extreme, and makes the word a physical extension of the body: "La Parole," he observes in *Albert Savarus*, "[est une] espèce d'arme à bout portant" (p. 109). The ways in which the narrator views his weapons—they are, after all, his own, although he may ascribe them to his creatures—fall roughly into two categories: phenomena of penetration and phenomena of crushing. In the first group, words are described as *barbelé, acéré, tranchant;* analogies are drawn between words and such objects as *poignards, flèches, épées, scalpels;* verbs associated with word-events are *percer, coup d'éperon, coup de hache, siffler comme une balle, piquer, coup de pistolet, feu de sarcasmes;* and of course such images as *ironie, pointe aigue, épigramme,* and *pointe envenimée* were more or less common. In the category of weighty weapons, we find adjectives such as *lourd* and *étourdi,* such nouns as *barre, massue, coup, boulet de canon,* and such verbs as *accabler,* and *aplatir.* The tendency to destructiveness is so strong at times that the very metaphorical formulation occasionally vanishes, leaving us with exaggerated reification: "Quoiqu'il eût le sang fouetté par ces petites phrases en forme de flèches, bien aigues, bien froides, bien acérées, décochées coup sur coup, Montriveau devait aussi cacher sa rage, pour ne pas tout perdre par une extravagance" (DL, 242). And, of course, the ultimate reification occurs in journalism. Lousteau explains to Lucien de Rubempré the mechanics of assassination by language: "Lorsque vous aurez une vengeance à exercer contre quelqu'un, vous pourrez rouer votre ami ou votre ennemi par une phrase insérée tous les matins à notre journal en me disant: 'Lousteau, tuons cet homme-là!' Vous réassassinerez votre victime par un grand article dans le journal hebdomadaire. Enfin, si l'affaire est capitale pour vous, Finot, à qui vous vous serez rendu nécessaire, vous laissera porter un dernier coup d'assommoir dans un grand journal qui aura dix ou douze mille abonnés" (IP, XII, 159). One can hardly imagine a balder statement of the reduction of words to real entities. The assassinations spoken of by Lousteau are by no means metaphorical within the framework of the novel. Lucien will discover that men can indeed die by the word, and the narrator will have converted a fanciful linguistic principle into a powerfully dramatic literary theme.[8]

[8] Such devices suggest that the word-event is a form of *Idée* rooted in calculation and logic. The great exception is *Le Lys dans la vallée,* where Monsieur de Mortsauf's use of words is as irrational as it is vindicative: "il épiloguait dans les plus minces détails, en concluant toujours par ces mots assassins: 'Si vos enfants retombent malades, vous l'aurez bien voulu' " (Lys, 189). It is not overinterpreting the novel to suggest that Madame de Mortsauf's death is due at least in part to her husband's verbal attacks. On the other hand, one must recognize in *Le Lys dans la vallée* a kind of benevolent cruelty on the part of Madame de Mortsauf towards Félix. He perceives many of her words as "des coups de poignard froidement don-

The *Comédie humaine* then, insofar as it deals with language, presents a somber view. Three works especially exploit the theme of the language battle: *La Cousine Bette, Béatrix,* and the section of *Splendeurs et misères des courtisanes* entitled *Où mènent les mauvais chemins. La Cousine Bette* is surely one of the cruelest novels in this respect. Between Lisbeth and Wenceslas, there exist moments of veritable war, a "duel de la parole" (p. 87); between Valérie and Baron Hulot a similar duel takes place on the occasion of her pregnancy, as Valérie converts the words "mon fils" into an annual income of twelve hundred francs (p. 286).[9] Other fights are waged between Bette and the Hulot family,[10] as well as among the various lovers of Valérie Marneffe.[11] Although each of these battles actually occurs, our sense of their force and destructiveness is largely a matter of the way in which the narrator translates the incidents into "linguistic" terms. Seen in this way, *La Cousine Bette* is the great novel of the transformation of events into words, and of words into word-events. And at the same time, it is as much a commentary on the kind of language possible under the July Monarchy as is *Illusions perdues* itself.

In *Béatrix,* language is the battleground of the passions. In various ways and in various degrees of intensity, Camille is pitted against Béatrix, Calyste du Guénic against his mother, Claude Vignon against Calyste. In the fight be-

---

nés aux endroits les plus sensibles" (Lys, 237), although they are intended to save both of them from an impossible involvement with each other. Between Félix and Madame de Mortsauf, language is a tool for bringing the young man to his fullest self-realization. When she sends him off, at the end, to finish his apprenticeship to life in Paris, one of her major concerns is, rightly, his ability to handle language.

[9]Parallel battles are fought between the unfortunate Hortense and her husband Wenceslas, who both give and receive dagger-blows (pp. 278 and 303).

[10]Victorin is quite aware of this. "Savez-vous," he asks Madame de Saint-Esteve, "que, par une seule phrase, cette femme a mis la vie et la raison de ma mère en danger?" (Be, 441).

[11]When Bixiou, Du Tillet, and Léon de Lora tell Montès de Montéjanos that Valérie is involved with Steinbock and Crevel, "ces trois phrases furent trois coups de pistolet que Montès reçut en pleine poitrine. Il devint blême et souffrit tant qu'il se leva péniblement" (Be, 451).

tween Béatrix and Camille, Calyste is caught in a cross-fire of word-events, having nothing to act upon except what people say. He is upset and disoriented, and hears disturbing words through a continual and annoying buzzing in his ears (B, 135). Between Camille and Béatrix there is an endless verbal duel described in fascinated detail by the narrator, "un duel sans trêve où elles firent assaut de ruses, de feintes, de fausses générosités, d'aveux mensongers, de confidences astucieuses, où l'une cachait, où l'autre mettait à nu son amour, et où cependant le fer aigu, rougi des traitresses paroles de Camille, atteignait au fond du coeur de son amie et y piquait quelques-uns de ces mauvais sentiments que les femmes honnêtes répriment avec tant de peine" (B, 172). They engage in an endless exchange of epigrams and hurtful words; Camille uses her most incisive witticisms and Béatrix fires "les flèches les plus acérées de son carquois" (B, 204). They are, moreover, very much aware of their verbal battles: "Lorsque le café fut servi, mademoiselle des Touches dit à son valet de chambre un 'Laissez-nous' qui fut le signal du combat" (B, 202). The theme is asserted very early in the novel by Calyste's mother, who feels that she can do little to protect her son from Mademoiselle des Touches except speak to him: "Vous allez encore aux Touches, mon Calyste? Elle appuya sur ce mot, *mon* Calyste" (B, 61). Despite her gentle persuasion, Calyste spends most of his time at the chateau of Les Touches, where he encounters several rivals for Camille's attentions, among them Claude Vignon, whose chief amusement is to inflict verbal wounds on the young country gentleman.[12]

Béatrix is a clear example of the ability of the Balzacian narrator to take a fairly pedestrian device and transform it

[12]The narrator continually uses the word "blesser" to characterize Vignon's effect on Calyste, for he knows that in the struggle for Camille's affections, words are the effective weapons: " 'je faisais votre éloge, dit Vignon, ce qui est bien plus facile que de vous faire la barbe.' 'J'ai une épée qui la fait à ceux qui l'ont trop longue,' répondit Calyste. 'Et moi je fais très bien l'épigramme,' dit en souriant Vignon, 'nous sommes français, l'affaire peut s'arranger' " (B, 121).

into a narrative technique of extraordinary drama. And it is not exaggerated to see this as one of his great contributions to the liberation of the novel from gothic horror. Language as a battle ground was by no means an original discovery with him, but the complexity and drama with which he endowed it in *Béatrix* was perhaps unmatched in the novel until then. One of the great advantages of seeing word-events as weapons in a perpetual human battle is that everyone speaks, and the field of conflict is immediately widened to include all mankind. With this broader perspective, the *Comédie humaine* acquires one of its characteristic qualities, and at the same time brings to the fore one of Balzac's most far-reaching observations: that violence and aggression are a function of man's deepest-lying neural and mental activities. Tragedy and conflict are no longer restricted to the princely dramas of an earlier age. All men participate in the human battle by the simple fact of speech. This is perhaps the most important way in which the novels express and transcend the Balzacian theory that "la pensée tue": thought in itself is a good deal less destructive than would at first appear, but speech as the embodiment of thought encountering the world (that is, the language of *Idée*) is the destructive principle *par excellence*.

The view of the language of *Idée* as the battlefield of humanity, and of words as weapons in the fight, touches upon the ever-present motif of criminality. Just as tragedy is now no longer the purview of "elevated" souls, so does criminality become universal. In a story appropriately entitled *Les Martyrs ignorés,* the archcriminal becomes Everyman: "Je pensais que l'assassin de grande route mené si pompeusement à l'échafaud n'était pas aux yeux du philosophe si coupable dans son égarement que bien des hommes qui donnent la question avec des mots poignants, qui, après avoir éprouvé, dans certaines âmes, les endroits que la noblesse, la religion, la grandeur rendent vulnérables, y enfoncent à tout moment leurs flèches" (MI, 141). Nowhere is this concept more fully exploited than in the final episodes of *Splendeurs et misères des courtisanes*. Tracked down, imprisoned, surrounded on every side by his enemies, unable to engage in any overt action, Vautrin is reduced to the weapons no one can take away from him: words. The prosecutor quite correctly realizes that his prisoner is withholding a "parole terrible" (SM, xvi, 90). In a situation limited almost entirely to its linguistic dimensions, every protagonist knows exactly what the stakes are; even the good but somewhat obtuse Camusot is not under any delusion very long. It is clear that the abbé Carlos Herrera is really Jacques Collin, and that he and Lucien are implicated in forgery, kidnapping, extortion, and murder. The whole structure of the novel is aimed at leading someone to say something that everyone knows, but which must be *said* before it is real. Lucien being the weaker of the two prisoners, the pressure is directed at him. Asie articulates the situation only too clearly: "si monsieur Camusot *l'interroge mal*, avec deux phrases il peut en faire un coupable" (SM, xvi, 62). The italics are hers, as she explains to Diane de Maufrigneuse and Madame de Sérisy that Lucien is not guilty unless he speaks maladroitly. The interrogating officials must therefore be prevented from asking the wrong questions. From this arises the extended playacting in the latter part of the novel, the elaborate pretense on everyone's part, and the maneuver designed to trap the suspects into an inadvertent word. Everyone, with only the possible exception of Lucien, understands the rules of the game in which language itself is the battleground. We are not really all that far from the whist players of *Modeste Mignon*. And the one who clearly takes the greatest pleasure in arranging the witticisms, the epigrams, the taunts, and all the other verbal exchanges is the narrator himself. He presents the whole drama as a struggle in which the cleverest talker is the winner. It is not by accident that novels such as these seem to move with more speed, seem fleshed out with more "life," than others. For once, the problems of the characters coincide exactly with his own: the formulation of word-patterns to generate meaning. The battle of words within the fictional framework was merely one form of the narrator's own struggle to assign significance and values to words.

The power of the word-event—whether that power be used for good or evil—raises certain further questions about the role of the narrator. It is, after all, he who marks word-events. And if they are viewed, as we have indicated, as elements of *his* language, they obviously move beyond their role as mimetic signs within the frame of the story and underscore the narrator's view of himself as *artifex symbolarum*, the image-maker. It is his chief way of conveying to us something of how he sees himself as a creator of values. To do this, he must face the ultimate problem of any narrator of fiction: he must establish his own position vis-a-vis what he is actually describing or telling. The fact that such an overwhelming proportion of his word-events are destructive tells us more, in a cumulative way, about the value system he is creating than any of the individual occurences to which those word-events refer.

The Balzacian narrator, with his commitment to the total rather than the elitist view, makes of the word-event the commonest of human devices. So common indeed, that he reifies the word-event at every level of the society he is describing, and at almost every turn in the plot. The wealth of Rosalie de Watteville ("dix-huit cent mille francs!"), is "embroidered" on her bodice (AS, 134); Eugénie Grandet literally sees the words of Charles' letter to Annette written on the walls around her (EG, 391); Louis Mongenod's words, "Votre compte s'élève à seize cent mille francs," form a halo around the head of Madame de la Chanterie (EHC, 239). Examples could be multiplied a hundred-fold. As early as the *Physiologie du mariage,* language is seen as spreading over the world; and in the world of the narrator the natural consequence is not only that words are objects and events, but that events and objects constitute a language. "Une antichambre est une espèce de préface qui doit tout annoncer, mais ne rien promettre" we read in *Une Double Famille* (p. 275). Madame Firmiani, when she is angry, can slam her doors in a way that constitutes a language for those who hear (Fir, 371). Such notions are connected, of course, with the old mystical tradition of the Book of the World, the *Liber mundi,* to which the narrator makes a specific reference in *La Physiologie du mariage* (p. 267). But for him the Book of the World is different from what it had been to Saint-Martin, Boehme, or Madame Guyon. The narrator of the *Comédie humaine* is not reaching by way of an ineffable Word for some mystical union with the Godhead. Even in the Swedenborgian *Séraphîta* he understands that what makes up his novelistic universe is simply a series of words that trace his effort to find meanings, values, and significances. His union with the Godhead, if one can use that terminology, would be not silence, but a most perfect language; and *Séraphîta* points consistently towards an ever more complete system of expression. That is the whole drama of *Séraphîta:* the attempt of the androgynous angel to communicate to human intelligence an immediate knowledge of the world. It is the old problem of the veil, and the narrator has, after all, nothing but words with which to deal with it. Despite his mistrust of language and his occasional desperation over its inadequacies, there was no other way.[13]

The world, Mallarmé was to say, is intended to end as a book; that vision is not far removed from the ideal of the Balzacian narrator. The reification of the word-event turns the Balzacian universe into a system of significances—into a

[13] It is interesting to note that although there are a few quixotic characters in the *Comédie humaine* (one thinks of Frenhofer), there are no Emma Bovarys falling victims to books. Nor are there any portraits of writers struggling to create. All the writers of the *Comédie humaine* are presented in "finished" portraits; successful or not, they have travelled their route and their intimate struggles are not known to us. Not even Louis Lambert is shown to us directly at work. That kind of paralanguage would have required a dimension of discourse with which Balzac was not prepared to deal, and which perhaps was simply closed to him, given the way in which he perceived the possibilities of narration in the France of Louis-Philippe. But the clues and indications are all there, and they will lead eventually to *Bouvard et Pécuchet,* and then, by way of Proust, to a broad movement in contemporary literature.

Book—of which these are only the most explicitly expressed elements. Language becomes, in Merleau-Ponty's happy phrase, a process of "singing the world,"[14] and this is exactly what happens in the *Comédie humaine*. The narrator's world is language, as Mozart's was music. His world is a system of signs that he sets up, and in *his* Book-of-the-World, the word most commonly written is "arriver," or some version of it. "Arriver . . . est la pensée générale! Pensée d'ailleurs écrite partout, jusque dans les lois" (EG, 367–68). Vautrin sees the same word at a critical juncture and he says so quite openly to Rastignac: "Ce jour-là vous êtes revenu avec un mot écrit sur votre front et que j'ai bien su lire: Parvenir! Parvenir à tout prix" (PG, 331). Very early in his development, the Balzacian narrator is not above poking some fun at the idea and the article on the grocer playfully connects the word-in-the-world with pseudocreativity: "Direz-vous que l'épicier ne peut rien créer? QUINQUET était un épicier; après son invention, il est devenu un mot de la langue, il a engendré l'industrie de lampiste" (Ep, 17). But the joke is short-lived. Modeste Mignon is utterly serious when she announces that the word "mépris" is engraved on the emotional armor that she has put on (MM, 86). Obviously the armor is metaphorical; the word engraved upon it even more so, being the ultimate hieroglyph, the metaphor within the metaphor. Quite logically, then, the narrator later picks up Modeste's own words ("elle arriva nécessairement à revêtir cette armure sur laquelle elle avait dit avoir gravé le mot *mépris*" [MM, 175]), and uses them to underscore the opaqueness and density of the language that constitutes his world.

Since the narrator tends to use word-events to render his language opaque—that is, real—it is not surprising to see him use them openly to communicate directly with the reader, and by so doing reach for a kind of universal validity. Father Niseron, the symbol of uprightness, patriotism,

[14]Maurice Merleau-Ponty, *Phénoménologie de la perception* (Paris, 1945), p. 217.

honesty, and integrity, is praised by protagonists and narrator alike in a typical linkage of word-events: "Pour couronne civique, cette belle vie *obtenait dans toute la vallée ces mots:* 'Le brave père Niseron! Il n'y a pas de plus honnête homme!' Pris souvent pour arbitre souverain dans certaines contestations, il réalisait *ce mot magnifique,* 'L'ancien du village!' " (Pay, 225; my italics). The first word-event is clearly within the story frame, the second is not. Together they tend to obliterate the line between fiction and reality. The same confusion is deliberately courted in the comments of abbé Taupin: "En voilà de la morale sociale! dit le curé qui avait tout observé et tout entendu *sans dire mot.* Sur cette épigramme ou plutôt *cette satire de la société, si concise et si vraie qu'elle atteignait chacun,* on proposa de faire la partie de boston. N'est-ce pas la vie comme elle est à tous les étages de *ce qu'on est convenu d'appeler le monde! Changez les termes,* il ne *se dit* rien de moins, rien de plus dans les salons les plus dorés de Paris" (Pay, 307; my italics). Again, the word-event leads the narrator to communicate directly with the reader over the heads, so to speak, of his characters. This technique is a perennial temptation to narrator, who frequently begins with the needs and motivations of his characters, and ends with his own.[15]

Ultimately the unleashing of power in the word-event could be, on the narrator's level, enough in itself. There are occasions when neither an explanatory second stage, nor even an overt appeal to the reader is present, but merely a kind of reveling in words—as if the word-event reminded the narrator that he, too, could play with language. The narrator renders his language opaque and forces us to look at it, as it becomes a word-event between himself and us. Such a moment occurs when the abbé Birotteau is told that his archenemy Troubert has moved

[15]One can find examples of this shift from inside to outside the story frame in almost every novel of the *Comédie humaine.* The curious reader might consult *La Fausse Maitresse,* p. 18; *Les Chouans,* p. 141; *Eugénie Grandet,* p. 420; *Ursule Mirouet,* p. 163; *Splendeurs et misères des courtisanes,* p. 126; *Le Curé de village,* p. 214.

into his old lodgings, the ones Birotteau had hoped to inherit from his friend Chapeloud and occupy for the rest of his life:

> 'L'abbé Troubert n'est plus là, monsieur le vicaire, il est dans votre ancien logement.' Ces mots causèrent un affreux saisissement au vicaire qui comprit enfin le caractère de Troubert, et la profondeur d'une vengeance si lentement calculée, en le trouvant établi dans la bibliothèque de Chapeloud, assis dans le beau fauteuil gothique de Chapeloud, couchant sans doute dans le lit de Chapeloud, jouissant des meubles de Chapeloud, logé au coeur de Chapeloud, annulant le testament de Chapeloud, et déshéritant enfin l'ami de ce Chapeloud, qui, pendant si longtemps, l'avait parqué chez mademoiselle Gamard, en lui interdisant tout avancement et lui fermant les salons de Tours (CT, 218).

There is nothing here that the reader has not known for a long time; what emerges is the crushing weight of the realization that finally dawns in Birotteau's slow mind. The narrator can tell us nothing more than he already has, in an objective sense; but he can turn a comedy into a tragedy by transferring the weight of Birotteau's suffering, so to speak, to the heavy cascading of his own prose. The cascade itself becomes the word-event whose mimetic transparency is darkened by its density as language, leaving us with what Bixiou calls "des phrases qui filent comme notre macaroni" (MN, 369–70).[16]

There was a danger in all this, of course: the danger that the narrator might exploit the device in obvious and irritating ways as a simple mechanism for moving his story along at the required pace. This does indeed occur, leading to what one can only call false word-events. Modeste Mignon is told by a wily admirer "Vous êtes charmante" principally, one suspects, so that the narrator can continue, "ce qui signifiait: 'Je suis toute à vous pour le service que vous

---

[16]Bixiou is prone to such macaroni sentences himself. Another example of this opacity, too long to quote in its entirety, but having to do with "le talent de la parole," can be found in *La Duchesse de Langeais*, p. 182.

venez de nous rendre' " (MM, 284). The alignment, or realignment, of loyalties is important in the development of the story, but the word-event cannot but strike us as an all-too-easy way of accomplishing it. The same sort of sleight-of-hand can be observed when de Marsay's suspicions that Lucien is having an affair with Esther Gobseck are used to move the story on: "*Aussi* le mot de Marsay . . . contenait-il plus d'une observation. Mais les dangers sousmarins de la position de Lucien s'expliqueront assez dans le courant de cette histoire" (SM, xv, 81). De Marsay's remark is only a guess, and the narrator's "aussi" is a totally unjustified deduction from his words.[17] This kind of maneuver was inevitable in a narrator as self-conscious as ours. For his self-consciousness could not exist in a vacuum; it demanded an audience. As emphatic as he made his language, it could not exist merely for himself in a solipsistic circle. On the other hand, the presence of the reader was a complicating rather than simplifying notion in an age when conventional norms of readership were falling apart. The Balzacian narrator therefore finds himself in a peculiar position, in which he is obliged to address his self-conscious prose not to one, but several kinds of readers. And this now leads us on to still another level of linguistic complication.

[17] A parallel instance can be found in *La Vieille Fille:* "Le mot prophétique du président du Ronceret: '*Du Bousquier est un homme très fort*' fut adopté par le pays" (p. 401). But du Ronceret's remark is "un horrible contresens" to Madame du Bousquier, who suffers endless conjugal indignities. The whole passage is written in the present tense, and is again directed by the narrator straight at the reader.

CHAPTER VII

The Narrator, The Reader, and the Abolition of the Veil

"L'Analyse ronge la société en l'expliquant. Plus le
monde vieillit, plus la narration est une oeuvre pénible"
(Lov. A168, F/151)

"Malheur en amour, comme dans les arts, à qui dit tout!"
(EB, 402). Such is the principle that Balzac ascribed to
Stendhal, the novelist he so admired and perhaps envied.
The remark sums up a good deal of the wrestling with
narrative problems that manifested themselves in such
techniques as the word-event. Obsession with rationality
and logic, and the seeming inability of French and English
philosophy—with a few rare exceptions—to deal with
problems of thought, language, and creativity in any other
terms, sharply limited the range of Balzac's theoretical
speculation. If he sensed in his own work, as every writer
sooner or later does, that certain aspects of the creative act
escaped logical analysis, it is not surprising that he should
be dissatisfied with theories based upon empiricism and
sensualism. Experience seemed to show that words were
treacherous as vehicles of thought; yet nowhere did faculty
psychology or sensualist aesthetics (insofar as sensualism
could be said to possess an aesthetics) account for this except in terms of malfunction. D'Alembert, writing in the
"Discours préliminaire" of the *Encyclopédie,* defined art as
an activity of the imagination which, however, he derived
from memory and reason. He held works of art to be imita-
tive constructions because imagination can create only objects similar to those it already knows directly.[1] Here
D'Alembert was only reflecting the traditional hierarchy
of the faculties. But the experience of writing obviously

[1] D'Alembert, "Discours préliminaire des éditeurs," *Encyclopédie,* I, xxix.

|189|

taught Balzac that problems of creativity were far more complex than sensualist or empiricist theory ever recognized.

Uncertainty about the types of intellectual operations involved in art led to equal uncertainty as to the authority of the artist with respect to his own work. Can the creator of a work claim any special ability to interpret it? Rational premises and a modicum of self-awareness would seem to indicate that he could. Yet it is a mark of Balzac's dissatisfaction with such theories that in the *Comédie humaine* there are no such happy possibilities. For if the creation of a work of art can escape conscious reasoning, then the creator may be no more aware of the totality of processes occurring than any outside observer. To no one does this apply more directly than to a fictional narrator, especially in the case of a first-person novel such as *Le Lys dans la vallée*. There the narrator, being presumably a participant in events and still bound to a nineteenth-century convention of omniscience, hardly knows how to speak of what is going on in the minds of other characters. This is especially vexing when he must tell us how he is viewed by other characters, and we occasionally get an uneasy form of discourse that sits well with neither the one voice nor the other: "En me parlant ainsi, Origet étudiait mon visage et ma contenance; mais il vit dans mes yeux la claire expression d'une âme candide" (p. 202). Or, at moments, it seems as if Félix can literally follow his words into the minds of M. and Mme de Mortsauf as he speaks in "une voix émue qui vibra dans ces deux coeurs où je jetai mes espérances à jamais perdues et que je calmai par l'expression de la plus haute de toutes les douleurs" (p. 246). True, Félix is telling the story retrospectively, but that does not make it any easier for the reader to accept his apparently effortless ability to step outside of himself and watch another watching him: "Elle usa de son pouvoir, elle en abusa dès qu'elle vit dans mon regard cette ardente expression qui s'y peignait aussitôt que commençaient ses sorcelleries" (p. 262).

These moments lead us directly to the most difficult of

all the problems faced by the narrator: his relationship to the reader. The reader is the one presence about whom the narrator can make no precise statements. He is the eternal absent, the one consciousness into which the narrator can never, under any circumstances, enter. If his difficulties with, say, Madame de Mortsauf suscitate repeated awkwardnesses, his problems with the reader are infinitely more complex. All prose narrative situates itself somewhere between monologue and dialogue; all narrators work endlessly to fill voids that are never reduced. Their language is intransitive in the most anguished way, and the doubling that Félix indulges in represents only an attempt to reach a hopeless and unattainable ideal.[2]

In its basic form, the narrator's problem boils down to the question of what he must say to the reader, and what the latter does or does not know already. In addressing himself to that projected "other"—to use existential terminology—the narrator has a choice of possibilities that lie along a spectrum ranging from a reader presumed totally ignorant to a reader presumed totally knowing. In the first case the novel would be impossible, since it would entail the establishment of a whole conceptual world. Balzac was not insensitive to the temptation, as the length and complexity of the *Comédie humaine* testify. In the second case the novel would be unnecessary, since the presumed reader already knows everything. In the former instance the product would be endless language; in the latter it would be silence. In practical terms, the pole of ignorance is characterized by language that is sequentially minute, painstaking, and highly explicative. As it moves toward the assumption of a knowing reader, language tends to lose its explicative qualities, to short-circuit logic and sequentiality, until at the theoretical extreme nothing is left.

[2]Wayne Booth, in *The Rhetoric of Fiction* (Chicago, 1961), has dealt with the "audience" of the narrator, and with the latter's own shifting trustworthiness. His criteria depend upon publicly verifiable standards of measurement; I am concerned rather with the effect of writing for an unknown reader upon the internal dynamics of the narrator's language, and especially with the mechanisms he uses to deal with this problem.

One of the most curious things about Balzacian texts is their uncertainty about which assumption they are making. The paradoxical situation arises from the conflicting ambitions of complete autonomy (the creation of an independent conceptual world that implies an ignorant reader), and of mimesis (the desire to record a real world with which the ideal reader would necessarily be familiar). Typically, of course, any piece of prose must carry us from the pole of ignorance to the pole of knowledge; but the interesting question is how to do this without eliminating the necessity of the text itself. In a world viewed quantitatively, as Balzac viewed it, the more one describes the less is left to describe. Yet somehow, in the *Comédie humaine,* the more the narrator describes, the more there is to describe.

The state of the reader with which the narrator must immediately contend is that of ignorance. To assume ignorance on the reader's part is to imply the necessity of explanation on the narrator's. Ignorance is really only a masked version of the narrator himself, and possibly does not so much call forth the explanation as justify its previously determined presence. Hence one may find the narrator deliberately creating occasions for descriptive prose. Having briefly identified a "panier à salade" on the first page of *Où mènent les mauvais chemins,* the narrator sets up a factitious narrative situation: "Il est peu de flâneurs qui n'aient rencontré cette geôle roulante; mais quoique la plupart des livres soient écrits uniquement pour les Parisiens, les Etrangers seront sans doute satisfaits de trouver ici la description de ce formidable appareil de notre justice criminelle." (SM, XVI, 3). There follows a long and detailed description of the vehicle, the purpose of which is not so much to delight the foreign reader as to establish certain things about the coming story: a feeling for the power, efficiency, and irresistible professional competence of the French judicial system. Even the slight irony with which the passage is laced is designed to support the idea of perfection in the administration of the law—an idea of central importance to the ending saga of Vautrin.

The assumption of an ignorant reader is primarily aimed at generating further prose—taking "further prose" to mean those pockets of narrative that answer the narrator's self-posed questions. These passages are diverse in character, ranging from out-and-out digressions to developments really quite essential to the story. But they always fulfill the function of asserting the presence of a reader. After the description of the "panier à salade" in the opening pages of *Où mènent les mauvais chemins*, the narrator devotes a lengthy passage to the Conciergerie. The strategem is again as frank and as straightforward as one can imagine: "Maintenant que les deux paniers à salade roulent sur les quais, l'intérêt de cette histoire exige quelques mots sur la Conciergerie pendant le temps qu'ils mettront à y venir" (SM, xvi, 15). The key here is the narrator's sense of a requirement to be filled; and indeed it is a requirement. On one level, of course, it is simply the indespensible novelistic delight in exploring a world—the revelation of the ins and outs of a conceptual space in which a story will unfold itself, and with which the reader may not be familiar. We are thus treated to four dense pages on the history of the Palais de Justice, and four additional pages on its contemporary layout. Strictly speaking, only the latter are "required" for the comprehension of Jacques Collin's entry, stay, and exit. But one of the main points about the Palais, and especially of the Conciergerie, is its symbolic presence as the heart of the French social structure. It is a building associated with the very origins of the French monarchy, with the development of her system of justice, and with the cultural stability against which the "energy" of Jacques Collin is in revolt. What the narrator has been driving at since the very beginning of the Vautrin novels has been the power of the antagonist against which the outlaw has pitted himself. It culminates here in the nerve center of the French judicial system: "cet espace est le sanctuaire de Paris; c'en est la place sacrée, l'arche sainte" (SM, xvi, 16). This description is the ultimate step in the gradual movement from the pettiness of Madame Vauquer's boarding house, where we first meet Vautrin, to the center of French society. Until this has been established, the reader is ignorant of the real dimensions of the ensuing battle. And so the stage is set for the supreme struggle between the forces of order and those of freedom. As the central symbol of the former, the Conciergerie deserves its looming presence in these opening pages; as the final step in the movement from ignorance to knowledge, the narrator's concern with this description seems quite understandable.[3]

But there is something besides solidity embodied in the Conciergerie. The "further prose" has purposes relative to the narrator himself: "Ce palais de nos rois," he writes, "était une merveille d'architecture; il l'est encore aux yeux intelligents du poète qui vient l'étudier en examinant la Conciergerie" (SM, xvi, 17–18). The hint can hardly be missed. In addition to being a "secretary to society," the narrator is a poet in the finest romantic sense: he is establishing a sentient selfhood, and he is endowing the materials of his world with artistic significance. He is also exercising intelligence and making choices; in a word, he is making something, as it is put in La Maison Nucingen, "out of nothing." He clearly wishes to establish his own credentials for putting aesthetic meaning where most people would have seen none, and has maneuvered the narrative in such a way as to make this self-authentification possible and even necessary. One might wonder, as a matter of fact, about a narrator who, far from taking his own authority as a given, is thus driven to create opportunities to demonstrate it. There is something defensive about the attitude, something that suggests the narrator's uncertainty about the authority of his text in the "real" world. The same uncertainty occurs in La Fille aux yeux d'or, where an unknown man is introduced, "que toutes les imaginations, depuis celles qui grellottent au Groënland jusqu'à celles qui suent à la Nouvelle-Angleterre, se peindront d'après cette

___

[3]There are many other instances of the same process; one might mention, as particularly interesting, the discussion of the faubourg Saint-Germain in La Duchesse de Langeais (p. 181 ff).

phrase: *c'était un homme malheureux.* A ce mot, tout le monde le devinera, se le représentera d'après les idées particulières à chaque pays" (FYO, 366). Logically, the proposition should end there and be sufficient. And yet it is not. "Malheureux" generates a considerable amount of further prose, whose purpose is partly to establish the extent of the pauper's misery, but more clearly to give scope to the narrator's poetic perceptions: "Mais qui se figurera son visage blanc, ridé, rouge aux extrémités, et sa barbe longue? Qui verra sa cravate jaunasse en corde, son col de chemise gras, son chapeau tout usé, sa redingote verdâtre, son pantalon piteux, son gilet recroquevillé, son épingle en faux or, ses souliers crottés, dont les rubans avaient barboté dans la boue? Qui le comprendra dans toute l'immensité de sa misère présente et passée?" (FYO, 366) Who? Simply the narrator, and through him, the sufficiently sensitive reader.

In such cases, the narrator's vision is constituted beforehand, and the question of how to render a certain scene already contains the description which is the answer. This places the narrator in a position to expand his descriptive passages ad infinitum, by successively describing "indescribable" objects. The insistence upon his authority is also a statement of it, and this combination of qualities often evokes his most striking and suggestive prose. The opening pages of *César Birotteau,* where Madame Birotteau, half awake, stares about for the missing César, is a case in point: "Par quels mots rendre les effroyables zigzags que produisent les ombres portées, les apparences fantastiques des rideaux bombés par le vent, les jeux de la lumière incertaine que projette la veilleuse dans les plis du calicot rouge, les flammes que vomit une patère dont le centre rutilant ressemble à l'oeil d'un voleur, l'apparition d'une robe agenouillée, enfin toutes les bizarreries qui effraient l'imagination au moment où elle n'a de puissance que pour percevoir des douleurs et pour les agrandir" (CB, 6). The problem of portraying Madame Birotteau's panic need hardly be stated any further; it has been resolved.

But the most common technique the narrator uses to

create and satisfy a necessary ignorance is that of definitions. When the narrator maintains that one of his definitions is written only "for etymologists" we may discount the remark (HA, 401). Definitions are clearly a function of *Idée,* and thus to be distrusted; in a very early text Balzac had put the matter succinctly: "Troisième axiome: A côté du besoin de définir se trouve le danger de s'embrouiller" (PE, 486). The suspicion remained with him, and he never quite trusted the technique, considered abstractly. Even when he wants us to take a definition seriously, the narrator often assumes a bantering tone: "Lorette est un mot décent inventé pour exprimer l'état d'une fille ou la fille d'un état difficile à nommer, et que, dans sa pudeur, l'Académie française a négligé de définir, vu l'âge de ses quarante membres" (HA, 401).

Why then does the narrator use definitions so frequently? Most importantly because they locate him as the central consciousness of the novel. One of the most striking instances of this self-establishment through definition occurs in *Le Deputé d'Arcis,* when Simon Giguet presents himself as a political candidate under the banner of progress:

Le Progrès, un de ces mots derrière lesquels on essayait alors de grouper beaucoup plus d'ambitions menteuses que d'idées; car, après 1830, il ne pouvait représenter que les prétentions de quelques démocrates affamés, ce mot faisait encore beaucoup d'effet dans Arcis et donnait de la consistance à qui l'inscrivait sur son drapeau. Se dire un homme de progrès, c'était se proclamer philosophe en toute chose et puritain en politique. On se déclarait ainsi pour les chemins de fer, les mackintosh, les pénitenciers, le pavage en bois, l'indépendance des nègres, les caisses d'épargne, les souliers sans couture, l'éclairage au gaz, les trottoirs en asphalte, le vote universel, la réduction de la Liste Civile. Enfin, c'était se prononcer contre les traités de 1815, contre la branche aînée, contre le colosse du Nord, la perfide Albion, contre toutes les entreprises bonnes ou mauvaises du gouvernement. Comme on le voit, le mot *progrès* peut aussi bien signifier: Non! que Oui! . . . C'était le réchampissage du mot *libéralisme,* un nouveau mot d'ordre pour des ambitions nouvelles" (DA, 305).

Such a definition of progress reflects very closely the warnings the narrator himself has issued about their danger. At the same time, definition places the narrator in the omniscient position from which alone his sarcasm could flow. More is at issue here than Simon's political ambitions and his use of a propagandistic word. The narrator is reducing Simon and his ambitions to an obviously inadequate set of terms. The result is not any useful definition of progress but a particular and biased interpretation of the character by the narrator. The latter is maneuvering his definition in order to control what, he thinks, the reader will see in it. The presumed ignorance of the reader is cleared up *in a certain way,* and the assumptions underlying the process are only thinly veiled.

Definitions consequently come to occupy a central position in the expression of basic themes. This happens with the definition of "rebouteur" in *L'Enfant maudit.* The "rebouteur", or folk-doctor, is defined as follows: "Cet homme était l'espèce de sorcier que les paysans nomment encore, dans plusieurs endroits de la France, un *Rebouteur.* Ce nom appartenait à quelques génies bruts qui, sans étude apparente, mais par des connaissances héréditaires et souvent par l'effet d'une longue pratique dont les observations s'accumulaient dans une famille, *reboutaient,* c'est-à-dire remettaient les jambes et les bras cassés, guérissaient bêtes et gens de certaines maladies, et possédaient des secrets prétendus merveilleux pour les traitements des cas graves" (EM, 359). The controlling elements of this definition correspond precisely to the place of the rebouteur in the novel. They center, on the one hand, around the awe-inspiring nature of his craft: he is at least one-half magician. The important words of the definition in this respect are "sorcier," "génie," "secrets," and "merveilleux." On the other hand "connaissance," "étude," "pratique," and "observation" establish his fundamental humaneness: he is also at least one-half country doctor. Thus the rebouteur is able to impose himself on the brutal and ignorant duke because of his mysterious and magical aura; at the same time he is able to earn the trust of the spiritual duchess and her son because of his humanity. The rebouteur becomes, in fact, a key character between the two opposing forces of the

|197|

novel, and his subsequent role unfolds from the microcosmic definition.

Definitions used in this way are a variety of the narrator's fondness for "laws" and generalizations, but colored by the particular dynamics of the texts in which they appear. The definition of "espion" that we are offered in *Une Ténébreuse Affaire* provides not a dictionary description of the word but an analysis of what a spy represents in this novel. "*L'espion* . . . a le front d'airain pour les injures, il marche à son but comme un animal dont la carapace solide ne peut être entamée que par le canon; mais aussi, comme l'animal, il est d'autant plus furieux quand il est atteint, qu'il a cru sa cuirasse impénétrable" (TA, 130). Obviously, not all spies conform to this pattern; the qualities enumerated do, however, apply directly to Corentin, and alert us to many subsequent incidents involving him.

The net effect is to dehyperbolize the tale. The narrator's basic caution with definitions makes him proceed with care and choose them as part of the general enterprise of establishing his authoritative position vis-a-vis the reader. This immediately reflects the purpose of the definition back onto the narrator himself. The "etymologists" and the "ignorant readers" are nothing but other versions of himself, which enable him to establish himself as the central spinner of words in a world made of nothing but words.[4]

But the reader cannot remain ignorant indefinitely. As his knowledge is recognized by the narrator, explanation becomes increasingly superfluous. In connection with cer-

---

[4]Among the literally hundreds of definitions in the *Comédie humaine*, a long passage on "bourguignon" in *Etude de femme* (p. 387), with a teasing play on the classical theme of love-as-fire, is particularly interesting. "Bourrier" in *Le Curé de Tours* (p. 236) is the subject of a long definition with touchingly pathetic overtones. Other definitions of special interest are "l'homme politique" (Be, 258); "Eureka" (RA, 331); "carotter" (B, 323); "candeur" (F, 120); "chiner" (CP, 119 and 121); "narette" (R, 430); "cagnard" (R, 408); "Vocation" (R, 277); "conscrit" (Ch, 10); "chuin" (Ch, 31); "tante" (SM, xvi, 179); "medecin des morts" (SM, xvi, 141); "préau" (SM, xvi, 160); "chevaux de retour (SM, xvi, 173); "rat" (SM, xv, 15–16); "brio" (Be, 101).

tain objects, persons, or themes, the narrator can quite easily assume, between himself and the reader, a common fund of cultural knowledge. The carriage known as *malle,* we read, "sert à emporter les effets de voyage, dirait un homme de l'école de Delille" (PMV, 15). Confidence in the literary sophistication of the reader shines through an allusion to Heine's description of love as "la maladie secrète du coeur" (PrB, 373), or the description of Maxime de Trailles' belly being borne about "au majestueux, suivant l'expression de Brillat-Savarin" (DA, 391). With such an attitude, definitions become less necessary; rather, the reader is drawn into a participatory relationship with the narrator in which words are accepted as unproblematical between them.

When this happens, explanatory language gives way to what the narrator calls "talismanic" language. It would be an endless process to catalogue the words of the Balzacian vocabulary that have special internal, conventional meanings. But it is surely enlightening to observe that "faire la cour" and "modestie" are singled out in *Modeste Mignon* (pp. 96 and 131); that "un bon mariage" is emphasized in *Le Médecin de campagne* (p. 216); that Rose Cormon, in *La Vieille Fille* has "la beauté du diable" (p. 311); that cousin Pons is "exploité" in the novel that bears his name (p. 27). The stresses given these words (sometimes through sheer typographical devices such as italicization) reflect major themes in the novels, and help establish the conceptual points of view from which their events are seen.[5]

The reader's awareness of the talismanic role of language results from the fact that when so used words sum up whole networks of thematic material without, however, specifically mentioning them. When Victurnien d'Esgrignon is floundering in the marshes of Parisian society, his rival de Marsay is delighted to see him "s'enfonçant" (CA, 74). The word is identified only as coming from the vocabulary of dandies, but its particular and unspoken malice

---

[5] In *Les Chouans* (p. 149) words are even said to possess their own "physiognomy," which the narrator assumes is understood by the reader.

in this context arises from the reader's awareness that it is de Marsay himself who is helping Victurnien's demise in no small measure. At the other end of the moral spectrum, the narrator need only metamorphose Madame Firmiani "en maison" for the reader to grasp immediately the warmth and friendliness of her hospitality (Fir, 357). The danger of talismans is that with overuse they can become hackneyed and possibly incomprehensible; but when they work as intended—that is, as concentrations of meanings under-stood and assumed—they contain a poetic potential of quite unusual power. Félix de Vandenesse expresses their fascination when he muses on the names of Madame de Mortsauf's two estates: "Ces noms possèdent les vertus talismaniques des paroles constellées en usage dans les évo-cations, ils m'expliquent la magie, ils réveillent des figures endormies qui se dressent aussitôt et me parlent, ils me mettent dans cette heureuse vallée, ils créent un ciel et des paysages; mais les évocations ne se sont-elles pas toujours passées dans les régions du monde spirituel?" (Lys, 120)

Behind definitions and talismans lies the double nature of knowledge on which the narrator depends: the common and conventional knowledge that he assumes in his reader, and the "knowledge" that he himself has provided through his narration. The interplay between them is a narrative puzzle Balzac and his narrator often refer to as the distinc-tion between "dire" and "exprimer." The alternatives are perhaps best formulated in La Femme abandonnée: "En ce moment, Gaston de Nueil se sentait poussé vers madame de Beauséant . . . par cette foule de motifs impossibles à dire, et que le mot de fatalité sert souvent à exprimer" (FA, 266). "Dire" is closely associated with Idée and its poetic inadequacies, with direct description and with language that tends toward silence; "exprimer" is associated with Pensée and a language able to convey aesthetic concepts beyond the powers of "dire."

As the narrator confronts his putative reader, he must find a kind of discourse that lies between the two theoreti-cal opposites. While his statements must be grounded in the mimetic qualities of *Idée* and its language of "dire," he must seek his ultimate meanings in *Pensée* and the language of "exprimer." Yet the mode of "dire " is most easily and directly available, even in the realm of art and aesthetics. Most of the artists of the *Comédie humaine*, through whom the narrator renders this problem explicit, discuss works of art in very "reasonable" ways. Frenhofer, the painter, is full of good sense about painting: "Parce que vous avez fait quelque chose qui ressemble plus à une femme qu'à une maison, vous pensez avoir touché le but . . . vous vous imaginez être des artistes merveilleux" (ChO, 9). Despite his famous formulation about "expression," it is only in a copyist's terms that he can talk about Porbus' canvas: "Non, mon ami, le sang ne court pas sous cette peau d'ivoire, l'existence ne gonfle pas de sa rosée de pourpre les veines et les fibrilles" (ChO, 7). Porbus' female figure, in his judgment, "ne vit pas." The same terminology characterizes Poussin's reaction to a painting of Adam by Mabuse. He is struck principally by its "puissance de réalité." Frenhofer agrees, remarking that "l'homme est bien vivant, il se lève et va venir à nous," although he regrets that "il manquait encore un peu de vérité dans le fond de la toile" (p. 16). And we ascertain with a certain surprise that Mabuse's great secret was "le secret du relief, le pouvoir de donner aux figures cette vie extraordinaire, cette fleur de nature, notre désespoir éternel, mais dont il possédait si bien *le faire*" (p. 20). As far as what these artists can *say* about a painting, we are not much advanced beyond the most elementary trompe-l'oeil.

Like Frenhofer, Gambara is trapped in the modalities of "dire" when speaking of his opera *Mahomet* to his patron the count. Although aided by a piano, Gambara's verbal description comes down to a catalog of leitmotifs linking tonalities to emotions in a way that suggests later Wagnerian practices, but which most musicians find profoundly unsatisfactory: "A travers ses plaintes, par une transition au temps relatif (*mi bémol, allegro quatre temps*) percent les cris de l'amoureux épileptique. . . . Cadhige annonce au peuple les entrevues du prophète avec l'ange Gabriel (maestoso sostenuto en fa mineur)" (Gam, 71).[6] Unable to communicate his perceptions through "dire," Gambara resorts to comparisons with nature. Indeed, he goes so far as to claim for music a kind of natural inevitability: "je dis que la musique est un art tissu dans les entrailles mêmes de la Nature. La musique obéit à des lois physiques et mathématiques. . . .Ce qui étend la science étend l'art" (pp. 61–62). But such metaphors fall just as short of accounting for the beauty of *Mahomet* as do the catalogues of tonalities.

The problem is clear enough: the beauty of the opera *Mahomet* is not questioned; merely the way in which Gambara tries to describe it. His lucid moments—those when he is most concerned with describing and explaining in the mode of "dire"—are the moments when he makes the least sense about it. Intentionality, will, and reason all fail him, as they fail other creative spirits of the *Comédie humaine.* Balthasar Claës is not destroyed by the Absolute itself, but by the supposition that the Absolute can be analytically and rationally sought in nature. The word used by the Polish soldier who first interests Balthasar in alchemy is "cherchable" —a fatal word that sets off the processes of ruin and disaster. Faith in the power of reason applied to the world leads Balthasar to describe his supreme experiments as "reproductions" of nature: "Je fais les métaux, je fais les diamants, je répète la nature!" (RA, 189) And this is exactly the ambition and the illusion of Frenhofer, who prides himself on having reproduced—in his portrait of La Belle Noiseuse—"la nature elle-même" (ChO, 25). Yet Balthasar

---

[6]Like so many other critics, Charles Affron analyses this passage to illustrate a type of what he calls artistic "failure" in the *Comédie humaine.* He rightly points out that the narrator's technique here is utterly ineffectual; but to conclude from that that "the Word, used imaginatively to describe the world, becomes reticent before art" is to ignore the whole point of this passage: namely, that only a *certain kind* of language—the mimetic language of *Idée*—is incapable of dealing with art. Other passages, where the narrator is speaking in his own right, amply demonstrate that language can indeed deal with art. See Affron, *Patterns of Failure,* p. 128.

stumbles upon the Absolute in an accidental way totally unconnected with his ruinous "experiments"; Gambara makes his most truly beautiful music when he abandons description, explanation, and all discursive categories in a drunken stupor; Frenhofer finally commits suicide rather than continue the hopeless competition with "nature," which is ruining, not creating, his masterpiece. True creativity, the narrator writes, goes beyond the limits of human reason, "emmenant la froide raison . . . à travers mille routes pierreuses où, pour [elle], il n'y a rien" (ChO, 19).

Yet after the Fauves, who would reject Frenhofer's canvas; after Stockhausen, who would object to Gambara's opera; after atom-smashers, who would still call Balthasar Claës crazy? None of these artists is "wrong" for having created as he did. But each surrenders to a mode of thinking in which he admits that his creation and real reality can be judged according to the same criteria; in which he admits, so to speak, a Turgotian system of naive realism. This weakness arises after the creation of the work, supplanting the heady exploration of *Pensée* with the descriptiveness of *Idée*. Having created, the artist stands before his work as simply another perceiver; his position is perhaps even more painful, for he knows what it has been like to create. But now his interpretations, like all hermeneutic acts in the *Comédie humaine,* must be conducted in the language of *Idée*, in the modalities of "dire." And submitted to formal analysis, the work "disappears."

The problems that destroy the artists of the *Comédie humaine*, however—and with few exceptions they end disastrously—do not destroy the narrator. *He* must go on; and he does so by assuming that to analyze the work of art merely as a picture of the world is to miss its significance entirely. He recognizes the danger of being diverted from the creation of significance and value to the mere description of form. Indeed , the narrator refrains entirely from writing a novel about literary creativity—a project that would have led him to engage in just the sort of descriptive analytics that he condemns in his characters.[7]

No matter how many times the narrator presents us with artistic or creative characters attempting to "explain" what they are doing, he always finds himself at an impasse. How then would it be possible to convey to his putative reader, without the interposition of a veil of descriptive language, some sense of the ultimate reality of his position, of the godlike joy of creation? The only recourse would be to some element within his language, not to some metalanguage outside it. The mode of discourse he calls "exprimer" has, in his view, such possibilities. "Exprimer" or "expression" is linked to the narrator's theoretical speculations about the "musicality" and the "energy" of primitive language. The speech of Genestas, for example, is "une expression pleine de sens comme l'est la parole du Sauvage" (MC, 8). Such sense is part of what Balzac's century was disposed to see as the direct access to primal truth possessed by the primitive, artistic, saintly, or emotionally impassioned mind, and it represents part of what the narrator is trying to achieve. When Gaston de Nueil writes a love letter to Madame de Beauséant, pleading with her to realize that "ce n'est pas une déclaration vulgaire ni intéressée, mais l'expression d'un fait naturel" (FA, 286), he is appealing to a kind of direct, unmediated truth, which he is not sure the mere words of his letter will convey. His doubts are well founded, for as he and Madame de Beauséant develop their relationship, as they "s'informèrent de la vérité de leurs expressions" (FA, 279), they find themselves engaged in a process that takes them "très loin en théorie." David Séchard finds himself in a similar situation with respect to Eve Chardon, when he realizes that nothing he can say

[7]The closest the narrator comes to this experiment is to say that d'Arthez' novel is designed to explore the resources of language—although he refrains, significantly, from giving us any examples of d'Arthez' work. Later novelists—one thinks immediately of Flaubert and Proust—were to discover methods of introspective analysis. I am not suggesting that Balzac anticipated their narrative discoveries, but rather that he clearly pointed out the narrative dead-end of "dire."

touches the essentials: "J'avais, hélas! le coeur bien lourd de sentiments que je ne pouvais ni savais exprimer" (IP, XI 285).[8] Similarly, Benassis suffers from not having "le droit d'exprimer les élans de [son] coeur" (MC, 218).

"Expression" thus represents some kind of ideal communication between speaker and hearer, between narrator and reader, but not a reach for mystical or ineffable union. The special nature of "expression" in contrast to "dire" seems to be that the former is unique in each case of its use. Within the general mode of human love, Benassis observes, emotional attachment becomes for each individual "une oeuvre unique où s'expriment ses sympathies" (MC, 220). He notes further that "l'expression de l'amour est tellement diverse que chaque couple d'amants n'a pas son semblable dans la succession des temps" (MC, 221). Where "dire" is the common coin of conventional language, reproducible from one situation to another and lying in the domain of *Idée,* "exprimer" is a mode of language that enshrines the esthetic uniqueness of each situation, which is incapable of repetition, and which lies in the domain of *Pensée.*

Just as *Pensée* was most clearly discernible in the antiquarian's art gallery, so "exprimer" is particularly characteristic of artistic language. This is not without its difficulties, however. "Il y a les poètes qui sentent et les poètes qui expriment" we are told in *Ferragus* (p. 26), and "les premiers sont les plus heureux." Notwithstanding this, the inevitability of "expression" in any work of art is insisted upon time and again, perhaps nowhere with such force as in the case of Frenhofer, who exlaims "La mission de l'art n'est pas de copier la nature, mais de l'exprimer!" (ChO 9) Here, "copier" is the precise equivalent of the poet's "dire"; that is, a phenomenon of *Idée* based upon the assumptions of naive realism. And Frenhofer spells out the choice quite precisely: "essaie de mouler la main de ta maîtresse et de la poser devant toi, tu trouveras un horrible cadavre sans

[8]The narrator had already observed that David "contenait sa passion au lieu de l'exprimer" (IP, XI, 242).

aucune ressemblance, et tu seras forcé d'aller trouver le ciseau de l'homme qui, sans te la copier exactement, t'en figurera le mouvement et la vie" (ChO, 9).[9] Another sage figure, the antiquarian of *La Peau de chagrin,* takes much the same view: "Ce que les hommes appellent chagrins, amours, ambitions, revers, tristesse, sont pour moi des idées que je change en rêveries; au lieu de les sentir, je les exprime, je les traduis" (Pch, 39). Here again, we observe that "exprimer" leads not to silence, but to communication—a kind of communication that the antiquarian equates with revery, but communication none the less. "Je les dramatise," he explains, "je les développe, je m'en amuse comme de romans que je lirais par une vision intérieure" (Pch, 39). Translation, dramatization, and development are all processes that are diametrically opposed to the functioning of "dire" and its analytical, reproductive bias. "Exprimer" has little to do with descriptive exactitude. When the narrator of *Pierrette* comes to grips with the difficulties of communicating to the reader a true understanding of the horrors he must relate, he remarks that "leur traduction algébraïque quoique vraie, est infidèle sous le rapport de la forme. Ces calculs profunds ne parlent pas aussi brutalement que l'histoire les exprime" (P, 89–90). There must be a necessary infidelity to "dire"; only by being formally unfaithful to experience can the narrator be essentially, that is, aesthetically, faithful. Into this unavoidable deviation pours everything he perceives and feels about Pierrette's fate, not to speak of all the unspoken cruelties of the story itself, which he, unlike the characters, must articulate.

The Balzacian narrator returns again and again to his most deeply-felt sense of what artistic creativity—hence his own activity—should be. The anonymous painter of *Visites* teases his client Mme ∗ ∗ ∗ by insisting that when a por-

[9]The distinction between physiognomonics and pathognomonics is quite clear in this passage. Yet although Frenhofer is recommending a change in the methods of art, he is not questioning the purposes of art. As it happens, however, the change in methods will alter the perceived purposes.

traitist works, "le talent du peintre fait parler les traits, mais son âme doit en trahir le langage" (V, 6). The poetic mind, he says elsewhere, "devant à un caprice de la génération intellectuelle la faculté rare d'exprimer la nature par des images où il empreint à la fois le sentiment et l'idée, il donne à son amour les ailes de son esprit: il sent, et il peint, il agit et médite, il multiplie ses sensations par la pensée" (SM, xv, 59). Here again, the essential ingredient is development; but it must be emphasized that the development in question is a function of the poet's *Pensée,* "ses sensations," and not a further extraction of data from reality. This does not mean, of course, that the poet abandons all contact with the objective world. It is, after all, in addition to his own sentient selfhood, a vision of the world and an interpretation of the human condition that he is aiming at. "Quand un artiste a le malheur d'être plein de la passion qu'il veut exprimer," says Capraja in *Massimilla Doni,* "il ne saurait le peindre, car il est la chose même au lieu d'en être l'image. L'art procède du cerveau et non du coeur. Quand votre sujet vous domine, vous en êtes l'esclave et non le maître" (p. 462).

But the action of the mind is capricious and uncertain. The hand must always be ready to obey the head, we read in *La Cousine Bette,* but "la tête n'a pas plus les dispositions créatrices à commandement que l'amour n'est continu" (p. 243). Yet in those privileged moments when the mind guides the hand in a process of "expression," there emerges a sense of plenitude and rightness that springs from the exact sufficiency of the form to artistic sensibility. "Je sens, ils expriment; je conçois, ils exécutent; ils me traduisent, ils me devinent, ils m'entrainent où je veux aller"; so speaks the painter of his feelings when he reads the great poets (V, 6). It is the fullest form of the contextuality that Balzac recognized as the only escape from the dilemmas of naive realism.

In a sense, then, the narrator-reader relationship might be defined as the progression, on the reader's part, from ignorance to knowledge; and on the narrator's part from "dire" to "exprimer." Both are versions of the general theoretical contrast of *Idée* and *Pensée*. Only the failed artists such as Pierre Grassou can reject the latter in favor of the former: "Inventer en toute chose, c'est vouloir mourir à petit feu; copier, c'est vivre" (PGr, 447). Such statements stand in clear opposition to the narrator's own position, which is that the option of "exprimer" or, as it is put here, "inventer," is not the artist's death, but his life. We are back to the lesson of *La Peau de chagrin*, in testimony to which we now have the accumulating texts of the *Comédie humaine* itself.[10]

Faced with the complexities of "expression," the temptation of any speaker to silence is great indeed. Benassis respects the reticence of his beloved on just these grounds: "Je finis par deviner que ce timide silence était le seul moyen qui pût servir à cette jeune fille pour exprimer ses sentiments" (MC, 219). But silence, however tempting for the lover, is a narrative dead end. "La beauté sans expression est peut-être une imposture," remarks the narrator of *Une Double famille* (p. 283). And yet there are concepts that defy expression, and for which the Balzacian narrator finds not silence but a form of expression he calls "virtualité."[11] "Les grands calculateurs," writes the narrator of *La Recherche de l'absolu*, "n'ont de respect que pour la virtualité empreinte dans un parfait accomplissement" (p. 113). This was a strange and paradoxical remark that establishes vir-

[10] Not every occurrence of the word "exprimer" is of significance, of course, but the fact that the narrator's constant return to this term is no mere tic, is demonstrated by its occurrence in a key sentence from the *Lettre addressée aux écrivains français:* "Ne constatons-nous pas les moeurs? La civilisation n'est rien sans expression. Nous sommes, nous savants, nous écrivains, nous artistes, nous poètes, chargés de l'exprimer" (p. 654).

[11] At the time Balzac was writing, "virtualité" was not a common term of either literary criticism or philosophy, although it had been used by Leibnitz in the *Nouveaux Essais* to indicate a kind of innate idea with predetermined contents that could be generated by the mind itself. This was in clear opposition to the Lockian concept of ideas as the products of *reactive* processes of mind. Balzac is known to have read Leibnitz as early as 1822, and there is every likelihood that he was struck by this argument levelled at the English philosopher he so admired. See his letter to Madame de Berny, *Correspondance,* edited by Roger Pierrot (Paris, 1960), I, 178.

tuality as the supreme expression of calculation, and the highest quality of the perfectly conceived work! But even men of reason must preserve in their relations with creative work—whether of art or science—the domain of the un-explainable, the element of mystery, the elusive quality that prevents its ever being totally explicated. Surfaces painted, things said, sounds played, experiments performed, never only challenge nature, but are also simply themselves—contextual networks of internal relationships infinite in number and variety. Only the false artist violates the work in order to impress his audience. He affronts it too brutal-ly, calculates the conditions of its existence even before it is fully born, refuses it a margin of aesthetic significance, and condemns it to remain in the domain of *Idée*. True virtual-ity endows the work of art with a profound calm (RA, 113). It is a potential; it is that aesthetic dimension of the work that allows the possibilities of varied interpretations with-out imposing any one of them; it is the quality which "com-prend toute une nature en germe plus virtuellement que la graine ne contient le système d'une plante et ses produits" (LL, 167).

It is therefore quite natural to see virtuality play its role among the true artists of the *Comédie humaine*. Joseph Brideau is one of a small group "occupés pendant des journées entières, dans le silence de leurs ateliers, à des travaux qui laissent jusqu'a un certain point la pensée libre" (R, 319). This contemplative state contrasts dramatically with the feverish activity of Claës, Frenhofer, and other failed artists. The true creator is characterized by "égalité d'humeur . . . indulgence et continuité de la pensée sub-lime dont il est l'interprète" (RA, 139). The failed artists do not understand this. Their willingness, even eagerness, to "construct" the work diverges clearly from the narrator's own position, which is that analytic thought during the process of creation risks destroying the work of art itself. Creativity, in his view, simply does not lie within the realm of the rational processes of mind. There must be, between the artist and his work, a pact of contemplation according to which the artist waits for the work as much as he seeks it. *La Théorie de la démarche* was an attempt to describe this necessary stage in the development of a work of art. Beginning with its initial existence as an *Idée,* the work moves through a series of transformations in the subliminal areas of *Pensée* to its eventual expression in a form that is partially unforeseen and unexpected even to the artist himself. Frenhofer instinctively locks his work away in his studio; Balthazar Claës forbids his family to enter his laboratory; Gambara retreats from the world into drunken stupors. And in such states, each achieves some partial success: Frenhofer does make miraculously beautiful pictures, Balthazar does synthesize some substances, Gambara does create lovely music, and admits that if music copies science, it does so "à son insu" (Gam, 59–60).

But the relationship of "virtualité" applies not only to the artist and his work; it applies as well to the work and the perceiver. "Virtualité" is one way to escape the silence imposed by the all-knowing reader, because it assumes in him not a totality of knowledge about the work of art, but the ability to read creatively and to move hermeneutic acts from the domain of *Idée* to the domain of *Pensée.* This may indeed be merely a matter of orders of complexity; but to allow the work of art a margin of mystery and potential is also to allow a diversity of interpretation.[12]

The narrator takes this stance with respect to the reader in a number of ways, of which the most characteristic is the reiterated warning that in this most realist of chronicles, nothing is real. We must abolish the competition with nature so that, paradoxically, nature may come through all the more clearly. The process is set up at the very begin-

[12] Later in the century, Mallarmé used the concept of "virtuality" to indicate precisely the multiplicity of the work of art that contains too many hermeneutic possibilities for human reason to encompass, and which therefore forces us to renounce mimeticism: "Au contaire d'une fonction de numéraire facile et représentatif, comme le traite d'abord la foule, le dire, avant tout, rêve et chante, retrouve chez le poète, par nécessité constitutive d'un art consacré aux fictions, sa virtualité" (from *Divagations;* cited by A. G. Lehmann, *The Symbolist Aesthetic in France* (Oxford, 1950), p. 156).

ning of many episodes of the *Comédie humaine* in peculiar and sometimes enigmatic "entrées en matière." *Splendeurs et misères des courtisanes* opens with a masked ball at the opera, where the fantastically costumed characters play on the mysteries of their identities, and so set the tone of a novel that explores, among other things, the nature of identity; an anonymous "rêveur" strolls about old Paris at the beginning of *L'Envers de l'histoire contemporaine,* engaged in a "double contemplation" (p. 216) and establishing the parameters of a novel concerned with questions of appearance and reality.

But certain of these entries into the world of fiction are accomplished by the narrator's questioning the relationship of his own language to objective reality. *Les Petits Bourgeois* opens with a lament on the disappearance of the rue du tourniquet Saint-Jean, which now has only an "existence typographique" (p. 3), located in the mind of a potential reader. *Le Père Goriot* begins with the precise description of an imaginary street, and the entry is accomplished by a word, *drame,* which, "en quelque discrédit qu'[il] soit tombé," is the word to describe all that will happen in the Pension Vauquer (PG, 221–22). A considerable part of the opening movement of *Eugénie Grandet* is devoted to the definition of the phrase "la maison à Monsieur Grandet," simply because that phrase contains so much of what the reader must know, not of any real Saumur, but of the complex relationships among certain concepts in the story; and *Le Cabinet des antiques,* to take a final example, proposes to tell a true story about a city and a family that cannot be named: "faites comme si d'Esgrignon était un nom de convention, sans plus de réalité que n'en ont les Belval, les Floricour, les Derville de la comédie" (p. 3). The narrator insists repeatedly upon the autonomous nature of his linguistic object. Over and over again, the romantic clichés of anonymous characters, mysterious scenes, insistently precise imaginary décors, distracted artists, and so on, become, through their explicit status as language, part of a flight into virtuality. The language of the *Comédie humaine* "irrealizes" best, to use Sartre's term, when it abandons the competition with nature.

The problem as it presents itself is, therefore, by no means a metaphysical abstraction, but a starkly practical difficulty. At certain critical moments, language seems to falter in its mimetic continuity; at that point the narrator raises the problem of description itself as if, by substituting a statement of his difficulties for the ostensible object of the narration, he might close the gap between himself and his reader.[13]

This was virtuality exploited to the fullest, and in successive novels, Balzac developed and extended the concept and technique. *La Femme de trente ans* uses the device with perhaps more consistency than any other part of the *Comédie humaine*. This novel turns the flight to virtuality a fundamental compositional device. Each of the four parts begins with the specific statement that the scene about to be evoked is a matter of the imagination. We are in a world of "teintes presque fabuleuses" (pp. 5–6); then immersed in a "monologue dont les mille pensées . . . sont intraduisibles" (p. 106); then transported into "féeries éloquentes" (p. 129); and finally placed in front of a "sublime et naïve composition" (pp. 148–49). These are not merely a romantic narrator's devices for excusing himself from the responsibilities of realistic verifiability, but radical departures from naive realism. Unlike certain of his characters, the narrator does not propose to compete with nature, but to present us with a record of perceptions. The distinction is important. For it means that the Balzacian narrator is not rejecting the real world; he is suggesting that language creates individual angles of vision on the world, no one of which can pretend to be objectively accurate. And if that is true, then his own text, in the eyes of the presumed reader,

[13]Balzac could surely not have failed to note in the *Tristram Shandy* he admired so much a suggestive remark: "no author who understands the just boundaries of decorum and good breeding, would presume to think all: The truest respect you can pay to the reader's understanding, is to halve this matter amicably, and leave him something to imagine, in his turn, as well as yourself" *(Tristram Shandy,* Book II, chapter 11, p. 83).

|212|

is but another object of interpretation. And so the narrator presents himself in the opening pages of *La Femme de trente ans* as writing from the vantage point of an eternal "aujourd'hui" (p. 6); he explicitly refers to himself as a poet *who one day might describe* the scenes which are about to be presented in the text (p. 21), or as a dreamer who accompanies the characters in their movements (p. 80). Again and again the narrator laments his inability to reach his reader with any certainty: "le langage ne suffirait pas . . . " (p. 50); "une confusion que rien ne saurait exprimer" (p. 177); "horribles souffrances, incroyables, sans langage!" (p. 210) He is driven to various devices in his attempts to close the gap: descriptions of landscapes that are then said to express inexpressible emotions (pp. 63 and 125); confrontations with the reader, and warnings that those who have not had parallel experiences cannot hope to understand (p. 51); and simply the insistence that some things are eternally beyond the power of words to convey (p. 85). Many of these maneuvres were not new. Diderot, among Balzac's immediate predecessors, had felt the occasional inability of language to convey thought;[14] but what is new is the consistency with which Balzac uses them to establish the basic tonality of his relationship with the reader. The end result, however, is not a breakdown in that relationship. Indeed, the narrator's complaints are the limiting case of a successful process. Complaints of noncommunicability take the place of silence, and enable the text to continue because of the way they oblige the reader to cope with the difficulties himself. If the words of the text are not viewed mimetically, and if the reader is drawn into the imaginative enterprise that is the novel, then theoretically the veil no longer exists, because it has no interlocutors between whom to exist.[15]

There is thus at the center of *La Femme de trente ans* a

[14]Especially striking is Diderot's observation that "on ne retient presque rien sans le secours des mots, et les mots ne suffisent presque jamais pour rendre précisément ce que l'on sent." Denis Diderot, *Oeuvres complètes*, edited by J. Assézat, Vol. XII: *Beaux-Arts* (Paris, 1876), 77.

[15]The point has been made with precision and in almost identical terms by Wolfgang Iser: "The literary text activates our own faculties, enabling

peculiar silence-in-words; a meditation on the limitations of language, in which the narrator obliges the reader to participate. But even making the reader participate in these problems was apt to be an unsatisfactory solution in the end. In a letter to Madame Hanska, Balzac observed that there was in this work "trop de pensées et . . . trop de drame pour qu'on puisse les mettre en dehors."[16] Balzac was never really satisfied with *La Femme de trente ans;* the problems of the veil reasserted themselves as fast as he thought he abolished them, and in 1836 he was still trying—vainly—to make certain aspects of the story more "probable."[17] Yet the very improbabilities of this novel are part of its strange charm. It was perhaps inevitable that the rejection of naive realism should leave the narrator in an ambiguous position reflected in the episodic, jerky, unconnected nature of the text. It is full of unexplained happenings, and has only the most casual linking of part to part. This is surely due to some extent to its curiously haphazard composition;[18] but Balzac's willingness to see it as a novel at all, and his repeated attempts to give it a satisfactory shape, suggest that there was something attractive in it. The interruptions in the narrative flow (here, to be sure, grossly and even annoyingly exaggerated) might have been the means, had he been able to handle them well, by which to co-opt

---

us to recreate the world it presents. The product of this creative activity is what we might call the virtual dimension of the text, which endows it with reality. This virtual dimension is not the text itself, nor is it the imagination of the reader: it is the coming together of text and imagination." See Wolfgang Iser, "The Reading Process: A Phenomenological Approach," *New Literary History,* III, no. 2 (1972), 284.

[16]*Lettres à Madame Hanska,* edited by Roger Pierrot (Paris, 1968), I, 240. The letter is dated probably around March 28, 1834, and refers to section II of the novel, which is characteristically entitled "Souffrances inconnues."

[17]A letter to Madame Hanska written in January 1836 refers to the departure of Hélène with the mysterious stranger, and calls the incident "presque vraisemblable" *(ibid.,* I, 384).

[18]On the composition and text of *La Femme de trente ans,* see Raymond L. Sullivant, "L'Edition Werdet de *La Femme de trente ans,*" *L'Année balzacienne* (1966), 131–42; and, by the same author, *"La Femme de trente ans:* Quelques emprunts de Balzac à la littérature anglaise," *L'Année balzacienne* (1967), 107–14.

the reader and draw him successfully—as he did elsewhere—into the narrative process.[19] If ever the veil was to be abolished, it would be in this way; the difficulty was that since the reader to whom the creative act is addressed can be nothing more than a projection of aspects of the narrator's own consciousness, the latter has no way of knowing whether or not he will succeed in ensnaring a real reader. In Balzacian narrative this puzzle tends to generate ever more language in an effort to maneuvre and manipulate that enigmatic absence. And so, paradoxically, complaints of the problematical nature of language are nearly swamped by the endless flow of language itself. But only nearly. Through the voluminous verbiage of the *Comédie humaine* the Stendhalian attitude does penetrate intermittently but insistently; and for the same reason that Balzac so admired his illustrious contemporary: "[il] laisse beaucoup à deviner."

[19]Iser observes that "whenever the flow is interrupted and we are led off in unexpected directions, the opportunity is given for us to bring into play our own faculty for establishing connections—for filling gaps left by the text itself" (Iser, "The Reading Process," pp. 284–85). For further treatment of the same idea, see by the same author "Indeterminacy and the Reader's Response in Prose Fiction," in *Aspects of Narrative*, edited by J. Hillis Miller (New York, 1971) pp. 1–45.

Texts

CHAPTER VIII

Illusions perdues and the Word Game

The ancient question of the object-thought-word relationship was, of course, not settled by Balzac. But his basic
maneuver of turning the difficulty into a source of novelistic invention led him to reject naive realism, thus liberating
the imagination, as Saussure was later to say. It is this revolutionary stance on Balzac's part that makes him such a
problem for new and not-so-new critics.[1] For all his old-
fashioned ways, Balzac took the first steps toward the contemporary self-consciousness of fiction, toward the breakdown of mimesis as the conscious and accepted mode of
narration. In discussing the mental revolution of which
Balzac's work was a part, Foucault concludes that "c'est
dans l'élément du discours que doivent être désormais
analysés la possibilité des objets, la présence d'un sujet, et
tout le déploiement positif du monde."[2] It would be foolish
to impute to Balzac a naively Whorfian position; but one
must surely recognize the extent to which an acute sense of
language presided over his response to the objective world.
Far from creating a factitious "realism," he created a discourse in which the debates of several centuries come to a
head. *Illusions perdues* is without doubt the novel in which

[1] It is clear, then, that I cannot accept Goldmann's interpretation of the
Comédie humaine as "la seule grande expression littéraire de l'univers struc-
turé par les valeurs conscientes de la bourgeoisie" *(Pour une sociologie du
roman* [Paris, 1964], p. 34). Individualism, power, and money are indeed
Balzac's chief theme, but to see a bourgeois work in the *Comédie humaine*
for this reason seems to me to revert to the "analyse de contenu" that
Goldmann himself is at pains to deplore. Barbéris' view of the *Comédie
humaine* as a moment of fruitful "waiting," during which the *meaning* of
the triumph of money becomes clear, seems to me to be much closer to the
mark. If Balzac's creatures are not always in opposition to the *status quo, the
narrator is;* and this leads us directly to a narrative structure in dialectical
conflict with its content.
[2] Michel Foucault, "La Grammaire générale de Port-Royal," *Langages,*
VII (1967), 15.

these issues are most clearly expressed; but before turning to a detailed analysis of that text, a few retrospective remarks on the major lines of speculation will enable us to orient our observations.

Since Port-Royal, and even before, the representational nature of language had been a central subject of philosophical speculation; the *Grammaire générale* as well as the *Logique* had assumed the existence of universal logic and language, and had focussed upon the nature of the sign. Port-Royal was much concerned with the nature of signs because the simple Renaissance model of additive analogy, according to which language referred to the real world and all sentences were constructed in parallel with previous examples, turned out to be inadequate.[3] The analogical or mimetic model was troublesome, indeed, even in the language-logic context. For if one assumes the existence of some perfect, universal, a priori logic toward which the mind strives, then the practical experience of verbalization demonstrates the inadequacies of language and forces the thinker back to theological solutions. Port-Royal understood the difficulty, and accepted the doctrine of divine origin, but saw grammar as a set of intermediary principles governing the construction of both discourse and reality.[4] In taking this position, Port-Royal created what Balzac called the veil. Words became the intermediaries between mind and world, and the very mechanism that made discourse possible also rendered it indirect and problematical.[5]

[3] Analogies formed, of course, an endless series of reflecting mirrors: "On sent peu à peu que ce déroulement indéfini du donné est une fuite à l'interieur du Ratio et qu'il faut chercher des relations plus abstraites qui expliquent le fonctionnement de la langue." Chevalier, "La Grammaire générale de Port-Royal," p. 28.

[4] *Ibid.*, p. 24.

[5] Michel Foucault's analysis of the Port-Royal doctrine is characteristically complicated, but comes down to the same thing: "Donner un signe à une idée, c'est se donner une idée dont l'objet sera le représentant de ce qui constituait l'objet de la première idée; l'objet du signe sera substituable et équivalent à l'idée de l'objet signifié." ("La Grammaire générale de Port-Royal," p. 10).

Port-Royal had pointed out, moreover, as had many other theoreticians, that the relationship of the signifier to the signified was conventional rather than natural.[6] What they did not say, of course, was that the world view derived from such a system might itself be conventional. The difficulty was avoided by keeping arbitrariness within the sign (it was, after all, Adam who named the animals), and by regarding both the processes of mind and the objects of the world as fixed. By thus papering over the contradictions of their doctrine, the Port-Royal thinkers were able to identify the Ratio with middle-class consciousness, taken as a theologically justified measurement of universal order. Through language, the bourgeoisie, "la classe dominante par le talent,"[7] attempted to reduce a painfully multiform reality to a state of submission.[8] But the paradoxes did not disappear for all that, and just about the time the young Balzac was laboring over his *Dissertation,* they were becoming increasingly visible. If grammar and logic, based on a theory of arbitrary signs, enabled Port-Royal to choose a certain world view, that very arbitrariness also made other world views possible. Perhaps it was a vague intuition of this possibility that lay behind Balzac's interest in the mysterious "faculté de faire des rapports."[9] For if Port-Royal had indeed solved the problem of mimesis, then there would have been no sense or purpose in Balzac's original ambition to "déchirer les derniers voiles de la nature." When Balzac was working on his *Dissertation* he could not yet have known of Biran's trenchant observation that if

[6] Saussure was not, of course, the inventor of the doctrines of arbitrary signs. Arnauld and Lancelot had not actually used the word "arbitrary," but the concept was clearly in the *Grammaire générale.* See Donzé, *La Grammaire générale et raisonné de Port-Royal* pp. 48–51. For an exhaustive study of this theory, see Eugenio Coseriu, "L'Arbitraire du signe: Zur Spätgeschichte eines aristotelischen Begriffes," *Archiv für das Studium der neueren Sprachen und Literaturen,* no. 24 (May 1967–March 1968), pp. 81–112.

[7] Chevalier, "La Grammaire générale de Port-Royale," p. 30.

[8] Lucien Goldmann has discussed this process with respect to Pascal and Racine in *Le Dieu caché* (Paris, 1955), pp. 13–31.

[9] See chapter I, pp. 30–31.

thinking were calculating, then genius would be redundant.[10] But it is clear that such must have been his view. Maine de Biran's radical psychology of the 1820s was a distinct break with what had gone before.[11]

This transition, fundamental to the nineteenth century, was part of an epistemological shift in focus from "general" man to "particular" man: in this instance from "animal loquens" to "homo parlans." It was a commonplace of eighteenth-century thought, expressed especially by Condillac, that signs originate with respect to particulars, and are extended by analogy to objects and occurrences similar to the original ones. The consequence of this view is that there are no genera in nature, but only in signs.[12] The breakdown in the idea of natural genera authorized that exploitation of the particular which Plato so regretted in the poet, and also justified a thoroughgoing challenge to the traditional assumption that one can move analogically from discrete instances to generalized categories. The Balzacian narrator not only tolerates, but seems to enjoy contradictions between particular cases and the "laws" he likes to draw from them. In ways that can sometimes only be called sly, he leads us through instances that seem to be adding up to an abstract statement about the human condition which, when it comes, turns out to be a vast generalization with only the most tenuous connections with what has come before.

Now if series of signs do not "add up" to abstract principles about reality, one can legitimately ask whether or not they function mimetically in their individual instances. The interest of the *Comédie humaine* in this respect is that it renders this problem of language explicit. It recognizes, as few

[10] Acton, "Philosophy of Language," p. 218.

[11] Michael Foucault has argued that language and logic were quite distinct at Port-Royal: "On voit combien il serait faux de caractériser la grammaire classique par une assimilation hative à la logique. Dans l'une, règles et fondements ne font qu'une seule et même chose; dans l'autre, ils ne sont pas de même niveau" ("La Grammaire générale de Port-Royal," p. 8). The early nineteenth century, however, did not take this view.

[12] Acton, "Philosophy of Language," pp. 203–204.

pieces of nineteenth-century fiction do, the difference between the mimetic and nonmimetic functions of language; or, in Balzac's terminology, the difference between *dire* and *exprimer*. This does not mean that his narration rejects mimesis; rather, it brings mimesis into a new relationship with what one might call "representation." In representation, the conventionality of words is still considered to be the product of repetition; but this repetition is sharply distinguished from the mimetic reproduction of an objective original. Rather, it is the constitution of a *simulacrum,* that is, a series of signs which need not have mimetic content.[13]

To say that we may have fictional signs without an original is not to beard the logician in his den, but simply to indicate that there may be no objectively verifiable referent for a sign that operates in a text as if there were such a referent. Every writer of fiction has his methods of making his signs sufficiently complex and intriguing for them to retain our interest as aesthetic objects. If the Balzacian narrator begins the story of Eugénie Grandet with a long passage on provincial towns and on Saumur especially, the reader can accept the words mimetically: there are towns that correspond to the description generally, and there is a place called Saumur. But as the words referring to Saumur recur, it becomes less and less important to know anything precise about the real city, and more and more important

---

[13]I am indebted to Niels Egebak for the terminology he develops in an important essay, "Représentation et Anti-Mimésis," *Orbis litterarum,* xxvi, no. 1 (1971), pp. 9–19. "Simulacrum" is his term for such series of copies "without originals," so to speak. The concept of the simulacrum brings together many of the themes we have been dealing with so far: the assimilation of the knowable into the known, the relationship of *Idée* and *Pensée,* the relationship of "dire" to "exprimer," among others. Ultimately it raises in particularly sharp ways the old debate over the referentiality of the fictional sign. Mikel Dufrenne makes essentially the same distinction between what he calls "représentation" and "expression," although he is not as systematic as Egebak. (Dufrenne, "Critique littéraire et phénoménologie," p. 212: "Ce que nous disons de la poésie peut se dire à quelque degré de toute oeuvre littéraire. Ce qui définit cette oeuvre, ce qui l'oppose aussi bien au reportage, à l'oeuvre scientifique ou au traité philosophique, c'est que le sens y reste immanent au langage et à la structure formelle de l'oeuvre.")

to accumulate knowledge about a city, a house, and a group of people all nonexistent in the real world. The information we now urgently require comes from the text itself and not from the real world, although allusions to the real world may continue. But the latter are not central: only for the briefest instant can *Eugénie Grandet* be considered a guide book to Saumur. Almost immediately, the internal significances begin to accumulate, and the inner, aesthetic structure of the work begins to emerge. To suppose that *Eugénie Grandet* is intended to teach us something historically or geographically verifiable about that city is to ignore the literariness of the text. Indeed, the novel is probably not based· upon Saumur at all, and so in the end we really only reach historical knowledge through aesthetic knowledge. No amount of historical or geographical description can make us understand the world views from which that history and that geography derive.

Eventually we come full circle, for by recognizing the aesthetic status of the text, we make of the novel an object in its own right: not a copy of something else, but an autonomous object whose structures of perception and consciousness are those of the age that produced it. Inevitably, then, it will return us to history, not by what it refers to, but by what it is, thus fulfilling Balzac's fondest dream.[14] This aesthetic appeal to the reader is made by "representation," as distinguished from "mimesis." Although texts might carry any number and kinds of significance—historical, political, sociological—they carry no literary significance other than that generated by the representation of the sign.[15]

[14]There is a large Anglo-American literature on the problem of mimesis, which takes world and mind as given, and concentrates on the logic of their relationship. Much of the discussion as it relates to literature is reviewed in David Lodge, *Language of Fiction* (New York, 1966).

[15]Jean Blot has put the position for referentiality neatly: "le romancier va se heurter à une particularité de l'instrument qu'il utilise: le langage est entièrement extériorité et renvoie toujours à autre chose qu'à lui-même. Contrairement à la couleur ou au son, il ne saurait être beau en soi parce qu'il ne trouve sa nature, ne cesse d'être bruit, qu'au moment où s'établit un rapport entre ce bruit actuel et virtuel et le monde auquel il fait

No one has put the sensible position better than Balzac himself: "Le verbe n'a rien d'absolu: nous agissons plus sur le mot qu'il ne s'agit sur nous: sa force est en raison des images que nous avons acquises et que nous y groupons" (LL, 62). This grouping, or "développement" as he elsewhere called it, enables us to assimilate what is knowable into what is known, and thus to recognize the conceptual structure that underlies the descriptions we are offered. In the creative process there first had to occur the initial *Idée*—the datum drawn from reality. But then there had to follow the famous second stage described in the *Théorie de la démarche:* the severing of the link to verifiability, so that the literariness of the text can emerge. Justifiably, Balzac could call himself both realistic and imaginative.

The most meaningful reading of Balzac is, therefore, not one that measures his descriptions against the criteria of objective reality.[16] That would tempt us to see divergencies from reality as "errors" rather than as symptoms of a specific world view. We must rather look to the texts themselves, for they alone tell us what the past actually was. When Merleau-Ponty remarked that language in use is thought, he was aligning himself with the old Balzacian notion that the presence and use of language overrides all theories about it. This is one Balzacian "law" to which we must bow, and we turn our attention to *Illusions perdues,* where we shall find a microcosm of the concerns we have found so widespread in the *Comédie humaine* as a whole.

It would, of course, be materially and mechanically im-

---

allusion" (Blot, "Le Roman et son langage," *Nouvelle Revue française,* no. 198 (1 June 1969), 1158). On the other hand, Bernard Vannier has argued that just such purely verbal techniques as alliteration, homophony, leximatic shifting, and so on, determine Balzac's processes of characterization. So completely does Vannier empty Balzacian characters of verifiability that they almost become what Greimas has called "actants." See Bernard Vannier, "Jeux du texte balzacien," *Europe,* xviii (October 1970), 167–81.

[16]The Chicago group of Balzacians, under the leadership of E. Preston Dargan and Bernard Weinberg, published a number of studies of this sort, collected in *The Evolution of Balzac's Comédie humaine* (Chicago, 1942).

possible to analyze the text of *Illusions perdues* in exhaustive detail. We can, however, isolate two themes that bear directly on the problem of language: perception, and the "word game." The first involves such matters as the reliability of perception and contrastive interpretations of reality; the second, the role of language in society. The importance of these themes in the *Comédie humaine* as a whole has, we hope, been well established by now; with care, their centrality to *Illusions perdues* can be shown without deforming the sense of the text.[17]

With a plot concerning literature in a materialist society, printing as both art and business, and language as the substance of social structure, *Illusions perdues* is indeed the backbone of the *Comédie humaine*. It opens with a typical Balzacian lexicon, based on the assumption that the reader is totally ignorant of the matters to be discussed, and designed to introduce the word game. Certain expressions must be made understandable: "faire gémir la presse," "la forme," "marbre," and especially "ours." From the last term the narrator draws the opening statement of the word game theme, because the "ours," that is, old Séchard, "en sa qualité d'imprimeur, . . . ne sut jamais lire ni écrire" (p. 172). This version of the word game, that is, divergence between the printed word as physical object in the world and its existence as an element of art, will run through the entire text of *Illusions perdues*. For old Séchard, printing is merely a business. He even maintains to David that "les gens qui achètent des livres ne sont guère propres à en imprimer" (p. 186).[18] It is curious then that he should send

[17]An elaborate justification of such linear selectivity can be found in Lodge, *Language of Fiction,* pp. 78–87.

[18]This bit of homely wisdom will be repeated to Lucien by Lousteau a-propos of publishers. Old Séchard's business origins are not very pretty. He had bought out the printing shop of his former employer's widow for half its value, and regularly snapped up stocks of paper from distressed paper merchants. He is wily enough to bargain with his customers by stressing, as occasion demands, the weight of the large type or the difficulty of picking out the small type; but he is not clever enough to buy up the second printer's license available in Angoulême in order to assure himself a monopoly.

his son to school "pour se préparer un successeur" (p. 174), seeing that he has done quite well for himself using hired compositors. To compound matters, he sends David to Paris to be further trained in the Didot shop, which, if anything, is less necessary than a lycée education to run a provincial print shop. We sense here the hand of the narrator, for "tout en apprenant son métier, David acheva son éducation à Paris. Le prote des Didot devint un savant" (p. 174). David's training and education are indispensable for the development of the word game, for he will come to embody the two attitudes that will be eternally at war in *Illusions perdues*. The necessities of the theme override the need for logic in the character of the ignorant and avaricious father.[19]

In the first passage of arms between the two approaches to printing, business clearly wins over art. David compounds his father's failure to monopolize the printing market in Angoulême by his own failure to take a political stance; in order to have any business, "il fallait opter entre la pratique des Libéraux et celle des Royalistes" (p. 188). David doesn't see printing that way; he sells off the *Journal de la Charente* which his father, surprisingly for such an ignorant man, had been able to put out over the years; he loses the business of the diocese without gaining the business of the liberals. In twoscore pages, the Cointet brothers have all but destroyed the printery, the old man has carried off most of the profits, and David is left with a large debt and a marginal income.

The word game having been launched, the narration now picks up the theme of perception, and suggests that it is based upon a continual process of comparison. Comparison is first emphatically put forward in the double portrait

[19]Old Séchard's status as an "ours" continues even after he leaves the printing business. He is an alcoholic, like "les véritables ours de l'Amérique" (p. 175; let us not quarrel with the narrator over natural science). Beyond the obvious sources of friction in business matters there are clear generational conflicts between father and son, although Balzac has avoided "Oedipal" overtones by dispatching Madame Séchard many years before the story begins.

of Lucien and David. Each young man is linked to the other by being the other's unfulfilled potential. Lucien is destined by a scientific father for a career in the sciences, but he finally enters literature; David really prefers poetry but is carried by training and circumstances towards the sciences. Each undertakes a course of action fundamentally at odds with his basic nature. It is Lucien who communicates to David an old idea of his father's about the production of cheap paper; it is David who reveals to Lucien the exciting new school of romantic poetry.[20] We are therefore invited to see them as a complimentary couple: "Lucien avait beaucoup lu, beaucoup comparé; David avait beaucoup pensé, beaucoup médité" (p. 199). And yet they are called "les deux poètes." Their true natures, as the story proceeds, will turn out to be more complex than a first glance would suggest.[21]

The problematical nature of perception is further stressed in the physical world surrounding the characters. The narrator makes much, for example, of the dirt and dilapidation of the Séchard house. The walls are cracked, the façade poorly built of disparate and unmatched brick and stone, the roof and window-fittings are rotten, and the whole structure seems to stay upright merely because its decayed components lean against each other (pp. 196–97). Yet when David and Lucien finish reading the Latouche edition of André Chénier, sitting in the courtyard of the collapsing house, everything is transformed: "Les pampres s'étaient colorés, les vieux murs de la maison, fendillés, bossués, inégalement traversés par d'ignobles lézardes, av-

[20]It must be emphasized that the double portrait is never naively schematic. If Lucien really does seem to be taking the wrong tack in going into poetry, David is much more subtly torn between his "génie," which is meditative, and his "goût," which is analytical (p. 194). This situation gives him, in surprisingly modern terms, "des nausées" (p. 198).

[21]There are also Lavaterian complexities. Although both young men are said to possess the physical exteriors appropriate to their inner selves, David nevertheless has "un caractère timide en désaccord avec sa forte constitution" (pp. 199–200); and although Lucien has a sharp, analytical—and presumably male—mind, he possesses "especially significant" feminine hips (pp. 198–99).

aient été revêtus de cannelures, de bossages, de bas-reliefs et des innombrables chef-d'oeuvre de je ne sais quelle architecture par les doigts d'une fée. La Fantaisie avait secoué ses fleurs et ses rubis sur la petite cour obscure. . . . La Poésie avait secoué les pans majestueux de sa robe étoilée sur l'atelier où grimaçaient les Singes et les Ours de la typographie" (pp. 201–202). This is the same house that so shames David and Lucien at other moments; yet now, when printing is supplanted by poetry, their perception of it is transformed.

Conditions now exist for the development of a story that depends upon the interaction of problematical perception and the deceptiveness of the word game. Nothing is certain, and the characters make a series of decisions based upon the most tenuous visions of reality. The Bargeton salon is an excellent example of the slipperiness of "reality" in this narrative. On the one hand, it is a collection of country fools, "les plus pauvres sires à vingt lieues à la ronde" (p. 220); on the other hand, the group has a "respectable attachement *quand même* aux Bourbon" and is compared to fine old silver (p. 221). Although they are constantly portrayed as provincial fools, they are somehow witty enough to pun endlessly on Lucien's name; and although they are presented as utter ignoramuses, they know enough to see a precedent for Lucien's reception in the fact that Duclos, Grimm, and Crébillon had been received by the nobility of a previous age. Louise herself is the subject of many uncertainties of interpretation. She is charming and seductive despite her "mâle éducation" (p. 210); she is an "exaltée," but only because she lives in intellectual isolation (p. 213); she is fundamentally sensitive, but exists in a perpetual state of emotional hyperbole.[22] For his part, Lucien seems to lose his analytical abilities when he enters her circle. He is now "trop jeune pour analyser sa maîtresse" (p.

[22]The portrait of Louise also illustrates to perfection the failure of Lavaterian methods to take into account the role of milieu in the formation of character. A good deal of Louise's character is attributable to her being confined to a mediocre milieu.

229), and will fall victim to illusion as easily as anyone else. Although the narrator is constantly deflating Louise's "belles tartines" and her "pompeuses expressions" (p. 233), Lucien sees her only as a Muse. When she suggests that she might be able to arrange for him to assume his mother's noble name, he is completely carried away: "A ces mots, Le Roi, la marquise d'Espard, La Cour, Lucien vit comme un feu d'artifice, et la nécessité de ce baptême lui fut pouvée" (p. 234). From our point of view as readers, we know that she has not the slightest idea of whether she can fulfill such promises; and the narrator lets pass no opportunity to undermine her words.[23]

Thus we really do not know—nor does the narrator appear to know—just what the "truth" is about these characters. For such descriptions there are no originals and no common-sense referentiality. The narration is involved in a process of focusing, like a cinema projector seeking an image of optimum clarity. A proper focus cannot be found until positions on both sides of the optimum have been tested. The descriptive variations in *Illusions perdues* represent the same kind of trial and error, with the difference that narrative focusing never reaches a single, precise, "correct" interpretation. Rather, it engages in a continuous process of self-propagation and self-correction.

When all these more or less introductory maneuvers have been executed, the narrative proceeds to two elaborate tableaux: Lucien's evening of poetry reading in Louise's drawing room; and the interview between Eve and David at precisely the same moment. The scene in Louise's salon mingles the themes of perception and the word game, and also elaborately exploits the devices of "varnish" and the word-event. Lucien arrives early, to find only Monsieur de Bargeton in the salon; the two engage in an absurd

[23]As if to multiply the complexity, the narrator also mocks one of his own most cherished terms, "génie," by attributing to Louise a mock version of theories he has elsewhere proposed seriously: "les grandes oeuvres que [les hommes de génie] devaient édifier leur imposaient un apparent égoisme. . . . Le génie ne relevait que de lui-même . . . il devait donc se mettre au-dessus des lois" (pp. 234–35).

mock exchange, since Monsieur de Bargeton speaks only "à la dernière extremité" (p. 250), for fear of revealing his intellectual nullity. As each pair of guests arrive they are presented in quick and sarcastic detail, with a lexicon of names and nicknames. The latter (Lolotte, Fifine, Zizine . . .) are clues to the qualities we soon are shown directly: Astolphe is "ignorant comme une carpe" (p. 258); Adrien bellows romances in the mïstaken belief he has a good voice,'and so on. The high point of the evening—and of the word 'game—comes with Lucien's reading of Chénier's poetry. Most of the guests have been attracted by "des mots . . . semblables aux trompettes, aux cymbales, à la grosse caisse des saltimbanques" (p. 265). None of them understand what transpires, but that is of little import: "Les mots beauté, gloire, poésie, ont des sortilèges qui séduisent les esprits les plus grossiers" (p. 265). This principle, echoing Louise's flaunting of "king" and "court," underlies much of what will later occur in the novel. It is the "varnish" effect used to the hilt. Without this principle, Lucien's career in journalism would be impossible. The soirée in Louise's salon is, in fact, presented as the first meeting of the Poet and the Philistines.

The rest of the evening is a microcosm of all the language themes that have been touched upon so far. Chénier is perfectly unknown in Angoulême. Any poem beyond a few stanzas in length is too much for these "esprits médiocres" (p. 266). Fifine has no opinion because poetry always puts her to sleep; Francis gets indigestion from poetry after dinner. Halfway through the evening Francis glances at Lucien's book and discovers that he is reading print. "C'est bien simple," smirks Amélie, "monsieur de Rubempré travaille chez un imprimeur. C'est, dit-elle en regardant Lolotte, comme si une jolie femme faisait elle-même ses robes" (p. 268). All the women conclude that Lucien must have printed the book, and Astolphe observes that everyone could just as well have read the verses for themselves. Learning that Lucien has not actually *written* the poems, they clamor for something unprinted—and presumably fresher—"le vin du cru" (p. 269). All this is accompanied by typically stupid dialogue on the nature of the French language ("se prête peu à la poésie"; "notre langue est très musicale," and so on). The scene is a clear and obvious parallel to the scene between David and his father, in which the same simple-minded distinction between word and print had been drawn.

The evening proceeds to a reading of Lucien's own ode "A Elle." Lucien's recitation is critical: Louise will be justified in the eyes of society only if Lucien is an authentic genius.[24] But his reading is followed by a barrage of snide remarks: "Après tout, c'est des phrases, dit Zéphirine à Francis, et l'amour est une poésie en action" (p. 272). French wit, that destructive weapon so deplored by the Balzacian narrator, is now brought out to destroy the upstart: "En un moment chacun s'entendit pour humilier Lucien par quelque mot d'ironie aristocratique" (p. 273). The culminating thrust is unwittingly given by the benevolent bishop, who has been misled by Francis into thinking that Madame Chardon helps her son with his poetry. He remarks, when told that Lucien's genius will have a difficult birth, that Madame Chardon, a midwife, "pourra vous aider" (p. 276).[25] There is a wave of malicious joy in the salon. This word-event is the final goad that sets Lucien on his fatal path: "Ce coup avait envoyé tout d'abord Lucien au fond de l'eau; mais il frappa du pied et revint à la surface, en se jurant de dominer ce monde. Comme le taureau piqué de mille flèches, il se releva furieux" (p. 277).

[24]In a moment of crisis the escape mechanism comes into play: "Naïs laissa échapper son secret aux yeux des femmes ... elle ne put s'empêcher de trembler pour Lucien" (p. 270). Had she been stronger, she might well have imposed Lucien on her friends; as it is, they fly to attack her at her weakest points.

[25]The bishop's remark is an excellent example of the word-event. It is prepared over quite a long stretch of text, during which time the context is carefully established. There had been much discussion of the "birth" of genius, and of Madame Chardon's profession as midwife. Everything is prepared for Lucien's maximum humiliation; the blow, when it comes, derives its destructive force from the context, for the words are innocent enough. In point of fact, Lucien's mother *does* help him with his career, but in ways imagined neither by the bishop nor the other guests.

The bishop's phrase marks a turning point, following which nothing can ever be the same again. To the very end, the evening is a battle of words. Louise, "à cheval sur ses grands mots qui n'ont ni queu ni tête" (p. 279), is narrowly watched by the others; whenever possible her words are mocked and derided (p. 280). There is not a moment of respite, and when Lucien walks home plucking out one by one "les traits envenimés qu'il avait reçus" (p. 280), he determines all the more firmly to carve out for himself a place in high society (p. 280). What the narrator does not yet tell us is why Lucien, having experienced the viciousness of that world, should have the least desire to be part of it.

While Lucien is being tortured in Louise's drawing room, David and Eve are having an interview that is the antithesis of Lucien's experience. With them, all is simplicity, understanding, and silence. "Quoique l'imprimeur se fût résolu à parler de lui-même," we read, "il ne trouva plus rien à dire. . . . Eve . . . trouva ce silence gênant" (p. 281). He tries to speak of his love "par analogie" by praising the beauties of the night (p. 282); Eve, always the "divineresse," understands that nature can untie the tongue of an embarrassed lover. But he speaks only a few moments of his love for her: "laissez-moi m'emparer de cette nature où je crois voir mon bonheur écrit en toute chose," he cries (p. 288); and then almost immediately he launches into a long explanation of paper-making.

This most curious discussion serves several purposes. On the one hand, it provides a natural subject for David, who is struck dumb when it comes to speaking of his emotions directly. Since Eve has admitted her love for him, he can now proceed to discuss other matters (chiefly Lucien and his future), which he finds easier to do. But in avoiding through this enormous "anti-phrase" the issue that touches him most directly, David moves into the subject that most concerns the narrator, the word game. It again appears in its most characteristic form as the opposition of printing and poetry. Indeed, the subject is so important that the narrator makes a digression of his own, taking over from the character an explanation too important not to handle himself: "David Séchard . . . donna [à Eve] sur la papéterie des renseignements qui ne seront point déplacés dans une oeuvre dont l'existence matérielle est due autant au papier qu'à la presse" (p. 289). Pointing to the printing-poetry relationship in terms of the very work he is writing, the narrator is in effect discounting the opinions of old Séchard and of Louise's group, who all agree that poetry and printing are antithetical. In the narrator's eyes the relationship is by no means adversary: between the abstract notion of art and the concreteness of typography there is a necessary symbiosis on which depends the existence of such words as *Illusions perdues* itself. The point may seem obvious, but it is central. We therefore get a capsule history of paper-making in which, typically, the first concern is the establishment of a lexicon. Raisin, Jésus, Colombier, Cicéro, Saint-Augustin, are presented as keys to an understanding of this section of the story.[26] The reason these papers are so important is that they are rag based and relatively permanent. David's problem is to find a paper that will be cheaper, although as durable as the old linen rag product. He is not attracted primarily by economic gain, nor even by the abstract interest of solving a scientific problem. Rather, he considers the cotton-based paper used to replace rag paper too fragile to survive more than a few years, thus placing in jeopardy the works of the mind imprinted on it: "Les chemises et les livres ne dureront pas, voilà tout" (p. 292). David consistently focusses on the symbiosis between printing and poetry: the book preserves the work of the mind, and that is its only function. His search is therefore undertaken to guarantee the survival of the works of the mind: "Aussi le problème à résoudre est-il de la plus haute importance pour la littérature, pour les sciences et pour la politique" (p. 292). Printing and poetry are one, and the very existence of *Illusions perdues* is at issue.[27]

[26]The narrator had already used the term "Gros Canon" in a conversation between David and his father without having explained it. Here the small mystery is cleared up.

[27]Historically speaking, the narrator has placed his character in exactly

Thus the two tableaux complement each other in a way that sets out the basic themes with utmost clarity. Neither words nor people can be descriptively fixed. Yet this is precisely the insight Lucien fails to achieve. The transition to the end of "Les Deux Poètes" is based upon his surrender to naive realism. His dream palace is a palace of words that he takes for reality. He is admired as a poet by all those around him, even to the point where it interferes with his more physical ambitions vis-à-vis Louise. Châtelet, who understands the importance of words and gestures in the provinces, realizes that it doesn't matter whether or not Lucien is "du dernier bien" with Louise; with proper care, saying can make it so: "Sixte voulait forcer madame de Bargeton à si bien se prononcer pour Lucien qu'elle fût ce qu'on nomme *perdue*" (pp. 309–10). As Raphaël de Valentin was persuaded in *La Peau de chagrin*, words determine reality: "Madame de Bargeton allait se trouver dans cette bizarre situation où se sont trouvées beaucoup de femmes qui ne se sont perdues qu'après avoir été injustement accusées" (p. 311). Du Châtelet, therefore, arranges for Stanislas de Chandour to surprise Lucien and Louise in a tête-à-tête. "En province," remarks the narrator, "une semblable aventure s'aggrave par la manière dont elle se raconte" (p. 316). The result is that to all intents and purposes, Louise *is* Lucien's mistress. A preposterous duel takes place between Monsieur de Bargeton and Monsieur de Chandour, and Louise contemplates flight. She who has until now been pompous and heavy in her speech suddenly

the right time and place to conduct his experiments. In the late eighteenth century the Didot factory at Essonne had seen the development of the first automatic paper-making machine, which marked the emancipation of printing from the quantitative restrictions of hand-made paper. The Didots continued to improve this machine, and David must surely have learned something about it during his apprenticeship. Just about the time Balzac was writing *Illusions perdues*, the price of linen rag was rising to a point where these machines could no longer be supplied economically with the quantities of pulp they needed. Thus the reflexivity of the novel extends to its real, physical existence. Along the way, David shows himself to be prophetic about the future of publishing, forecasting something like the Pléiade editions, and predicting the current storage problems of libraries.

becomes eloquent and effective in bedazzling Lucien with prospects in the capital. "Ne le voulez-vous pas?" she asks her stunned admirer. That remark is a word-event of far-reaching implications, for it sparks in Lucien the vision that finally destroys him: "Lucien, hébété par le rapide coup d'oeil qu'il jeta sur Paris, en entendant ces séduisantes paroles, crut n'avoir jusqu'alors joui que de la moitié de son cerveau; il lui sembla que l'autre moitié se découvrait, tant ses idées s'agrandirent" (p. 329). Next to this blinding vision nothing counts. Just before leaving, Lucien comes upon Eve and Madame Chardon kneeling in prayer. David warns Lucien never to forget the scene. "L'imprimeur jugea sans doute ces graves paroles nécessaires" (p. 334); he could not know that other words had already created the world in which Lucien was determined to live.

Part II, "Un Grand Homme de province à Paris," opens with the somewhat disappointing circumstances of the trip to Paris, which Lucien had thought of as a romantic elopement, but which turns out to be a rather expensive and disagreeable voyage. The young man, who until now has been a "jeune poète" suddenly is no longer quite so poetic. What come out in him now are naiveté and loquaciousness. Louise, who had been a creature of exaggeration and hyperbole, now frowns on his flights of fancy. Where did she learn that his behavior is not "de bon ton"? The transformation leads us to the further development of the basic themes of Part I. Only by subjecting his characters to a radical shift in milieu could the narrator show how the structure of reality is rooted in language and perception. "Un Grand Homme de province à Paris" turns out to be a kind of narrative experiment in epistemology.

The ensuing text is based once again upon a series of tableaux. Châtelet sets the mood at the very beginning by telling Louise to remain distant from Lucien, "un jeune homme que vous n'avez encore comparé à personne" (p. 6). As we move through Part II, comparison will become not just a matter of descriptive juxtaposition but the basis for value judgements. Whether Louise and Lucien are

charming lovers or gawky country bumpkins, or a combination of both, depends almost entirely upon the progression of local perceptions and contexts; that is, upon comparison.

The first cold shower of comparison floods in on Lucien
on his very first morning in Paris. He and Louise have slept
late—in separate apartments—to recover from the ardors
of the trip. When Lucien sees her again in the morning, in
one of those "ignobles chambres qui sont la honte de Paris"
(p. 4), she is quite changed. Louise is one of those persons
who, in an altered habitat, "n'ont plus ni le même aspect ni
la même valeur" (p. 4). Lucien finds the change baffling; he
does not see that there is no "true" Louise but only a changing woman in changed circumstances. On her side, she has
just had a conversation with du Châtelet, who has revised
all her ideas by talking "la langue du monde à une femme
du monde" (p. 8). This transformation of Louise is not
really magical; she belongs to the central normative group
of the *Comédie humaine*, and is merely moving into her
natural milieu. The same is true of Lucien; what is altering
is the relationship between the two. Louise still sees the
handsome young man in Lucien; but she now observes that
he is "ridiculement mis" (p. 8). Her new ability to judge
style comes from a comparison with Châtelet: "Les yeux
comparent avant que le coeur n'ait rectifié ce rapide jugement machinal" (p. 8). Although she has had plenty of
opportunity to make this comparison before, she is now
doing it in the context of Paris. She will not indulge in a
love affair with a man who now seems to be a country
bumpkin. She explains "les lois du monde" (p. 8) to Lucien,
who begins to understand that he is no longer the Lucien
of Angoulême; then she goes off to her sumptuous new
apartment, leaving Lucien in the miserable hotel room,
"qu'il ne put s'empêcher de comparer au magnifique
apartement de Louise" (p. 10). Each of them tries repeatedly to discover what Paris *is;* they think it is a thing
that can be possessed, a state of being that can be "entered." In the end they realize that there is no single Paris,

but rather a kaleidoscope of conceptual worlds of bewildering complexity and variety. This, in turn, enables them, and the narrator, to examine rival systems of values from which the ultimate shape of the novel will emerge.

These strands come together in the first formal tableau, the evenings at the theater and the opera, where Lucien and Louise have the opportunity of judging each other in the first stages of their respective transformations. Lucien compares Louise to "plusieurs jolies Parisiennes si élégamment, si fraîchement mises" (p. 14), and condemns her outmodishness. "Va-t-elle rester comme ça?" he wonders. In the provinces, the narrator observes, "il n'y a ni choix ni comparaison à faire" (p. 15); but here everything is different: "Les yeux de Lucien faisaient la comparaison que madame de Bargeton avait faite la veille entre lui et Châtelet" (p. 15). The narrator, however, does not allow his reader much certitude either. He takes the opportunity to remark that in the month of June, no one who counts is in Paris, and that theater boxes are consequently filled with vulgar, unknown people. Do we have waves of "deliciously" dressed Parisiennes, or a sea of dowdy ladies dressed, as he says, like worn-out carpets (p. 11)? It all depends, apparently, upon the angle of vision.

In the case of Lucien, we are equally beset with uncertainties. He arrives with the "bel habit bleu" (p. 13) that had been his pride; but in very short order the narrator is talking about "le sac bleu qu'il avait cru jusqu'alors être un habit" (p. 20). Such rapid shifts in the Balzacian narrator have often been noticed and deplored as errors in his omniscient stance. But he is not merely playing games with us; he would, after all, have to be incapable of reading his own text and devoid of the shortest memory span in order not to be aware of such apparent contradictions. As a matter of fact there is much more at stake here. Since there is no "real" blue suit to be checked, no "real" audience in the theater that night, the narrator is free to shift the data of perception in order to make an essential point: the *value* to be attached to the blue suit or to the nature of the audience varies from person to person and moment to moment, in terms of local narrative needs. This is the process of *Pensée* —the reflexive focussing and scanning, out of which will emerge not an objective rendition of reality, but a "simulacrum" of reality.

In this sea of uncertainty, Louise makes a few last efforts to remain loyal to Lucien. Forgetting her own supercili-ousness, she defends his muteness during the theatrical soirée: "Les hommes qui ont tant de choses à exprimer en de belles oeuvres longtemps rêvées professent un certain mépris pour la conversation, commerce où l'esprit s'amoindrit en se monnayant" (p. 16). Her concern is equivocal: in Angoulême she had told Lucien that "poetic" conversation ought to be the aim and the satisfaction of all superior minds. Is she, along with the narrator, regretting the "old" conversation and deploring the new "monetiza-tion" of words? Perhaps; but she herself is already halfway to condemning Lucien for his lack of wit. We cannot tell, for everything is in a state of flux, and the firm opinions of one moment will be rejected in the next. Du Châtelet urges her to reserve final judgement. "De grâce," he insists, "at-tendez et comparez!" (p. 16).

The themes of the theater scene are pursued in the out-ing to the opera. When Louise first sees Lucien in his newly acquired finery ("frisé comme un Saint Jean de procession, bien gileté, bien cravaté," according to the narrator [p. 22]), she is enchanted. She whispers her approval to him (p. 24), although it will not take long for everyone to see that even in his new clothes he is still ridiculous. She, for her part, has not yet received her new clothes; seen by Lucien she is still "grande, sèche, couperosée, fanée, plus que rousse, an-guleuse, guindée, précieuse, provinciale dans son parler, mal arrangée surtout!" (pp. 24–25). Local contexts have already begun to affect Lucien, for he sees in Louise what the Parisians do: "la pauvre Anaïs de Nègrepelisse, la femme réelle, la femme que les gens de Paris voyaient" (p. 24). As soon as the four dandies, de Marsay, Vandenesse, Montriveau, and Canalis, enter the box, Louise forgets her scruples about conversation and is swept away by their sparkling talk: "une parole vibrante où se trouvait le positif de cette époque, mais doré de poésie" (p. 30). Much of this gold exists only in her mind, for the narrator insists repeatedly on the cruelty, the impertinence, and the destructiveness of what is being said. But it is enough for Louise: "Lucien ne fut plus rien." Clearly this Paris is not the Paris for a young poet. Lucien is too attracted to reject it, but he cannot find a footing among its contradictions and mutual deceptions. As before, his reaction is to flee to another world in order to find himself.[28] In a burst of naive enthusiasm, he throws himself into work, into the "comparaison et instruction" (p. 49) from which alone a system of values could come.

In his period of work and study, Lucien is again confronted with the printing-poetry choice. The narrator gives us a tableau in which the business of literature is set over and against the art of literature. On the fatal day when Lucien must put his manuscript under his arm and approach the publishers along the Quai des Augustins, he finds, as it were, the fundamental choice: the row of shops, or the waters of the Seine "comme si un bon génie lui conseillait de se jeter à l'eau plutôt que de se jeter dans la littérature" (p. 57). Actually the choice is more apparent than real—though Lucien does not know it yet—for the literature into which he eventually casts himself will be a moral suicide.

The scenes at the publishers pick up the theme of the

---

[28]On two occasions, voices signal Lucien's awakening understanding. His first horrible deception over Louise had sparked two voices: "Une voix lui cria bien: 'l'intelligence est le levier avec lequel on remue le monde.' Mais une autre voix lui cria que le point d'appui de l'intelligence était l'argent" (p. 21). Now, having been definitively rejected by Louise, he hears them again: "De l'or à tout prix! se disait Lucien. Non! lui cria sa conscience, mais la gloire, et la gloire c'est le travail" (p. 41). Bernard Schilling has pointed out that even Lucien's determination to work is an illusion, since he merely wants to buy his way into high society. In his typically weak way, he accepts the advice of one "voice," but only to fulfill the ambitions of the other. See Bernard N. Schilling, *The Hero as Failure: Balzac and the Rubempré Cycle* (Chicago, 1968) p. 120.

word game that underlay most of Part I. David's account of the disappearance of the great linen papers explains how Vidal and Porchon can regard the verbal work of art as an item of consumption to be used up and replaced. The economics are arranged that way: "les livres étaient comme des bonnets de coton pour les bonnetiers, une marchandise à vendre cher, à acheter bon marché" (p. 60). The old lexicon of great papers and great works is now replaced by a commercial jargon Lucien can barely understand; horrified and repelled by the "brutal et matériel aspect que prenait la littérature" (p. 60), he flees to Doguereau's establishment. There he finds essentially the same thing: "Le père Doguereau . . . tenait par l'habit, par la culotte et par les souliers au professeur de belles lettres, et au marchand par le gilet, la montre et les bas" (p. 61). The latter parts naturally dominate.

Naive and innocent as he appears to be, Lucien has paid attention to David's political mistakes in Angoulême. He describes his novel, wherever he goes, as a study of the religious wars in which he favors the Catholics. He instinctively avoids talking about the work's merits as literature, although Doguereau finds in it an excellent style and a rich imagination (p. 64). But for all that, the publisher offers only a paltry sum, and the insult suscitates in Lucien an escaped gesture, "un geste plein de superbe" (p. 66), which signals his encounter with d'Arthez and his group.

D'Arthez' famous speech of advice to Lucien recommends that novels open with descriptions, rather than with the "diffuses causeries" charcteristic of Walter Scott (p. 72). He calls for dialogue that would be "la conséquence attendue qui couronne [les] préparatifs" (p. 72). This recommendation has obvious roots in the narrator's concern for the "new" conversation that has replaced the old fire-side talk, and also reflects his own techniques, in which initial descriptions and lexicons make possible the later condensed, tight negotiations between father and son. This was "expression" at its best, and approached what d'Arthez calls the "antagonisme nécessaire à toute oeuvre dramatique" (p. 72). Clearly, then, d'Arthez views novels as much more than the mere record of political maneuvering. Only once does he touch upon political considerations, when he remarks that history has failed to do justice to Catherine de Medicis (p. 73). He talks of human passions rather than of party politics: "La passion a des accidents infinis. Peignez donc les passions" (p. 73). History is still there, of course, and the historical novelist must pay attention both to the "moeurs brillantes du catholicisme" and the "sombres figures du calvinisme"; but we have learned, if nothing else, that history is largely what we make it.

Lucien's novel is therefore only potentially good, and to clarify what is meant the narrator must move on to discuss d'Arthez' own much more advanced work. D'Arthez believes absolutely that metaphysics is the basis of all genius: "Il voulait, comme Molière, être un profond philosophe avant de faire des comédies" (p. 74). He is passionately interested in the dialectic of mind and world: "Il étudiait le monde écrit et le monde vivant, la pensée et le fait" (p. 74). This equation is another version of the printing-poetry linkage, but on an infinitely more sophisticated level. Part I had talked about the preservation of the works of the mind by means of the book, which was a symbolic way of asking how *Pensée,* as distinguished from *Idée,* can be expressed in the real world. This is the problem that d'Arthez confronts; it ought to be the problem Lucien confronts. Above all, it is the problem the narrator confronts, when he explains how d'Arthez conducts his inquiry: "D'Arthez avait une oeuvre d'imagination, entreprise *uniquement pour étudier les ressources de la langue. . . .* C'était une oeuvre psychologique et de haute portée *sous la forme du roman"* (p. 74; my italics). Compared to this confluence of imagination, language, philosophy, linguistics, and narration, the question of taking political sides in the interpretation of history is a feeble issue indeed.

The history that the narrator makes is consequently of an entirely different order of importance. It is the record of his own search for values. In d'Arthez' Cénacle, which represents his ideal, there are no absolutes. The narrator goes to great pains to make clear that the nine extraordinary men who compose the group hold quite different and sometimes utterly opposing views. Free of envy and jealousy, acutely aware of the relativity of truth, they discuss issues calmly and contemplatively. Theirs indeed is a "new" conversation, which transforms the old crudities into new insights: "Les conversations pleines de charmes et sans fatigue, embrassaient les sujets les plus variés. Légers à la manière des flèches, les mots allaient à fond tout en allant vite" (p. 80). Once again, everything depends upon the angle of perception and the nature of context. Whether arrows wound or stimulate depends upon how and when they are shot. These young men possess the inner calm that renders possible the total, straight, and uncomplicated expression of ideas.

D'Arthez and his friends are aware of the troublesome nature of expression. D'Arthez warns Lucien of the dangers of the language of *Idée:* "Qui peut tout dire, arrive à tout faire! Cette maxime est de Napoléon et se comprend" (p. 90). But "tout dire" can mean many things, and even the narrator worries about its implications. The Cénacle, however, rises above the problem of expression: "ils pouvaient tout penser et se tout dire sur le terrain de la science et de l'intelligence" (p. 81). It is the one instance in *Illusions perdues* where language functions freely and perfectly in a human counterpart of the ideal idiom described by Séraphîta.

Lucien's encounter with the Cénacle remains enshrined in the center of *Illusions perdues* as a moment of potential purity. Through d'Arthez, the possibilities of narration as art are rendered explicit, and this gives Lucien his one chance to save himself. Needless to say, he is unable to respond to the challenge. Perhaps such ideals are by definition unattainable. Whatever the ultimate cause of his weakness, Lucien rejects the advice of the Cénacle, and undertakes to carve out for himself a career in journalism.

The following tableau shifts us from the domain of the

word as art back to the domain of the word as commerce. Lucien meets the Parisian counterparts of old Séchard, again selling words at so much per centimeter and haggling over the number of characters per line (p. 93). In their eyes, print has no significance except its convertibility into money. At all levels, from the petty bribery of a milliner buying subscriptions in order to obtain favorable articles (p. 96), to the auctioning of great political power to the highest bidder, the principle is the same.[29] Confronted with such standards, Lucien's only concern is to align himself with "les plus forts" (p. 103). The choice is between classicists and romantics, liberals and royalists; d'Arthez' alternative of letting art rise above politics does not even come under consideration. Lucien's eagerness leads Lousteau to speak candidly—and painfully—of the realities of a journalist's life. He is not trying to save Lucien from an unpleasant fate; his is simply the cry of the trapped man, torn and brutalized by the system in which he is imprisoned.

Lousteau's declamation, his "effroyable lamentation" (p. 111) is an extraordinary piece of writing. It is marked with the passion of a literary voice protesting the degradation of

[29]One can easily understand Marx's fascination with such aspects of the *Comédie humaine*. *Illusions perdues* pinpointed the monetization of words just before Marx began formulating his theory of the process. In "The German Ideology," Marx observes of words that "from the start the 'spirit' is afflicted with the curse of being 'burdened' with matter, which here makes its appearance in the form of agitated layers of air, sounds, in short, of language. Language is as old as consciousness, language is practical consciousness, as it exists for other men, and for that reason is really beginning to exist for me personally as well" ("The German Ideology," in *Marx's Concept of Man,* edited by Erich Fromm [New York, 1961], p. 203). During the July Monarchy the material aspect of language, to use Marx's term, was exploited in the interests of power, and the "practical" consciousness of language as a mediator between men was turned into an interpersonal weapon. During this scene of *Illusions perdues*, indeed, Giroudeau informs Lucien that an editor is not one who writes himself, but who exploits the writing of others (p. 99). Lukács picked up Marx's interpretation when he observed that *Illusions perdues* is concerned with the "transformation of literature (and with it of every ideology) into a commodity" George Lukács, *Studies in European Realism,* translated by Edith Bone (London, 1950), p. 49.

the instrument with which it creates. Who can miss the ring of authenticity in Lousteau's cry of pain: "Ah! ceux pour qui . . . [la réputation] est, pour moi jadis, pour vous aujourd 'hui, un ange aux ailes diaprées, revêtu de sa tunique blanche, montrant une palme verte dans sa main, une flamboyante épée dans l'autre, tenant à la fois de l'abstraction mythologique qui vit au fond d'un puits et de la pauvre fille vertueuse exilée dans un faubourg, ne s'enrichissant qu'aux clartés de la vertu par les efforts d'un noble courage, et revolant aux cieux avec un caractère immaculé, quand elle ne décède pas souillée, fouillée, violée, oubliée, dans le char des pauvres: ces hommes à cervelle cerclée de bronze, aux coeurs encore chauds sous les tombées de neige de l'expérience, ils sont rares dans le pays que vous voyez à nos pieds, dit-il en montrant la grande ville qui fumait au déclin du jour" (p. 111). Only Lucien, already deaf and blind, can remain unmoved by this last, supreme warning coming from Lousteau, whose usual mode is detached and ironic. We hear through this most unlikely instrument the voice of *Pensée,* the protest of the text—of the narrator—in revolt against the degradation of language and art. The prose affirms itself against the obstinacy, foolishness, and weakness of Lucien in a phrase that reaches across the *Comédie humaine* to the ideas of the *Avant-Propos:* "Oui, vous écrirez au lieu d'agir, vous chanterez au lieu de combattre . . . mais quand vous aurez réservé vos richesses pour votre style, votre or, votre pourpre pour vos personnages, que vous vous promenerez en guenilles dans les rues de Paris, heureux d'avoir lancé, *en rivalisant avec l'Etat Civil,* un être nommé Adolphe, Corinne, Clarisse ou Manon, que vous aurez gâté votre vie et votre estomac pour donner la vie à cette création, vous la verrez calomniée, trahie, vendue, déportée dans les lagunes de l'oubli par les journalistes, ensevelie par vos meilleurs amis" (pp. 113–14).

The forecast is accurate enough: Lucien will succumb, and all the things predicted here will come true. It will happen partly because Lucien thinks he knows how reality is structured, and thinks he can see where power lies. Thus he would never conduct the kind of philosophical-linguistic-artistic experiment that d'Arthez undertakes precisely to investigate such epistemological problems. Lucien is under the impression that he already possesses the knowledge that d'Arthez seeks.[30]

The foolishness of Lucien's attitude is made clear in the next great tableau, which is concerned with his visit to the Galerie-de-bois in Lousteau's company. Typically, the physical entity no longer in existence at the time of redaction is "painted" for us (p. 123); the ensuing description is unrolled in long, rhythmic sentences, in urgent and obsessive rhetoric, obliterating with its incantation the sordidness of the subject. There is a sick fascination in the narrator's detailed description of the ugliness of his subject: "Les boutiques éclairées sur le jardin et sur la cour étaient protégées par de petits treillages verts, peut-être pour empêcher la foule de démolir, par son contact, les murs en mauvais plâtras qui formaient le derrière des magasins. Là donc se trouvait un espace de deux où trois pieds où végétaient les produits les plus bizarres d'une botanique inconnue à la science, mêlés à ceux de diverse industries non moins florissantes. Une maculature coiffait un rosier, en sorte que les fleurs de rhétorique étaient embaumées par les fleurs avortées de ce jardin mal soigné, mais fétidement arrosé. Des rubans de toutes les couleurs ou des prospectus fleurissaient dans les feuillages. Les débris des modes étouffaient la végétation; vous trouviez un noeud de rubans sur une touffe de verdure, et vous étiez déçu dans vos idées sur la fleur que vous veniez admirer en apercevant une coque de satin qui figurait un dahlia" (p. 124). Is there any incongruity, then, in the attempt of the two young men to sell Lucien's *Marguérites*—those

---

[30]That Lucien could have misread so many signs so consistently is indeed amazing. Along with the spoken word, Parisian society employs a whole gamut of stylized gestures to indicate who is acceptable and who is not. Schilling points out a veritable language of the lorgnon, which both depresses and enrages Lucien. (Schilling, *The Hero as Failure,* pp. 119—120).

equivocal flowers—in this most doubtful flower-market? Words and illusions are the basic stock-in-trade of the Galeries-de-bois: *maculature, rhétorique,* and *prospectus* crown the real plants of the garden, but they are false flowers, thrown carelessly on a rank and repulsive growth. Even as he describes, the narrator rejects the world he is evoking, by focussing on the dirt and filth of this literary market-place. The discarded proof-sheets that lie on the rose bushes embody everything that the voice of *Pensée* abhors, and terms of revulsion fill this passage: "ignoble . . . baraques . . . huttes . . . sale . . . méphytique . . . sale . . . mauvais plâtras . . . avorté . . . fêtidement arrosé . . . débris . . . saleté . . . salissait . . . infâme . . . nausébonde . . . horrible choses . . . sinistre amas de crottes . . . " (pp. 124–26).

The mixture of businesses that inhabit the galleries is again symbolic: "Il n'y avait là que des libraires, de la poesie, de la politique et de la prose, des marchandes de modes, enfin des filles de joie qui venaient seulement le soir" (p. 126). Even the milliners are merchants of words rather than hats, since the latter remain on their hooks twenty years at a stretch. The sales ladies are possessed of "paroles astucieuses," of "le langage de la Halle," of "langue[s] déliée[s]," of a "vocabulaire fécond" (p. 127), but one wonders to what purpose all this language is put, since the hats never appear to be sold. Above all, "les libraires et les marchandes de modes vivaient en bonne intelligence" (p. 127), and the remark suffices to make us realize that the one thing that could never be sold there is *Illusions perdues*.

The theme of printing and poetry return us quite naturally to the theme of reality and illusion. Alongside the Galerie-de-bois we see the Galerie-Vitrée, where "se trouvent les commerces les plus singuliers" (p. 128). These businesses are all linked by a common quality: they sell illusion. Ventriloquists, magicians, fake side-shows, Cosmoramas, automata all take up their abode there, selling deception to a credulous public. Mixed up with all this are the peddlers of novels and the young poor who come to read *Smarra, Pierre Schlemihl, Jean Sbogar, Jocko,* and to find—who can tell?—their own illusions in their own ways. The ultimate illusion of this infernal scene arises at dusk, when the local prostitutes appear. What is true and what is false in this picture? People move "comme . . . au bal masqué" (p. 129), and in Dauriat's shop all talk is of buying and selling, of discounts and of profit-margins. Prostitution is the main business both inside and outside. Dauriat proclaims that those who are ruining the publishing business are Byron, Lamartine, Hugo, Delavigne, Canalis and Béranger! (p. 139). Everything here is quicksand; "tout est hasard, vous le voyez" (p. 142) remarks Lousteau. Is it any surprise that Lousteau considers d'Arthez to be "dangerous"? Or that, after the gathering in Dauriat's shop, he should drag Lucien off to that other house of illusions, the Panorama-Dramatique?

In the backstage area of that somewhat sleazy house, Lucien and Lousteau encounter the same play-acting that had taken place in Madame d'Espard's box. The underlying principle could have come directly from Moreau de la Sarthe: "Allons, ne manque pas ton effet, ma petite. . . . Précipite-toi, haut la patte! dis-moi bien: *Arrête, malheureux!* car il y a deux mille francs de recette. Lucien stupéfait vit l'actrice se composant et s'écriant: *Arrête, malheureux!* de manière à le glacer d'effroi. Ce n'était plus la même femme" (p. 145). Lousteau drives home the parallel: "C'est comme la boutique des Galeries-de-bois et comme un journal pour la littérature, une vraie cuisine" (p. 145).

The more the theater is explored, the more parallels are made with the Galerie-de-bois. All backstage talk has to do with which journalist is selling himself to which paper, which actress is prostituting herself to which Russian prince, and especially to whom Florine belongs or is to be sold. The façade in front of all this corruption is a façade of language. When Matifat takes offense at a line in Florine's role ("Je ne vous aime pas") he is ridiculed for having taken the language of sham for a reality—although the words are in fact literally true. Illusion and reality are confused until the stage bell rings and everyone prepares for the supreme illusion of the performance. What hope for mimesis can a narrator find in this "mélange de hauts et de bas, de compromis avec la conscience, de suprématies et de lâchetés, de trahisons et de plaisirs, de grandeurs et de servitudes" (p. 151)? What possibility is there for anything but approximations?

The final tableau of this remarkable series takes place at the party following the performance. The choices Lucien faces are made unavoidably clear by Blondet, Finot, and Vignon as they discuss the realities of the journalist's life. "Tout journal est . . . une boutique où l'on vend au public des paroles de la couleur dont il les veut" says Vignon (p. 184). Vignon still retains some respect for language: "Les idées ne peuvent être neutralisées que par des idées . . . . La terreur, le despotisme peuvent seuls étouffer le génie français dont la langue se prête admirablement à l'allusion, à la double entente" (p. 184). But he has little faith in "le peuple hypocrite et sans générosité" (p. 185). If, according to him, newspapers are "ces mauvais lieux de la pensée" (p. 186), it is because they reflect the society within which they exist: "Nous savons, tous tant que nous sommes, que les journaux iront plus loin que les rois en ingratitude, plus loin que le plus sale commerce en spéculations et en calculs, qu'ils dévoreront nos intelligences à vendre tous les matins leur trois-six cérébral; mais nous y écrirons tous, comme ces gens qui exploitent une mine de vif-argent en sachant qu'ils y mourront" (p. 186). Lucien now has all the alternatives placed before him, and must make his choice. He has seen, the narrator says, "the truth" about journalism and literature (p. 187). But even this assertion of what is "true" cannot remain uncontradicted. "Au lieu d'être saisi d'horreur à l'aspect du coeur même de cette corruption parisienne . . . Lucien jouissait avec ivresse de cette société spirituelle" (p. 187). The journalists can be even more brilliant than the members of the Cénacle. As if to underscore the complexity of things, the narrator repeatedly uses the word "littérature" to refer to the terrible world of the journalists into which Lucien has fallen.

This orgy is the last "set" scene. Part II comes to a close with a series of variations on comparison and the relativity of judgement. "Les idées sont binaires," observes Blondet, "Janus est le mythe de la critique et le symbole du génie. Il n'y a que Dieu de triangulaire!" (p. 248). He is seconded by Claude Vignon, who maintains that "c'est en effet la contradiction qui donne la vie en littérature" (p. 269). The others all agree that the same thing is true in politics and, indeed, in life itself. But Lucien is incapable of understanding the importance of that insight. He is only bemused by journalists who can write one thing on one day and its contradiction on the next. He believes himself clever enough to dominate them all, and mistakes a series of illusions for reality.

Our position, however, is quite different. In each tableau of Part II, the narrator has been at some pains to build into his prose a kind of reflexivity that enables us to perceive the deceptive illusions. The issues raised in connection with d'Arthez' novel are precisely those with which the narrator himself is constantly dealing. Lousteau's lamentation emerges from the entrails of a narrator who has reached this point—*Illusions perdues*—after passing through, but transcending, similar experiences. The sordidness of the Galerie-de-bois or the backstage of the Panorama-Dramatique are described in a way that emphasizes the discontinuity between the object of description and the mode of description. In these cases, the narrative voice clearly refuses to accept what it is describing. It will not *be* what it describes. Those repellent realities must be evoked, but *Illusions perdues* both englobes and transcends them. In each instance, we hear the voice of *Pensée* protesting against the prostitution of the instrument of its own existence. Moreover, the voice of *Pensée* rebels against the notion that reality is fixed and identifiable. It protests everywhere—in the Cénacle, in the Galerie-de-bois, in the Panorama-

Dramatique—against naive realism, against the monetization of words. We are shown a world that is a hall of mirrors—a world where virtue has never entered and from which art is excluded. Everywhere we turn, the process of comparison leads to "simulacra": signs without verifiable originals for either the characters within the story or for ourselves as readers. To say that Part II of *Illusions perdues* challenges mimesis is not to say that it flies off into clouds of fantasy; but rather that it challenges standards of a priori judgement in its characters, and of objective discourse in itself. Obviously, the very fact that we see illusions as illusions implies a stance on the narrator's part. But if his stance is omniscient it is not thereby necessarily consistent, and we have seen enough contradiction and paradox in the way he handles his materials to understand that he too is puzzled over the problems of narration. Although there is no question as to where his sympathies lie among the values represented by various characters, he offers no easy solutions. There is no clear-cut punishment of the wicked or reward for the virtuous, for he is fascinated by them all. The narrator suggests that the world he is evoking is full of evil, yet he pulls up short of suggesting alternatives. He is engaged in that process of pointing, juxtaposing, questioning and waiting that characterizes all narrators sensitive to the demands of *Pensée*. For him as for his creatures, the assumption of a stable reality and of a universally acceptable system of values may be the greatest illusion of all.

Part III, "Les Souffrances de l'Inventeur," opens with the retracing of Lucien's voyage to Paris. Having been both liberal and royalist, poet and journalist, Lucien has flitted from one world view to another without ever taking up a view of his own. The consequence is that he is crushed between the conflicting forces and sent back to Angoulême in poverty and disgrace. The lesson seems to be that if all worldviews are relative, the only way to survive is to choose the one that one considers most moral, and to remain with it even though one must admit that the choice is ultimately arbitrary. The drama of David Séchard will illustrate the point.

The situation in which David now finds himself is thoroughly discouraging. The noble optimism of Part I is now much diluted, replaced by the dubious and paradoxical idea that cheap paper might somehow channel the course of French civilization into more conservative and salutary directions (p. 373). This curious principle tends to empty David's search of its purely intellectual joy and convert it into a much more practical and business-like endeavor. After all that the narrator has told us about the nature of contemporary society, he ascribes to David the desire to analyze the development of the popular press "dans ses conséquences matérielles" and to align it with the major trends of the century (p. 373). The story moves away from the great intellectual themes of Parts I and II, in order to concentrate on the commercial aspects of paper-making. Little does David realize the extent to which he comes to resemble his father, despite his continued protestations of idealism.

Part III seems, as a result, relatively flat. The spirit of paradox and contradiction that animated the story until this point is now gone. There is not a single dramatic tableau. We are mostly concerned with the web of intrigue spun by the Cointet brothers around David in order to steal his secret. The narrator is so carried away by the details of the plot that everything is sacrificed to it. Here, as before, we sense behind the obsessive detail a lived experience; the trouble is that the mechanics of commercial competition, bankruptcy, and so on, have for us nothing like the interest they hold for the narrator. He seems aware of this difficulty: "Quatre-vingt-dix lecteurs sur cent," he claims, "seront affriolés par les détails suivants comme par la nouveauté la plus piquante. Ainsi sera prouvée encore une fois la vérité de cet axiome: 'Il n'y a rien de moins connu que ce que tout le monde doit savoir, *la loi*!" (p. 410). Despite the narrator's breezy optimism, few readers are charmed by the case-book on commercial law that follows. The narrator's maneuver here is one he had already used of course: the discussion of law is merely a lengthy "antiphrase." Like the digression on paper-making in Part I, the discussion of French banking practices and the detailed descriptions of protested notes of hand are a way of talking around the true subject: the preservation of the best works of the mind in a dependable physical medium. The narrator has not lost interest in his basic theme, but he obviously faces in David's experiments the same descriptive difficulties he faced with d'Arthez' novel. Here, however, he has failed to find an exciting and suitable counterpart. He attempts, as before, to englobe and transcend the subject by insisting upon the sordidness of the Cointet's machinations, in order to underscore the nobility of David's undertaking. But the business maneuvers lack drama; weariness rather than fascination is the result, and the text never quite succeeds in justifying itself as the transcendence of the disreputable maneuvers it is describing. There are numbers of possibilities, however. Petit-Claud, one suspects, might well have developed into a provincial Lousteau, serving as the voice of *Pensée* while leading his victim to destruction. He has all the proper qualities: ambition, sensitivity, and a dormant sense of morality. For whatever reason, he remains simply another element in the vast conspiracy, determined to profit as much as he can from David's discomfiture.

We are now plunged directly into the details of the Cointet's plot. The narrator vouches for the authenticity of the events by asserting that he has copied the papers (pp. 418–19), and shows us a bill of twenty two items whereby David's original debt of 1000 francs is augmented by an additional 1,046 francs of legal expenses. All this lacks direct connection with the printing-poetry theme of the novel, although it does touch on the general opposition of philistines and poets. David is incapable of verbalizing in a way that would clarify the theme; the best he can tell Petit-Claud is that he works for love alone (p. 424). Like other inventors of the *Comédie humaine,* he makes the discovery he had been looking for by sheer accident, as he pensively chews on a branch of nettle one day (pp. 424–25). His discovery is totally independent of his business embroilments; it has a kind of conceptual purity, a tranquil inevitability that marks David as potentially the great poet of *Illusions perdues*. But the narrator fails to exploit the incident except to remark rather lamely that "ces hasards-là ne sont rencontrés que par les audacieux chercheurs des causes naturelles!" (p. 425)

This rapid brush with really serious issues almost brings the narrator to the realization that he cannot devote his whole tale to the legal history of these suits and countersuits (pp. 432–33). But it is only for a moment. He continues his endless analyses of commercial law, pursuing issues which, however interesting they may be to him, lack the relationship to the main story that was so clearly visible in the history of paper-making and in the description of the Galerie-de-bois.

Eventually, the machinations of the Cointet brothers reduce David to the necessity of hiding himself—the ultimate act of the creative spirit defending itself from the world of calculation. In making one last effort to move his father, David confronts again the world of *Idée*. "Toutes les lois de la nature," observes the narrator, "ont un double effet, en sens inverse l'un de l'autre" (p. 454); but the principle that had first been enunciated by Blondet and Vignon at the end of Part II as the theoretical explanation of everything that had happened to Lucien, now serves merely to point up the contradiction of paternity and greed in old Séchard.

On the other hand, the narrative concern with Lucien does continue the themes of perception and the word game that had buttressed Parts I and II. Shortly after his arrival back in Angoulême Lucien is surprisingly and mysteriously serenaded beneath his windows, is the subject of a flattering article in the local paper, and receives an invitation to dine with Louise and du Châtelet, now man and wife. None of these events is genuine, and it takes the narrator six and a half pages to explain the hidden motivations behind them and their connection with the conspiracy against David

Séchard. But Lucien accepts them all at face value. He is even convinced that he can revive the fires of love in Louise, and sends to Lousteau for a suit of fashionable clothes so he can "appear" in Angoulême society. Everything around him is sham, but he perceives it all as real. Although he now considers the Hôtel de Bargeton to be a dingy country house instead of the opulent palace he had thought it to be ("Comme Paris vous change les idées!" he muses [p. 519]), he still cannot judge people or their motives for what they are. He is again caught up in the word game. The final irony is his belief that his letter to David has brought the latter out of hiding, whereas it is Cérizet's forgery that has turned the trick and landed David in debtors' prison. In the one case where he is quite right about his general responsibility for David's suffering, he is wrong about the precise circumstances. This final misapprehension makes him determine on suicide precisely when he might have exculpated himself.

It is Jacques Collin, in the guise of the false abbé Carlos Herrera, who must point the moral to this foolish, naive, weak, young man, and at the same time draw together all the strands of the narrative. With his appearance the text suddenly takes on new life and new energy; old familiar themes reemerge and we find ourselves in another of the great dramatic tableaux that had characterized earlier parts of the novel. Carlos Herrera begins with the basic principle of two forms of history: a lying, official version *ad usum delphini;* and a true, secret, and shameful history (p. 537). He does not take long to deflect Lucien from his proposed suicide by pointing out to him that reality, like history, has only the value the observer attaches to it: "Une destinée vaut tout ce que l'homme l'estime, et vous n'évaluez votre avenir que douze mille francs" (p. 537). Collin's own story is in itself an example of the relativity of valuative processes, for he is no more a Spanish priest than Lucien is a great poet. One illusion substitutes for another in a novel composed of mirrors in front of mirrors.

The discourse of Herrera is, nevertheless, an accurate

mirror of everyt! ing that has been going on in *Illusions perdues*. His cynical speech repeats, in effect, the speech of Lousteau initiating Lucien into the secrets of success in Paris. But now Lucien has had his own experiences of that world, and Herrera's arguments find quick roots (pp. 541–42). Herrera is merely working on a grander scale: his world is not that of Parisian journalism, but of the nation itself. In exposing the secret springs of European history, Herrera is touching on the very principles that animate the story of *Illusions perdues:* history is but an illusory façade. Reality is what one makes it, morality and ethics are political. What more pithy summing-up can one imagine to this distressing novel than Herrera's formulation: "Le fait n'est donc plus rien en lui-même, il est tout entier dans l'idée que les autres s'en forment" (p. 543). Inevitably, then, the final comment on the printing-poetry theme is noncommittal. The narrator ultimately declines to decide whether David's invention will preserve the best works of the mind, or merely foster personal ambition (his much-decried "égoisme"); he restricts himself to observing that the discovery was quickly absorbed into French industry like a nourishing food (p. 581). David himself is increasingly concerned with production costs and with the possibility of enriching his family—or at least providing them with a comfortable income. He seems to have lost the original intellectual curiosity that had impelled him; as a matter of fact, he seems also to have lost sight of the fact that his process, while cheap, is based upon vegetable fibres, of whose durability he has no assurance at all. What, we wonder, has become of his concern for the works of the mind? We can make of it what we will.

In many complex ways, then, the theme of relativity undermines not only what the novel tells us about the world, but the value we should attach to the novel itself. Despite all the troubles and difficulties of the story, it turns out to be a most agreeable world. There are no real victims: everyone is left more or less comfortable. Virtue is rewarded but so is villainy. The clichés of the romantic novel, which we had expected to be deflated, have in fact been fulfilled. *Illusions perdues,* which for a considerable time, seemed to exist on a level of synthesis passing beyond the summed-up possibilities of its elements—which seemed, indeed, to give the narrator his words back—falls finally into easy solutions. Part III adopts all the formulas of its age, and fails to work through the implications of its opening pages. What was to be the role of creativity and art in a society where material inventions could turn out to be either blessings or curses? For all his perspicacity, the narrator is no soothsayer, and he leaves us floating in an unresolved situation that contains many possibilities but no solutions.

David becomes a simple land owner. The Cointet brothers become millionaires. Petit-Claud and Cérizet make their careers in politics. The further adventures of Lucien have nothing to do with literature and the arts, although he continues to be both a purveyor of, and a victim of, illusion. *Illusions perdues* therefore stands as a unique, if somewhat flawed, moment of reflexivity at the heart of the *Comédie humaine*—a privileged moment when the narrative asserts itself as a statement of the problems of writing novels in a world where those problems are systematically avoided. For the narrator to write his novel in this way was the only way to display the problem in all its dialectical complexity. It is an act that carries him far beyond the double exposition of the problem by d'Arthez and by David, into a narrative mode that englobes their experiences and, with greater or lesser success, demonstrates what kind of narrative can both state their problems and attempt to resolve them.

Does this make of Balzac a realist or a visionary? The distinction, we said at the outset, is probably not very helpful. Either one could contain elements of the other, and Balzac himself claimed to be both. Clearly every novelist writes about the real world; just as clearly, he is not concerned with being a sociologist or an historian in a direct and technical way. The "message" of Balzac, as of all novelists, is imbedded in, and transcends, his description of reality.

But this does not mean that the *Comédie humaine* is in the

least disconnected from reality. The narrator of this vast panorama looks *at* his language as much as *through* it; each activity impinges on the other, and in the end we arrive at some sense of the only reality that matters in a novel: the situation of a creative mind composing its work in a specific historical situation. Only this way of looking at the text as an historical artifact in itself, can lead us to an understanding of the history it is trying to portray. All the devices we have observed are addressed to the problem of closing the gap between narrator and reader. Whatever tale he happens to be telling, part of the narrator's story is always the problem of the telling itself. The ideal of perfect communication is, of course, just that, an ideal. The narrator is always reaching for some better mode of narration; he is always overflowing with more than he can say; he is certain only that *this* book will not fulfill his expressive ambitions. The abolition of the veil leads to the discovery of a multifarious, not a stable, reality.

Yet *this* book is all he can offer us. In a peculiar way, his pains over the deceptiveness of language are pointless, for the work he offers us is inevitably a product of the age he wishes to describe. The novels about Catherine de Medicis tell us as much about the July Monarchy as do the novels about Lucien de Rubempré. Everywhere in the *Comédie humaine* we find signs of the deepest conceptual structures of the July Monarchy: the struggle between the vision of a fixed, quantifiable reality and the vision of one that is amorphous, relative, and ever-changing. If the contents of the *Comédie humaine* show us the triumph of the philistines, of money and political power, its design shows us their failure. It is an adversary text, minutely describing and yet condemning what it describes. Hidden—but not very deeply—beneath the much vaunted unity of the work, is the surprising assertion that although man lives in a physical world, he can make of it what he wishes. That function of free choice, of *Pensée,* is reserved for the narrator, for whom alone representation is possible. From the deepest levels of his experience come both the protestation against the degradation of art, and the affirmation that art will not be silenced. All the great creators in the *Comédie humaine* are flawed, if not failures; but from their failure arises the triumph of the narrator, who succeeds in creating the book we now hold in our hand.

Afterword

Balzac's use of adjectives . . . is a sign not simply of lack of analytic power . . . but of a tendency of all feelings to reduce themselves to their simplest elements."[1] With this broadside, one of the best-known English critics of French literature dismisses the creator of the *Comédie humaine*. His attack touches on the very juncture of language, psychology, and art that we have been examining in the preceding chapters. One must certainly admit that in many respects Balzac's narration no longer challenges contemporary sensibilities; yet one must also recognize that it is full of drama, passion, and violence. And even if it does not always display the fully-developed analytic sophistication that modern readers ask for, it is clearly moving in that direction. Freud remarked on more than one occasion that he was merely codifying insights that creative artists had always had; and his remark applies to no one as much as to Balzac. Without trying to turn him into a precursor of Freud, one can justifiably claim for him the first sustained effort in France to express in fiction the problems of creating fiction. As broad and as elementary as his psychologizing may now strike us, he nevertheless explored the concept of the subconscious, the relationship of word to thought, and the whole puzzle of creativity. Indeed, psychologists such as Merleau-Ponty find it quite appropriate to turn to Balzac for illustration and confirmation of their ideas.

Because the flaws and virtues of the *Comédie humaine* meet precisely in its fascination with language, most attacks on Balzac's style seem beside the point. At the end of our inquiry, there can be little question that Balzac's interest in problems of language was sustained and complex, and that linguistic theories and themes are the very kernel of his work. There is an amazing tenacity in his use of a relatively small number of devices from the earliest potboilers down

[1]Martin Turnell, *The Novel in France* (New York, 1950), p. 226.

through the final episodes of the *Comédie humaine.* The problem of the linguistic "veil" appears in the *Dissertation sur l'homme,* and subsumes all the others. The early novels interpret this problem in terms of premonitions, voices, and the "escape" mechanism; *La Peau de chagrin* examines the double nature of thought and its potential destructiveness. Subsequently the *Comédie humaine* explores the implications of these theories by working into its dramatic texture the thought-word controversy and the relationships of characters, narrator, and reader to each other. The solutions Balzac evolved—"Balzacian prose," "the word-event," and others—were not always satisfactory, but when they succeed in inducing us to accept them as real and true, they carry unparalleled force of conviction.

Clearly, then, language in the *Comédie humaine* touches upon issues altogether more important than mere style. It places us squarely before the ancient puzzle of epistemology. How, indeed, was one to eliminate that veil of language which, by interposing itself between mind and world, or mind and mind, rendered knowledge problematical and imperfect? On many occasions the Balzacian narrator longingly contemplates the possibilities of "completeness": both the complete evocation of French society, and the complete and immediate union with the reader. Some characters manage what neither author nor narrator can do. Raphaël de Valentin and the cashier Castanier are able to do all, see all, and understand all. They possess infinitely powerful minds, able to see immediately the furthermost results of their thought. But their conceptual universality is entirely a matter of *Idée,* and is derived from the inherent tautology of logic. All ideas contain all possible extensions of themselves, and for minds of such power the results of immediate perception is an immense lassitude and, finally, the renunciation born of total boredom.

But such characters are rare. Most Balzacian creatures are ordinarily "incomplete," and this accounts for their very lives. Only "incomplete" creatures experience desire, and therefore possess the dynamics of life. Total satisfaction may produce harmony, as it does for Félix de Vandenesse, but it also produces sterility. In the striking phrase of the narrator, desires "veulent être seuls, ils étouffent tout ce qui n'est pas eux" (FE, 92). By the same token, desire is dangerous; incomplete happiness is "le plus grand élément des mauvaises actions secrètes" (Pay, 127). Here, in a nutshell, is the drama and tragedy of the *Comédie humaine*. Incomplete destinies are the lot of all men, and the source of the energy that drives them toward whatever goals they may seek.

Geniuses, however, have a chance to escape from the limitations of "completeness" because their domain is *Pensée*, not *Idée*. For them there is no boredom. *Pensée* allows them to preserve their freedom: "Aussi les grands artistes, les poètes complets, n'attendent-ils ni les commandes, ni les chalands, ils enfantent aujourd'hui, demain, toujours" (Be, 248). For the poet, there is no end to language. "Dire" may embroil him in tautology, but "expression" involves him in infinite regression. Those who reject mimeticism face the frontierless domain of free creativity. The narrator's position is similar. His constant dissatisfaction stems from his acute awareness of the impossibility of ever reaching the outer limits of his work. He understands that he can never say everything, although the temptation to describe society "totally" remains the lodestar of his activity. Like the geniuses he speaks of, he is "incomplete" in a way that has nothing to do with the historical or sociological rendition of an existing society.

Nevertheless, the abstract ideal of completeness remains. Most writers believe they are describing the world "as it is," and our changing sense of the world in no way alters that ambition. Balzac was no different, except that he understood the impossibility of descriptive "completeness." He aimed, rather, at complete communication with a reader whom he might induce to accept the statements of his fictional construct as no less valid and verifiable than statements about the real world. All his linguistic techniques are designed to move us imperceptibly from the known to the possible, from *Idée* to *Pensée,* from *dire* to *expression.*

Ultimately one wonders at the persistence of such obsessions. From almost his first word to his last, and despite his own lack of illusions, the Balzacian narrator seeks an aesthetic ideal of total expression. Ultimately, moreover, the search for aesthetic perfection is simply the translated version of a search for moral perfection in a world manifestly flawed. Because linguistic "incompleteness" is the lot of all mankind, not merely his own, and because it is the manifestation of unfulfilled desire, language becomes the vehicle of evil. The position is thus surprisingly orthodox, but it is the essence of Balzac's humaneness: if he could just for an instant achieve a perfect language, even at the price of ennui, he would have demonstrated the possibility of good. Thus language, in his view, is not merely a set of arbitrary signs through which men make their thoughts about a stable reality known to each other. It is the constituent vehicle of that reality, and at the same time the very substance of morality. A perfect language would mean perfect men, and Balzac's comedy would then no longer be human but celestial. This is the naive yet dazzling perspective to which the *Comédie humaine* leads us, even if the path must necessarily cross the here-and-now of our present jungle.

The Text of the *Dissertation sur l'homme*

The text of this essay was deciphered by abbé Henri Gauthier and myself at the Chantilly archives, and published by him in *L'Année balzacienne*, 1968. His study of its dating and sources can be consulted there. My own analysis of its psychological and linguistic themes appear in *L'Année balzacienne*, 1969, and forms the basis of what is now chapter 1 of the present work. Since the *Dissertation* is such an obscure work and has appeared in print only in *L'Année balzacienne*, and since it is so germane to the issues raised here, I am reproducing its text.

La Dissertation sur l'homme

En jetant un coup d'oeil sur les travaux de l'homme, un profond sentiment d'admiration nous saisit en faveur de nous-mêmes et grandit le dernier individu de notre espèce. La terre a été labourée presque toute entière et nous avons forcé ses moindres substances d'obéir à nos besoins comme à nos caprices les plus désordonnés; nous l'avons embellie d'une foule de cités où brillent des chefs-d'oeuvre rivaux de ceux de la nature et chacun d'eux nécessite plusieurs sciences et la coopération du monde; l'intérêt a fait éclore la civilisation, les lois et la guerre qui comprennent toutes les sciences et le luxe qui renferme tous les arts. Aussitôt la mer aperçue, elle est traversée; son indomptable mobilité, loin d'être un obstacle, [devient] un nouveau lien de notre univers; la science de la Marine transporte des Villes et le commerce, autre science, réunit les deux bouts du globe étonné; les cieux mêmes, que la nature dérobait à nos dévorantes mains sont mesurés, ses feux sont comptés et le géomètre semble parcourir leur étendue et deviner leurs lois.

Après toutes ces merveilles l'homme a fait plus, il les a célébrées, et, semblable à Dieu, s'est donné l'immortalité. Les accents du poète [ont] retenti. Alors à l'admiration que l'on éprouve, se mêle une invincible curiosité. On veut surprendre les secrets de la Nature et savoir la cause de ces créations et de tous ces efforts successifs par lesquels l'homme est parvenu à ce faîte de grandeur. Mais le savant interrogé répond que cette cause est le génie, et paye notre curiosité par un mot.

On a fait des livres entiers pour expliquer ce qu'est le génie, de même que l'on en produit encore pour chercher le mystère de la création.

Certes si les sciences humaines avaient eu dès leur origine l'unité et la progression toujours croissante de force et de rapidité que nous observons dans les fleuves qui courent vers la mer, nous serions plus avancés dans la vaste route entreprise depuis bien des siècles; mais il semble, en étudiant l'histoire des sciences, apercevoir au bout de leur carrière une puissance jalouse de leur accroissement. A des torrents de lumière, elle oppose un ou deux siècles de barbarie pendant lesquels tout se perd insensiblement, et c'est ainsi qu'elle préserve les mystères dont elle paraît inquiète, tandis que l'homme étonné se voit sans cesse obligé de reconstruire le palais des sciences avec ses propres ruines, jusqu'à ce que le génie, ayant thésaurisé ses inventions, ait pu pénétrer un sanctuaire inconnu, l'objet de ses efforts.

Alors l'homme se connaîtra peut-être, alors l'essence de son âme, et le feu du génie, et les causes premières ne seront plus des secrets. Je doute que maintenant l'on puisse résoudre le problème que nous offre le génie. C'était à Corneille, c'était à Racine, au divin Homère, au cygne de Mantoue qu'il fallait demander les mystères de leurs talents. La tombe garde leur réponse, et leurs ouvrages sont des monuments admirables dont on peut faire le tour sans pouvoir deviner les secrets de l'architecte.

Ce n'est qu'en tremblant que j'ose présenter quelques réflexions sur un pareil sujet, mais la contradiction évidente de la question, les hérésies littéraires qui peuvent en découler ont attiré mon attention; et, pour éviter toute obscurité, je dois remonter à des principes et les établir. Commençons d'abord par expliquer le mot génie, considérons ensuite le génie en général et sachons enfin si le génie, pris comme essence, est différent de lui-même, ce qui doit nous conduire au génie poétique.

Le langage est un art par lequel l'homme dépeint à l'homme par les sons tous les objets qu'il aperçoit, toutes les sensations qu'il éprouve et les rapports qui existent entre ses sensations. [Le langage[parvient à son but à l'aide du son modifié, ou mots qui sont au discours ce que le chanvre est au tissu. L'existence d'un langage demande tant de travaux et de réflexions à l'esprit humain qu'elle recule pour un temps indéfini un mystère que les almanachs rapprochent avec une sagacité si rare. Les mots ont d'abord réprésenté les objets matériels qui s'offrent à nous, tels que le cheval, l'homme, l'arbre. Ces mots ont pour fondement des substances apercevables. Puis on a créé des mots pour dépeindre les rapports qui existent entre ces objets, tels que les mots grand, petit.

Enfin il est une troisième espèce de mots qui n'ont pour cause aucune substance apercevable, aucun rapport entre les substances. Ces mots représentent des collections plus ou moins nombreuses d'idées.

Nous chercherons plus tard comment naissent les idées qui donnent lieu à ces mots. L'idée est une opération intérieure, le produit immédiat d'une sensation, et la sensation est un mouvement de nos cinq sens, excité par les substances qui nous environnent. Ainsi, la sensation étant la cause de l'idée et l'idée la cause du mot qui la représente, il est arrivé que l'on a compris sous un mot des collections entières de sensations et d'idées. Les mots génie, science, esprit, goût font partie de ces sortes de mots.

Les mots qui dépeignent des objets matériels peuvent être appelés mots simples. Les mots qui représentent des rapports seront nommés mots mixtes et la troisième espèce, mots abstraits. Il est facile de sentir que les mots simples et mixtes n'ont pas besoin de définition parce qu'on voit la substance qui sert de fondement aux premiers, de même que l'on aperçoit les rapports qu'indiquent les seconds.

Mais les mots science, vertu, génie, étendue, infini, esprit, goût sont des mots abstraits et ces mots demandent pour être entendus des définitions plus ou moins savantes. Il est évident que l'on conçoit l'idée que représente [le] mot arbre et le mot grand plus facilement que la collection d'idées du mot génie. On voit la substance arbre, on aperçoit le rapport qu'il y a entre un arbre grand ou petit et l'on ne voit pas le génie; on ne conçoit pas l'infini tout d'un coup. C'est une véritable science que la définition de la collection d'idées que renferment ces mots.

Il est des peuplades dont le langage est borné à des mots simples. Un seul homme de ces peuplades a une somme de science égale à celle de toute la nation.

Il est d'autres peuples qui ont peu de mots abstraits; il en est enfin qui en ont beaucoup. Les nations d'Europe ont presque toutes une langue dont les mots sont multipliés, mais il n'a jamais existé de langue assez riche pour exprimer toutes les sensations et les idées de l'homme par des mots.

Ces principes posés, il faut chercher la signification la plus étendue et la plus comprise du mot génie. Ce n'est qu'en enlevant toute équivoque sur de tels mots que l'on peut raisonner clairement.

Il est une puissance dans l'homme; cette puissance naît, s'accroît et meurt avec lui; elle meurt avec lui parce que nous en voyons les effets commencer, s'accroître et diminuer et que, voyant l'homme périr, il est naturel de penser que la puissance qui a suivi ses différentes phases, périt avec lui. Il en a l'exercice à l'instant qu'il a les yeux ouverts au jour, à l'instant où il mange, à l'instant où il bronche en marchant. La lumière qui le frappe, le lait qu'il aspire et le caillou qu'il rencontre, excitent en lui un effet quelconque. Cet effet, je le nomme sensation; cette sensation, produite par une substance qui n'est pas lui, est transportée avec une extrême célérité au siège de la puissance et produit une impression qui s'y grave par des caractères inconnus qui ont une propriété immense et qui montrent tout d'un coup ce que peut la nature.

Sur cette impression transmise à ce point intangible de l'homme où gît la puissance, elle forme un jugement. Ce jugement, je l'appelle idée simple.

Mais il existe une seconde opération. C'est l'autre sorte d'idée que [font] naître la comparaison de deux idées simples et les rapports qui sont entre elles. On peut la nommer idée composée, tout en observant que cette nouvelle idée a pour fondement non plus une substance externe qui n'est pas nous, mais l'impression qu'elle a produite en nous. Et si l'on considère l'impression comme une modification de cette puissance, on peut regarder l'impression comme faisant partie de nous, puisqu'elle est gravée par ces caractères supposés. Alors on voit que la seconde idée est pour ainsi dire une sensation de cette puissance elle-même; le domaine de cette sorte d'idée devient bien plus vaste, car si les substances qui nous donnent les sensations, causes des idées simples, sont nombreuses, les rapports qui existent entre elles sont bien plus nombreux aussi. Il existe donc deux sortes de sensations: [la] sensation corporelle qui produit l'idée simple, et la sensation intellectuelle qui est l'idée composée. Ces deux espèces de sensations se passent également en nous, mais la première agit sur le corps et sa puissance interne, au lieu que la seconde n'agit que sur et dans la puissance. Et c'est à la faveur de ces trois êtres, la sensation, la puissance et l'idée, que l'homme a composé la science, et de la manière dont se construisent en lui ces trois êtres, il porte dans la science soit du génie soit peu de talent.

Tous les hommes possèdent cette puissance. Si cette puissance est un sixième sens plus exquis, plus vaste, plus étendu que les autres, elle est matérielle, ainsi que ses sensations qui ne sont pas moi, car si l'on accorde que le son et l'instrument soient deux êtres séparés, le sens et la sensation, l'âme et l'idée sont deux êtres séparés. Quoi qu'il en soit cette puissance est un genre qui contient des espèces et, de la défectuosité de ces espèces, dépend[ent] l'organisation et la manière d'être du genre.

Ces espèces sont la mémoire, la volonté, l'imagination et le jugement et la faculté d'inventer des rapports; mais remarquons que ces cinq espèces, ainsi tracées au milieu de cette puissance pour pouvoir la définir et s'en rendre compte, ne sont pas la puissance elle-même: elles en sont des propriétés, sans en être l'essence. C'est ainsi que l'on environne le globe et l'univers entier de lignes imaginaires pour le faire parcourir pas à pas à l'esprit humain et en rabaisser l'immensité vers nos petits organes.

Le corps humain, la sensation, les idées simples et composées, cette puissance interne et ses cinq espèces ou propriétés sont tellement subordonnés les uns aux autres et se mêlent dans leurs diverses opérations avec une telle rapidité que beaucoup de philosophes ont, dans leurs dissertations, confondu leurs effets et leurs causes; de là les hérésies et les sectes philosophiques. Mais jusqu'à présent chacun doit, je crois, reconnaître ce que je viens de poser. Je n'ai raisonné que sur des faits. Personne ne peut nier la puissance décrite, la sensation éprouvée, l'idée qui en est la suite, et l'idée composée qui est le dernier degré de combinaison dans notre esprit. Quant aux cinq propriétés de la puissance interne, qu'il me plaît nommer âme, nous allons les examiner avec l'oeil sévère d'un pyrrhonien.

Cet examen nous conduira à la recherche de la différence qui existe entre toutes les âmes et à la définition du génie, de l'esprit, de la médiocrité, de la sottise, de la folie que l'on peut avoir.

La Nature qui a fait tous les chênes semblables et différents, toutes leurs feuilles pareilles et variées, a mis la même ressemblance et la même diversité dans les animaux, dans les grains de sable, dans toutes les substances, enfin dans l'âme, les propriétés de l'âme et la conformation de l'homme. On en a cherché la raison bien loin, elle est à nos côtés, devant nous. C'est ainsi que l'on court à la fortune aux Indes, quand elle est à la porte du logis.

Si tous les hommes et tou[s] les produits de la nature étaient semblables à un tel point qu'en les superposant par la pensée les uns sur les autres, on trouvât les mêmes figures et les mêmes accidents, c'est alors que la nature entière pourrait être plus raisonablement l'effet du hasard; mais cette variété singulière prouve une autre puissance et donne en même temps la raison d'une foule de phénomènes.

En effet s'il est une vérité qui n'a jamais eu de contradicteurs, c'est la différence de taille qui existe entre les organes des hommes. Il est encore évident que l'homme qui habite dans tel climat est autrement affecté que l'homme qui habite dans tel autre; que, dans chaque climat, il est une portion d'hommes qui a des habitudes selon la température. L'homme du Mexique et l'homme du Labrador sont deux êtres totalement distincts et cette distinction sensible entre eux devient moindre entre les autres hommes selon leurs patries, sans cesser néanmoins d'exister. On dira que je renouvelle le système des climats. Si ce que je dis est vrai, si vous l'accordez, qu'importe qu'une chose soit nouvelle, soit ancienne! Est-elle vraie, adoptez-la; est-elle fausse, niez; mais ici l'évidence est trop forte pour contester.

Ces différences de taille, d'organes, de constitution existent donc entre les peuples. Mais, chaque nation prise séparément, il est encore d'autres .ariétés. L'organe visuel, le toucher, l'odorat sont diversifiés dans chaque individu d'une nation, outre la grande différence entre chaque peuple.

Or nos sens étant les seuls organes institués par la nature pour recevoir des sensations, il est vraisemblable de croire que toutes les sensations que nous éprouvons se ressemblent et diffèrent entre elles dans la proportion indiquée par le climat pour la nation et, pour les individus d'un même climat, par la différence de leurs conformations.

Il ne s'ensuit pas de là que toutes nos idées soient pareilles et dissemblables dans cette proportion. Cela peut être probable pour les idées simples, mais les idées composées ne doivent pas entrer dans ce système et cela par des causes naturelles. Nous ne sommes pas maîtres de nos sensations corporelles; nous le sommes un peu plus de nos sensat[ions] intellect[uelles].

Le fait de la sensation dure un moment; le moment passé, la sensation n'existe plus et mes organes ne résonnent plus, après avoir transporté la sensation au siège de la puissance. Mais il reste le jugement porté par cette puissance et ce jugement, cette idée, est par conséquent différente chez tous les hommes, puisque la puissance de chaque homme juge à sa manière. C'est sur ces idées simples et non plus sur les sensations que la puissance opère en imaginant les rapports qui sont les idées composées, comme nous l'avons vu.

Alors de la manière dont se grave l'idée simple dépendent les idées composées; et le plus ou moins de perfection dans les cinq propriétés de la puissance influe sur le mode de trouver les rapports: ce qui jette une telle différence dans les puissances que, bien que les idées simples soient presque toujours pareilles, les idées composées n'ont presque pas de ressemblance.

C'est dans la faculté de bien juger de la sensation et de fidèlement conserver le souvenir du jugement, de manière à se le représenter sur-le-champ, ainsi que les rapports entre les idées, que consiste ce que j'appelle la mémoire, qui n'est que le nom générique sous lequel je comprends une foule de sensations dont la marche est la même dans cette puissance interne. En effet l'opération qui fait que je me rappelle la dureté du bois que j'ai touché, est une sensation pour ma puissance interne; et cette sensation étant différente selon ce que je me rappelle, la mémoire est un composé de sensations de la seconde classe que nous avons établie plus haut. Et la mémoire est la première condition du génie.

L'imagination est une espèce de mémoire; si la mémoire est la souvenance des idées, l'imagination est la souvenance des images et les images sont ces rappels et des idées [*sic*] qu'ont excitées les substances des sensations et les sensations des substances elles-mêmes, c'est-à-dire que la puissance interne de l'homme a réuni une foule de sensations, d'idées et de substances sous une même catégorie, que j'appellerais volontiers choses. Entre deux choses il existe des rapports, ces rapports forment des images et l'imagination consiste à les rappeler. Une tour qui croule, un grand empire qui tombe, un arbre que la foudre abat, voilà trois choses; l'empire qu'une révolution renverse subitement, comparé à l'arbre que la foudre abat, voilà une image. La mémoire au contraire ne rappelle que les idées simples. La mémoire a rappelé l'arbre, la tour, la foudre. L'imagination a rappelé des choses, a trouvé leurs rapports. La mémoire tient aux idées simples, l'imagination tient aux idées composées; et c'est ici la démarcation entre l'homme et les animaux. Je crois, soit dit en passant, que les animaux ont leurs sensations, forment une idée simple, ont par conséquent la mémoire; et n'ayant pas une puissance assez forte pour former des idées composées parce que leurs organes sont moins bien construits, ils se sont arrêtés, sans même faire d'effort pour aller au-delà, tandis que l'homme n'imite pas cette réserve et s'irrite d'avoir plus qu'eux, parce qu'il sent ce qui lui manque.

* * * * *

Le Langage est un art par lequel l'homme dépeint à l'homme les objets qu'il aperçoit, les sensations qu'il éprouve et tous les rapports qu'il peut découvrir entre divers objects, entre plusieurs sensations.[1]

Le langage parvient à ce but difficile à l'aide du son modifié dont les divers modes ont formé les mots qui sont au discours ce que le fil est au tissu.

La création d'un langage a demandé tant de travaux à l'esprit humain, il a dû s'écouler tant de siècles avant qu'un

[1] Like all Balzac's manuscripts, the *Dissertation* is an extremely complex collection of papers, much amended, corrected and over-written. It is not clear whether this section is an abortive first attempt to open the discussion of language, or a second try that was dropped in mid-stream.

homme ait pu prononcer le mot d'amour ou de religion et se faire entendre, que l'on a trouvé plus simple de croire qu'un premier homme parlait une langue céleste dont il n'existe plus de vestiges. Il est inutile pour la question qui nous occupe de suivre l'homme pas à pas, ainsi que les systèmes des savants à ce sujet. Examinons seulement l'état du langage. Il est natural de croire que les premiers mots inventés furent ceux qui représentent les objets de nos sensations, tels qu'un cheval, un arbre, une plante. Ces mots ont pour fondement des substances apercevables: je les nomme mots simples. Puis on aura cherché des termes pour indiquer les rapports qui existent entre les objets, comme le font les adjectifs grand, petit, etc., les verbes périr, naître, aimer, etc. Ces rapports sont encore apercevables, sans néanmoins établir cette sorte de mots sur une réalité aussi matérielle que celle des premiers, d'abord parce que ces rapports sont sujets à varier selon les organes des hommes, ensuite ils demandent une opération intérieure que l'on ne voit pas physiquement. Et c'est la nécessité même de cette opération qui démontre que ces mots ne furent trouvés qu'après les autres. On peut appeler cette seconde espèce, mots mixtes. Enfin le dernier effort de cet art fut la création d'une troisième espèce de mots, l'aliment éternel des disputes. Ces mots n'ont pour cause aucune substance réelle, aucun rapport visible. Ils éveillent en nous des collections plus ou moins nombreuses de rapports, mais des rapports bien éloignés de la simplicité des fondements des mots simples et mixtes. Ce sont les termes génie, vertu, science, infini, Dieu, etc.

Bibliography*

Aaron, R. I. *John Locke*. Oxford, 1955.

Abraham, Pierre. *Créatures chez Balzac*. Paris, 1931.

Acton, H. B. "The Philopsophy of Language in Revolutionary France." *Proceedings of the British Academy*, XLV (1959), 199–219.

Affron, Charles. *Patterns of Failure in the Comédie humaine*. New Haven, 1966.

d'Alembert, Jean le Rond. "Discours préliminaire des éditeurs." *Encyclopédie ou dictionnaire raisonné des sciences, des arts et des métiers par une société de gens de lettres*. 3rd ed., Geneva and Neuchâtel, 1778–1779, I, i–ixxxi.

Allemand, André. *Unité et structure de l'univers balzacien*. Paris, 1965.

Alston, William P. "Meaning and Use." *Philosophical Quarterly*, XIII (1963), 107–24.

Amar, Marisol. "Le Néologisme de type hapax: quelques exemples et leur usage chez Balzac." *L'Année balzacienne* (1972), pp. 339–45.

Apel, Karl Otto. "Die Idee der Sprache in der Tradition des Humanismus von Dante bis Vico." *Archiv für Begriffsgeschichte*, VIII (1963), 377–80.

Arnauld, Antoine, and Lancelot, Claude. *Grammaire générale et raisonnée de Port-Royal*. Ed. M. Petitot. Paris, 1803.

Arrigon, L. J. *Les Débuts littéraires d'Honoré de Balzac*. Paris, 1924.

Bailey, Richard W. "Language to Literature; A Rejoinder." *Style*, I (1967), 221–24.

*As a general practice I have not given publishers' names, since place and date of imprint sufficiently identify my sources. I have, however, made an exception in the case of Balzac's own works, all published in Paris, where the names of publishers and editors are the only way to distinguish among multiple editions of the same title.

Baker, William, "Literary Criticism and Linguistics." *Style,* II (1968), 1–5.

Baldensperger, Fernand. *Orientations étrangères chez Honoré de Balzac.* Paris, 1927.

Balzac, Honoré de. *Annette et le criminel.* Paris, 1824; repr. 1963.

————. *Béatrix.* Ed. Maurice Regard. Paris, Garnier, 1962.

————. *Le Cabinet des antiques.* Ed. P. G. Castex. Paris, Garnier, 1958.

————. *Le Centenaire ou les deux Beringheld.* Paris, 1822; repr. 1962.

————. *Clotilde de Lusignan ou le beau juif.* Paris, 1822; repr. 1962.

————. *La Comédie humaine.* Bibliothèque de la Pleiade. Paris, Gallimard, 1935–37.

————. *Correspondance.* Ed. Roger Pierrot. Paris, Garnier, 1960–69.

————. *Les Chouans.* Ed. Maurice Regard. Paris, Garnier, 1957.

————. *Le Cousin Pons.* Ed. Anne-Marie Meininger. Paris, Garnier, 1962.

————. *La Dernière Fée.* Paris, 1823; repr. 1963.

————. *L'Envers de l'histoire contemporaine.* Ed. Maurice Regard. Paris, Garnier, 1959.

————. *Falthurne.* Ed. P. G. Castex. Paris, Corti, 1950.

————. *Eugénie Grandet.* Ed. P. G. Castex. Paris, Garnier, 1965.

————. *L'Heritière de Birague.* Paris, 1822; repr. 1961.

————. *Histoire des treize.* Ed. P. G. Castex, Paris, Garnier, 1966.

————. *Illusions perdues.* Ed. Antoine Adam. Paris, Garnier, 1956.

————. *Jean-Louis ou la fille trouvée.* Paris, 1822; repr. 1961.

————. *Lettres à Madame Hanska.* Ed. Roger Pierrot. Paris, Delta, 1967–71.

————. *Louis Lambert.* Ed. Jean Pommier and Marcel Bouteron. Paris, Corti, 1954.

————. *Le Lys dans la vallée.* Ed. Moise Le Yaouanc. Paris, Garnier, 1966.

————. *La Maison du chat-qui-pelote; Le Bal de Sceaux; La Vendetta.* Ed. P. G. Castex. Paris, Garnier, 1963.

————. *Oeuvres complètes.* Ed. Marcel Bouteron and Henri Longnon. Paris, Conard, 1912–40.

————. *Oeuvres complètes.* Edition nouvelle établie par la Société des études balzaciennes. Paris, Club de l'honnete homme, 1956–63.

————. *Oeuvres complètes.* Ed. J. A. Ducourneau. Paris, Bibliophiles de l'originale, 1965–.

————. *Les Paysans.* Ed. Jean-Hervé Donnard. Paris, Garnier, 1964.

————. *Pensées, sujets, fragmens.* Ed. Jacques Crépet. Paris, 1910.

————. *Le Père Goriot.* Ed. P. G. Castex. Paris, Garnier, 1963.

————. *Les Petits Bourgeois.* Ed. Raymond Picard. Paris, Garnier, 1960.

————. *Splendeurs et misères des courtisanes.* Ed. Antoine Adam. Paris, Garnier, 1967.

————. *Sténie ou les erreurs philosophiques.* Ed. A. Prioult. Paris, Courville, 1936.

————. *Le Vicaire des Ardennes.* Paris, 1822; repr. 1962.

————. La Vieille Fille. Ed. P. G. Castex. Paris, Garnier, 1957.

————. *Wann-Chlore.* Paris, 1825; repr. 1963.

Bar, F. "La Notion de langue litteraire." *Revue des sciences humaines,* no. 106 (1962), pp. 273–84.

Barbéris, Pierre. *Balzac et le mal du siècle.* Paris, 1970.

————. *Aux Sources de Balzac: les romans de jeunesse.* Paris, 1965.

Bardèche, Maurice. *Balzac romancier.* Paris, 1940.

————. *Une Lecture de Balzac.* Paris, 1964.

Barrière, Pierre. *Honoré de Balzac, les romans de jeunesse.* Paris, 1928.

Barthes, Roland. *Le Degré zéro de l'écriture.* Paris, 1965.

————. *S/Z.* Paris, 1970.

Baym, Max I. "The Present State of the Study of Metaphor." *Books Abroad,* xxxv (1961), 215–19.

Beebe, Maurice. *Ivory Towers and Sacred Founts: The Artist as Hero in Fiction from Goethe to Joyce.* New York, 1964.

Béguin, Albert. *Balzac lu et relu.* Paris, 1967.

Behler, Ernst. "The Origins of the Romantic Literary Theory." *Colloquia Germanica, Internationale Zeitschrift für Germanische Sprach-und Literaturwissenschaft,* ii (1968), 109–26.

Behrmann, Alfred. *Einführung in die Analyse von Prosatexten.* Stuttgart, 1967.

Bémol, Maurice. "La Représentation imagée de l'esprit et l'expression de l'inexprimable." *Revue d'esthétique,* xv (1962), 139–65.

Benachévitch, N. "Le Mot 'roman' dans les romans de Balzac." *Le Français moderne,* xxxi, no. 2 (1963), 81–93.

Bérard, Suzanne. *La Genèse d'un roman de Balzac: Illusions perdues.* 2 vols. Paris, 1961.

Berg. R. F. "On the Origin of Verbal Thinking." *Linguistics,* xxviii (December 1966), 5–45.

Bergmann, Gustav. "Meaning and Ontology." *Inquiry,* v (1962), 116–42.

Bertault, Philippe. *Balzac et la musique religieuse.* Paris, 1929.

———. *Balzac et la religion.* Paris, 1942.

Bilodeau, François. *Balzac et le jeu des mots.* Montreal, 1971.

Block, Haskell M. "The Concept of Imitation in Modern Criticism." *Proceedings of the 4th Congress of the International Comparative Literature Association.* Ed. François Jost. The Hague, 1966, ii, 704–20.

———. *Mallarmé and the Symbolist Drama.* Detroit, 1963.

———. "Theory of Language in Flaubert and Joyce." *Revue de littérature comparée,* xxxv, no. 2 (1961), 197–206.

Blot, Jean. "Le Roman et son langage." *Nouvelle Revue française,* no. 198 (1 June 1969), 1157–63.

Boehme, Jacob. *L'Aurore naissante.* Paris, 1800.

Bonald, Louis de. *Législation primitive.* 3d ed. Paris, 1829.

Bonnet, Charles. *Oeuvres.* Copenhagen, 1760.

BIBLIOGRAPHY

Booth, Wayne, *The Rhetoric of Fiction*. Chicago, 1961.

Borelli, Giovanni Alfonso. *De Motu animalium*. 2 vols. Rome, 1680–81.

Brekle, Herbert E. "Die Bedeutung der Grammaire générale raisoneé . . . für die heutige Sprachwissenschaft." *Indogermanische Forschungen,* LXXII (1967), 1–21.

——. "Semiotik und linguistische Semantik in Port-Royal." *Indogermanische Forschungen,* LXIX (1964), 103–21.

Le Breton, André. *Balzac, l'homme et l'oeuvre*. Paris, 1905.

Brombert, Victor. "Balzac and the Caricature of the Intellect." *French Review,* XXXIV, no. 1 (October 1960), 3–12.

Brooks, Peter. "Melodrama and Metaphor." *Hudson Review,* XXII (1969), 213–28.

Brown, Roger L. "Some Sources and Aspects of Wilhelm von Humboldt's Conceptions of Linguistic Relativity." *Dissertation Abstracts,* XXV (1965), no. 6607.

Bruneau, Charles. *La Langue de Balzac*. Paris, 1953.

Brutyan, G. A. "The Philosophic Bearing of the Theory of Linguistic Relativity." *ETC: A Review of General Semantics,* XXII (1965), 207–20.

Buchón, José L. M. "El artista literario y su creación." *Revista de ideas estéticas,* XXIII (1965), 3–28.

Burrows, David. "Art and the Structure of Thinking." *ETC: A Review of General Semantics,* XXIII (1966), 51–58.

Burton, J. M. *Honoré de Balzac and His Figures of Speech*. Princeton, 1921.

Carmody, François J. "Originalité et verbalisme." *Proceedings of the 4th Congress of the International Comparative Literature Association*. Ed. François Jost. The Hague, 1966, pp. 1270–76.

Cassirer, Ernst. *Philosophie der symbolishchen Formen*. Darmstadt, 1953; repr. 1964.

Castex, P. G. *Le Conte fantastique en France de Nodier à Maupassant*. Paris, 1951.

Chanet, Pierre. *Traité de l'esprit de l'homme et de ses fonctions*. Paris, 1649.

Chatman, Seymour. "On the Theory of Literary Style." *Linguistics,* xxvii (1967), 13–25.

Chevalier, J. C. "La Grammaire générale de Port-Royal et la critique moderne." *Langages,* vii (1967), 16–33.

Chomsky, Noam. *Cartesian Linguistics.* New York, 1966.

―――. *Language and Mind.* New York, 1968.

Condillac, Etienne Bonnot de. *Cours d'études pour l'instruction du prince de Parme: La Grammaire.* Paris, 1798.

―――. *Essai sur l'origine des connaissances humaines.* Paris, 1798.

―――. *Traité des systèmes.* Paris, 1798.

Coseriu, Eugenio. "L'Arbitraire du signe: Zur Spätgeschichte eines aristotelischen Begriffes." *Archiv für das Studium der neueren Sprachen und Literaturen,* no. 24 (May 1967–March 1968), pp. 81–112.

Cousin, Victor. *Cours d'histoire de la philosophie moderne.* Paris, 1846.

Cresson, André. *Descartes, sa vie, son oeuvre.* Paris, 1957.

Curtius, Ernst-Robert. *Balzac.* Trans. Henri Jourdan. Paris, 1933.

Dagneaud, Robert. *Les Elements populaires dans le lexique de la Comédie humaine d'Honoré de Balzac.* Paris, 1954.

Dargan, Preston E. and Weinberg, Bernard, eds. *The Evolution of Balzac's Comédie humaine.* Chicago, 1942.

Davie, Donald. "Language to Literature: The Long Way Round." *Style,* i (1967), 215–20.

Day, J. P. "Artistic Verisimilitude." *Dialogue* (Montreal), i (1962), 163–87.

Delattre, Geneviève. "L'Imagination balzacienne au travail: la lecture créatrice." *Cahiers de l'Association internationale des études françaises,* nos. 15–16 (1963), pp. 395–406.

Delhomme, Jeanne. "Expression et langage." *La Revue d'esthétique,* xv (1962), 189–96.

Derrida, Jacques. *De la Grammatologie.* Paris, 1967.

―――. "La Forme et le vouloir-dire." *Revue internationale de philosophie,* xxi (1967), 277–99.

Descartes, René. *Oeuvres.* Ed. Charles Adam and Paul Tannery. Paris, 1905; repr. 1964.

Destutt de Tracy, Antoine Louis. *Elémens d'idéologie.* Paris, 1827.

Dictionnaire de grammaire et de littérature. Liège, 1789.

Diderot, Denis. *Oeuvres complètes.* Ed. J. Assézat. Paris, 1876.

Donzé, Roland. *La Grammaire générale et raisonnée de Port-Royal.* Berne, 1967.

Dufrenne, Mikel. "L'Art est-il langage?" *Rivista di estetica,* XIII (1968), 161–77.

————. "Critique littéraire et phénoménologie." *Revue internationale de philosophie,* XVIII (1964), 193–208.

Durant, R. G. "Notes sur le système verbal et le point de vue dans le récit." *Modern Language Notes,* LXXXV (1970), 490–95.

Duron, Jacques, *et al. Le Livre du centenaire.* Paris, 1950.

Egebak, Niels. "Représentation et Anti-Mimésis." *Orbis litterarum,* XXVI, no. 1 (1971), 9–19.

Engel, S. M. "Thought and Language." *Dialogue* (Montreal), III (1964), 160–70.

Engler, Rudolf. "Théorie et critique d'un principe saussurien: l'arbitraire du signe." *Cahiers Ferdinand de Saussure,* XIX (1962), 5–66.

Escarpit, Robert. "Les cadres de l'histoire littéraire." *Proceedings of the 4th Congress of the Comparative Literature Association.* Ed. François Jost. The Hague. 1966, II, 195–202.

Escarpit, Robert, and Robine, Nicole. "Enquête préliminaire sur le vocabulaire de la critique littéraire." *Revue de littérature comparée,* XXXV (1961), 91–101.

Evans, Henri. *Louis Lambert et la philosophie de Balzac.* Paris 1951.

Fanger, Donald. *Dostoievsky and Romantic Realism.* Cambridge, Mass., 1965.

Fargeaud, Madeleine. "Dans le sillage des grands romantiques: S. H. Berthoud." *L'Année balzacienne* (1962), pp. 213–43.

Ferguson, Louis A. "Henry James and Honoré de Balzac." *Dissertation Abstracts,* XXIX (1968), no. 1537A.

Fernandez, Ramon. *Balzac.* Paris, 1943.

Fischler, Alex. "Rastignac-Télémaque: The Epic Scale in *Le Père Goriot.*" *Modern Language Review,* LXIII, no. 4 (1968), 840–48.

Forest, H. U. *L'Esthétique du roman balzacien.* Paris, 1950.

Foucault, Michel. "La Grammaire générale de Port-Royal." *Langages,* VII (1967), 7–15.

————. *Les Mots et les choses.* Paris, 1966.

Frappier-Mazur, Lucienne. "Espace et regard dans la *Comédie humaine.*" *L'Année balzacienne* (1967), pp. 325–38.

Frye, Northrup. *Anatomy of Criticism.* Princeton, 1957.

————. "Mythos and Logos." *Yearbook of Comparative and General Literature,* XVIII (1969), 5–18.

Gall, Franz-Joseph, and Spurzheim, Johann Christoph. *Anatomie et physiologie du système nerveux en général et du cerveau en particulier.* Paris, 1810.

Garelli, Jacques. "Wittgenstein et l'analyse du langage." *Les Temps modernes,* XVIII, no. 205 (1963), 2269–78.

Gauthier, Henri. "La *Dissertation sur l'homme.*" *L'Année balzacienne* (1968), pp. 61–103.

Gert, Bernard. "Wittgenstein and Private Language." *Journal of Philosophy,* LXV (1964), 700.

Gipper, Helmut. "Denken Ohne Sprache?" *Wirkendes Wort,* XIV (1964), 145–56.

————. "Wilhelm von Humboldt als Begründer moderner Sprachforschung." *Wirkendes Wort,* XV (1965), 1–19.

Giraud, Raymond. *The Unheroic Hero in the Novels of Stendhal, Balzac and Flaubert.* New Brunswick, N.J., 1957.

Glinz, Hans. *Ansätze zu einer Sprachtheorie.* Düsseldorf, 1962. [Beihefte zum *Wirkendes Wort,* no. 2.].

Gode, Alexander. "Language as Culture." *Babel,* X (1964), 23–25.

Goldmann, Lucien. *Le Dieu caché.* Paris, 1955.

————. *Pour une sociologie du roman.* Paris, 1964.

Gombay, André. "Philosophy of Language: Types of Implication." *Journal of Philosophy,* LXI (1964), 698–99.

Greimas, A. J. "The Relationship between Structural Linguistics and Poetics." *International Social Science Journal* (UNESCO), XIX (1967), 8–16.

Grenier, Jean. "L'Aspect négatif de la création." *Nouvelle Revue française,* XIII (June 1965), 1004–15.

———. "Aspects de la création." *Nouvelle Revue française,* XI (December 1963), 981–1000.

Grimsley, Ronald. *Maupertuis, Turgot et Maine de Biran sur l'origine du langage.* Geneva, 1971.

Grossvogel, David I. "Perception as a Form of Phenomenological Criticism." *Hartford Studies in Literature,* I (1969), 83–88.

Guise, René. "Balzac et Dante." *Année balzacienne* (1963), 297–319.

Guyon, Bernard. "Balzac et le mystère de la création littéraire." *Revue d'histoire littéraire de la France,* L, no. 2 (April-June 1950), 168–91.

———. *La Pensée politique et sociale de Balzac.* Paris, 1947.

———. "Sur la première philosophie de Balzac." *Revue d'histoire de la philosophie et d'histoire générale de la civilisation,* no. 20 (15 October 1937), pp. 369–92.

Guyon, Jeanne-Marie. *Cantique des cantiques.* Lyon, 1689.

———. *Moyen court et très facile pour l'oraison.* Grenoble, 1685.

Hampshire, Stuart. "Vico and the Contemporary Philosophy of Lanugage." *Giambattista Vico: An International Symposium.* Ed. G. Tagliacozzo and Hayden V. White. Baltimore, 1969, pp. 475–81.

Hankamer, Paul. *Die Sprache, ihr Begriff und ihre Deutung im 16. und 17. Jahrhundert: Ein Beitrag zur Frage der literaturhistorischen Gliederung des Zeitraums.* Hildesheim, 1927; repr. 1965.

Harding, D. W. *Experience into Words.* London, 1963.

Harrah, David. "The Adequacy of Language." *Inquiry,* III (1960), 73–88.

Harvey, Roland. "Noch Einmal: Sprache und Musik." *Poetica,* I (1967), 556–66.

Hasan, R. "Linguistics and the Study of Literary Texts." *Etudes de linguistique appliquée,* V (1967), 106–21.

Hayden, Donald E., *et al. Classics in Linguistics.* New York, 1967.

Helvétius, Claude-Adrien. *Oeuvres complètes.* Liège, 1774.

Hertz, Peter D. "Language and the Poetic Process." *Topic,* XVIII (1969), 5–10.

Hester, Marcus B. "Metaphor and Aspect Seeing." *Journal of Aesthetics and Art Criticism,* XXV (1966), 205–212.

Hill, Archibald A. "Analogies, Icons and Images in Relation to the Semantic Content of Discourses." *Style,* II (1968), 203–27.

Hoffman, Frederick J. "Searching for Reasons: The 19th Century Novel and 20th Century Literature." *Journal of General Education,* XV (1963), 221–29.

Hohendahl, Peter U. "Bemerkungen zum Problem des Realismus." *Orbis litterarum,* XXIII, no. 3 (1968), 183–91.

Horélek, Karel. "Sprache, Denken und Kultur." *Linguistics,* no. 17 (1965), pp. 5–10.

Humboldt, Wilhelm von. *Uber die Verschiedenheit des menschlichen Sprachbaues und Ihren Einfluss auf geistige Entwicklung des Menschengeschlechts.* Berlin, 1836; repr. Bonn, 1960.

Hunt, Herbert J. *Balzac's Comédie humaine.* London, 1959.

Iknayan, Marguerite. *The Idea of the Novel in France.* Geneva, 1961.

Ingarden, Roman. "Artistic and Aesthetic Values." *British Journal of Aesthetics,* IV (1964), 198–213.

Iser, Wolfgang. "Indeterminacy and the Reader's Response in Prose Fiction." *Aspects of Narrative.* Ed. J. Hillis Miller. New York, 1971, pp. 1–45.

———. "The Reading Process: A Phenomenological Approach." *New Literary History,* III, no. 2 (1972), 279–99.

Jefferson, D. W. "Tristram Shandy and the Tradition of Learned Wit." *Essays in Criticism,* I (1951), 225–48.

Jones, Howard M. "The Nature of Literary History." *Journal of the History of Ideas,* XXVIII (1967) , 147–60.

Josephs, Herbert. *Diderot's Dialogue of Language and Gesture.* Columbus, 1969.

Juliard, Pierre. *Philosophies of Language in Eighteenth Century France.* The Hague, 1970.

Kagan, M. "Die Kunst und die Wirklichkeit." *Kunst und Literatur,* XIII (1965), 765–85.

Kanes, Martin. *L'Atelier de Zola.* Geneva, 1963.

————. "Balzac and the Problem of Expression." *Symposium,* XXIII, nos. 3–4 (Fall-Winter 1969), 284–93.

————. "Balzac et la psycholinguistique." *L'Année balzacienne* (1969), pp. 107–31.

————. "Logic and Language in *La Peau de Chagrin.*" *Studi Francesi,* no. 41 (1970), pp. 244–56.

————. "The Mythic Structure of *La Peau de Chagrin.*" *Studi Francesi,* no. 46 (1972), pp. 46–59.

Knowleson, James R. "The Idea of Gesture as a Universal Language in the XVIIth and XVIIIth Centuries." *Journal of the History of Ideas,* XXVI (1965), 495–508.

Kuhlmann, Walter. "Vom Normcharakter der Sprache." *Zeitschrift für Phonetik, Sprachwissenschaft und Kommunikations-forschung,* XVI (1963), 113–15.

La Mettrie, Julien Offroy de. *Oeuvres philosophiques.* Berlin, 1764.

Lämmert, E. *Bauformen des Erzählens.* Stuttgart, 1955.

Laromiguière, Pierre. *Leçons de philosophie.* 2nd ed. Paris, 1820.

Laubriet, Pierre. *L'Intelligence de l'art chez Balzac.* Paris, 1961.

Lavater, G. *L'Art de connoitre les hommes par la phisionomie. Nouvelle édition augmentée d'une Exposition . . . par Moreau de la Sarthe.* 5 vols. Paris, 1820.

Lecuyer, Maurice. *Balzac et Rabelais.* Paris, 1956.

Lefebvre, Henri. *Descartes.* Paris, 1947.

Lehmann, A. G. *The Symbolist Aesthetic in France.* Oxford, 1950.

Leonard, S. A. *The Doctrine of Correctness in English Usage, 1700–1800.* Madison, 1929. [Chapter 2 reproduced as "The Philosophical Basis of Eighteenth-Century Language Theories," in *Classics in Linguistics.* Ed. D. E. Hayden, E. P. Alworth, and G. Tate, London, 1967, pp. 28–41.]

Leroy, G. *La Psychologie de Condillac.* Paris, 1937.

Levin, Harry. *The Gates of Horn.* New York, 1963.

Le Yaouenc, Moïse. *Nosographie de l'humanité balzacienne.* Paris, 1959.

Locke, John. *Essai philosophique concernant l'entendement humain.* Trans. Pierre Coste. 4th ed. Amsterdam, 1750.

————. *An Essay Concerning Human Understanding.* Ed. Alexander Campbell Fraser. Oxford, 1894; repr. New York, 1959.

Lodge, David. *Language of Fiction.* New York, 1966.

Lord, Albert B. "The Influence of the Fixed Text." *To Honor Roman Jakobson.* The Hague, 1967, ii, 1199–1206.

Lotman, J. M. "Sur la délimitation linguistique et littéraire de la notion de la structure." *Linguistics,* no. 6 (1964), pp. 59–72.

Lotringer, Sylvère. "La Structuration romanesque." *Critique,* xxvi (1970), 498–529.

Lovenjoul, Charles Spoelberch de. *Histoire des oeuvres d'Honoré de Balzac.* 3d ed. Paris, 1888.

Lugli, Vittorio. *Dante e Balzac, con altri Italiani e Francesi.* Naples, 1952.

Lukács, George. *Studies in European Realism.* Trans. Edith Bone. London, 1950.

Lyotard-May, André. "A propos du langage des images." *La Revue d'Esthetique,* xxii (1969), 29–36.

Maine de Biran, Francois-Pierre-Gonthier. *Oeuvres.* Ed. Pierre Tisserand. Paris, 1939.

Malebranche, Nicolas. *De la recherche de la vérité.* Ed. G. Rodis-Lewis. Paris, 1945.

Man, Paul de. "The Crisis of Contemporary Criticism." *Arion,* vi (1967), 38–57.

————. "Literature and Language: A Commentary." *New Literary History,* iv, no. 1 (1972), 181–92.

Mandiargues, André Pieyre de. "Le Supplice de la peau." *Nouvelle Revue française,* iv (April-June, 1966), 930–37.

Mannheim, Leonard F. "The Problem of the Normative Fallacy." *Problems of Literary Evaluation.* Ed. Joseph Strelka. University Park (Pa.), 1969, pp. 129–39.

Mareschal, Lazare-François. *Essai d'une grammaire latine élémentaire et raisonnée.* Paris, 1808.

Martin-Demézil, J., and Portel, Charles. *Balzac à Vendôme.* Tours, 1949.

Marx, Karl. "The German Ideology." *Marx's Concept of Man.* Ed. Erich Fromm. New York, 1961.

Mauro, Tullio de. "Giambattista Vico: From Rhetoric to Linguistic Historicism." *Giambattista Vico: An International Symposium.* Ed. G. Tagliacozzo and Hayden V. White. Baltimore, 1969, pp. 279–95.

May, Georges. *Le Dilemme du roman au XVIIIe siècle.* New Haven, 1963.

Mayer, Gilbert. *La Qualification affective dans les romans d'Honoré de Balzac.* Paris, 1940.

Mayr, Franz K. "Philosophie der Sprache seit ihrem griechischen Anfang." *Philosophisches Jahrbuch der Görres-Gesellschaft,* no. 17 (1965), pp. 5–10.

McCloskey, H. J. "The Philosophy of Linguistic Analysis and the Problem of Universals." *Philosophy and Phenomenological Research,* XXIV (1964), 329–38.

McMaster, Juliet. "Experience to Expression: Thematic Character Contrasts in *Tristram Shandy.*" *Modern Language Quarterly,* XXXII, no. 1 (1971), 42–57.

Merleau-Ponty, Maurice. *Phénoménologie de la perception.* Paris, 1945.

————. *Sens et non-sens.* 5th ed. Paris, 1966.

Metastasio, Arthur Paul. "Vico and French Romanticism." *Dissertation Abstracts,* XXIV (1963), no. 1619.

Meyer, Herman. "Der Zitierende Roman." *Jahrbuch der Deutschen Akademie für Sprache und Dichtung* (1961), pp. 9–23.

Mitterand, Henri. "L'Analyse du lexique littéraire. Perspectives et problèmes." *Annales de Bretagne,* LXXII (1965), 542–44.

————. "A Propos du style de Balzac." *Europe,* nos. 429–30 (1965), pp. 145–61.

Moeller, Charles. "Art et travail dans le roman européen du XXe siècle." *La Revue nouvelle,* XLV (1967), 358–69.

Moore, Will G. "Une Question mal posée: le style de Balzac." *Langue et littérature,* CLXI (1961), 275–76.

Moravcsik, J. M. E. "Linguistic Theory and the Philosophy of Language." *Foundations of Language,* III (1967), 209–33.

Moulinié, Henri. *De Bonald.* Paris, 1916.

Mowatt, D. G. and Dembowski, P. F. "Literary Study and Linguistics." *Canadian Journal of Linguistics,* XI (1965), 40–62.

Mudrick, Marvin. "Character and Event in Fiction." *Yale Review,* no. ᵕ (1960), pp. 202–18.

Mueller, Hugo. "On Re-reading Humboldt." *Problems in Semantics.* Ed. F. P. L   Washington, D.C., 1966. pp. 97–107.

Mylne, Vivienne. *The Eighteentn Century French Novel: Techniques of Illusion.* New York, 1965.

Nacquart, Jean-Baptiste. *Traité sur la nouvelle physiologie du cerveau, ou exposition de la doctrine de Gall sur la structure et les fonctions de cet organe.* Paris, 1808.

Nietzsche, Friedrich. *The Genealogy of Morals.* Trans. and ed. Walter Kaufmann. New York, 1967.

Nist, John. "The Ontology of Style." *Linguistics,* XLII (1968), 47–57.

Norton-Smith, J. "Auerbach on Literary Language." *Medium aevum,* XXXVI (1967), 159–67.

Nykrog, Per. *La Pensée de Balzac dans la Comédie humaine.* Copenhagen, 1965.

Onimus, Jean. "Poétique de l'aphorisme: En marge de René Char." *Revue d'esthétique,* XXII (1969), 113–20.

Paci, Enzo. "Ricerche per una fenomenologia del linguaggio." *Rivista di estetica,* VI (1961), 313–23.

Penn, Julia M. *Linguistic Relativity versus Innate Ideas. The Origins of the Sapir-Whorf Hypothesis in German Thought.* The Hague, 1972.

Percival, Keith. "The Notion of Usage in Vaugelas and in the Port-Royal Grammar." *Papers from the Fourth Regional Meeting of the Chicago Linguistic Society.* Chicago, 1968, pp. 165–76.

Pfohl, Gerhard, ed. *Das Epigramm: Zur Geschichte einer inschriftlichen und Literarischen Gattung.* Darmstadt, 1969.

Politzer, Robert L. "On Some Eighteenth Century Sources of American and German Linguistic Relativism." *Weltoffene Romanistik: Festschrift Alwin Kuhn.* Ed. G. Plangg and E. Tiefenthaler. Innsbruck, 1963, pp. 25–33.

Posner, Rebecca. "Linguistique et littérature." *Marche romane,* XIII (1963), 38–56.

Prioult, A. *Balzac avant la Comédie humaine.* Paris, 1936.

Pugh, Anthony. "Balzac's Beethoven: A Note on Gambara." *Romance Notes,* VIII (1966), 43–46.

———. "Interpretation of the Contes philosophiques." In *Balzac and the Nineteenth Century: Studies in French Literature Presented to Herbert J. Hunt.* Ed. D. G. Charlton, J. Gaudon, and Anthony R. Pugh. Leicester, 1972, pp. 47–56.

Rao, Raja. "The Writer and the Word." *Literary Criterion,* VII, (1965), 76–78.

Revesz, Geza, *Thinking and Speaking.* Amsterdam. 1954.

Rhodes, Enid H. "Concerning a Metaphor." *St,* XIII (1968), 295–310.

Richard, Jean-Pierre. *Etudes sur le romantisme.* Paris, 1970.

Riffaterre, Michel. "Fonctions du cliché dans la prose littéraire." *Cahiers de l'Association internationale des études françaises,* XVI (1964), 81–95.

Rodis-Lewis, G. *Nicolas Malebranche.* Paris, 1963.

Rohovit, D. D. "Metaphor and Mind: A Reevaluation of Metaphor Theory." *American Imago,* XVII (1960), 289–309.

Roques, Mario. "La Langue de Balzac." *Le Livre du centenaire.* Paris, 1952, pp. 246–57.

Rudich, Linda. "Une Interprétation de *La Peau de chagrin.*" *Année balzacienne* (1971), pp. 205–33.

Saint-Martin, Louis Claude de. *De l'esprit des choses.* Paris, an 8.

———. *L'homme de désir.* Lyon, 1790.

Salper, Donald. "The Imaginative Component of Rhetoric." *Quarterly Journal of Speech,* LI, no. 3 (1966), 307–10.

Sartre, Jean-Paul. *Search for a Method.* Trans. Hazel Barnes. New York, 1967.

————. *Situations I.* Paris, 1947.

Schankweiller, Ewald. "Wilhelm von Humboldts historische Sprachkonzeption." *Wissenschaftliche Zeitschrift ᵈᵉr Humboldt-Uniersität zu Berlin: Gesellschafts- und Sp. ʰwissenschaftliche Reihe,* IX (1959–60), 512–14.

Schilli.ｇ Bernard. *The Hero as Failure: Balzac and the Rubempré Cycle.* Chicago, 1968.

Schroder, Maurice Ẑ. "Balzac's Theory of the Novel." *L'Esprit créateur,* VII (Spring 1967), 3–10.

Seidler, Ingo. "Reale und Ideale Schichten des Sprachkunstwerks?" *Neophilologus,* LII (1968), 355–61.

Seylaz, Jean-Luc. "Reflexions sur Gobseck." *Etudes de lettres,* I (1968), 295–310.

Smith, Colin. "Destutt de Tracy and the Bankruptcy of Sensationalism." In *Balzac and the Nineteenth Century: Studies in French Literature Presented to Herbert J. Hunt.* Leicester, 1972, pp. 195–208.

Snyder, Georges. *La Pédagogie en France aux XVII et XVIII siècles.* Paris, 1965.

Souriau, Etienne. "L'Art est-il un langage?" *Revista di estetica,* XIII (1968), 5–20.

Stafford, Jean. "Truth in Fiction." *Library Journal,* XCI (1966), 4557–65.

Starobinski, Jean. "Remarques sur le structuralisme." *Ideen und Formen,* XLII (1965), 275–78.

Steiner, George. *Tolstoi or Dostoievsky.* London, 1959.

Sterling, Elwyn F. "An Overview of French Theories of Narrative Techiniques: 1630–1830." *Mosaic,* IV, no. 1 (1970). 63–77.

————. "The Theory of Verisimilitude in the French Novel prior to 1830." *French Review,* XL (February-May 1967), 613–19.

Sterne, Laurence. *Tristram Shandy.* Ed. Ian Watt. New York, 1965.

Stewart, D. H. "Linguistic Limits." *Rendez-vous,* III (1968), 1–13.

Sullivant, Raymond L. "L'Edition Werdet de *La Femme de trente ans.*" *L'Année balzacienne* (1966), 131–42.

―――. "*La Femme de trente ans:* Quelques emprunts de Balzac à la littérature anglaise." *L'Année balzacienne* (1967), 107–14.

Tanner, Michael. "Wittgenstein and Aesthetics." *Oxford Review,* no. 3 (1966), pp. 14–24.

Togeby, Knud. "Littérature et linguistique." *Orbis litterarum,* xxii (1967), 45–48.

Turgot, Anne Robert Jacques. "Etymologie." *Encyclopédie ou dictionnaire raisonné des sciences, des arts et des métiers par une société de gens de lettres.* 3rd ed. Geneva and Neuchâtel, 1778–1779, xiii, 323–47.

Turnell, Martin. *The Novel in France.* New York, 1950.

Valéry, Paul. "Poésie et pensée abstraite." *Variété V.* Paris, 1945, pp. 127–62.

Välikangas, Olli. *Les Termes d'appellation et d'interpellation dans la Comédie humaine d'Honoré de Balzac.* Helsinki, 1965.

Vannier, Bernard. *L'Inscription du corps. Pour une sémiotique du portrait balzacien.* Paris, 1972.

―――. "Jeux du texte balzacien." *Europe,* xviii, no. 498 (1970), 167–81.

Verstraelen, Eugene. "Language Analysis and Merleau-Ponty's Phenomenology of Language." *Saint Louis University Research Journal,* iv (1966), 325–42.

Viertel, John. "Concepts of Language Underlying the 18th Century Controversy about the Origin of Language." *Problems in Semantics.* Ed. F. P. Dineen. Washington, D.C., 1966, pp. 115–18.

Waelhens, Alphonse de. "Perspectives sur le langage." *Les Temps modernes,* xviii, no. 205 (1963), 2279–89.

Wais, Kurt. "Die *Divina Commedia* als dichterisches Vorbild im xix und xx Jahrhundert." *Arcadia,* iii (1968), 27–47.

Wells, George A. "Vico and Herder." *Giambattista Vico: An International Symposium.* Ed. G. Tagliacozzo and Hayden V. White. Baltimore, 1969, pp. 93–103.

Welty, Eudora. "Words into Fiction." *Southern Review,* I (1965), 543–53.

Whyte, L. L. *The Subconscious before Freud.* New York, 1960.

Wurmser, André. *La Comédie inhumaine.* Paris, 1964.

Yates, F. *The Art of Memory.* Chicago, 1966.

Yücel, Tahsin. *Figures et messages dans "La Comédie humaine.* Tours, 1972.

Zola, E. "Causerie." *La Tribune,* 31 October 1869.

Index

Aaron, R. I., 20 n
Abraham, Pierre, 157 n
Acton, H. B., 21 n, 22 n, 174 n, 222 n
Affron, Charles, 8, 8 n, 202 n
d'Alembert, Jean le Rond, 30 n, 31 n, 189, 189 n
Allem, Maurice, 66 n, 82 n
Allemand, André, 3 n
Amar, Marisol, 129 n
animal loquens, 148, 222
anti-phrase, 233, 253
Apel, Karl Otto, 26 n
aphorisms, 78, 78 n
Arago, Dominique François, 71
Aristotle, 6
Arnauld, Antoine, 17, 17 n, 155, 221 n

Baker, William, 130 n
Baldensperger, Fernand, 7 n
Balzac, works of: *Albert Savarus*, 164, 177, 183; *Album*, 65, 65 n, 66, 66 n, 70, 72 n, 77–79, 85, 91; *Annette et le criminel*, 42, 57, 59, 60, 63, 140 n; *Avant-propos*, 106; *Les Aventures administratives d'une idée heureuse*, 72; *Béatrix*, 112 n, 114, 116, 120, 136, 149, 168, 168 n, 179–82, 180 n, 198 n; *La Bourse*, 111–112; *Cabinet des antiques, Le*, 131–32, 176–78, 199, 211; *Catéchisme social, Le*, 102, 113 n; *Centenaire, Le*, 42, 50–56, 56 n, 57, 62; *César Birotteau*, 109, 111, 145, 148, 149 n, 161, 161 n, 165, 166, 195; *Chef d'oeuvre inconnu, Le*, 201, 202, 203, 205, 206; *Chouans, Les*, 134, 139–40, 142 n, 186 n, 198 n, 199 n; *Clotilde de Lusignan*, 42, 54; *Comédie humaine, La*, nonsequentiality and incompleteness of, 9; *Comédiens sans le savoir, Les*, 134, 151 n; *Cousin Pons, Le*, 115, 119, 136, 144, 144 n, 160 n, 168, 177, 198 n, 199; *Cousine Bette, La*, 112, 124–25, 133, 142 n, 144–45, 146 n, 151, 166, 172, 176, 179, 179 n, 198 n, 207, 263; *Curé de Tours, Le*, 111, 145, 162, 187, 198 n; *Curé de Village, L*, *143, 150, 186 n*; *Début dans la vie, Un*, 66 n; *De la propriété littéraire*, 109; *Député d'Arcis, Le*, 132, 136, 196, 198, 199; *Dernière Fée, La*, 42, 57, 59, 62; *Dernière Incarnation de Vautrin, La*, 140, 167, 168 n; *Des Artistes*, 111, 119, 120, 123; *Des Mots à la mode*, 108; *Deux Amis, Les*, 163 n; *Dissertation sur l'homme, La*, 4, 4 n, 8, 15, 15 n, 16, 19, 19 n, 20–22, 24–27, 29–33, 35–37, 39–40, 43–44, 47, 52, 56, 61, 65, 67, 69, 72 n, 82, 95, 101–102, 113, 152, 221, 265–274; *Double Famille, Une*, 183, 208; *Duchesse de Langeais, La*, 52 n, 109, 114–17, 117 n, 119, 131, 134, 164, 175, 178, 187 n, 194 n; *Du Gouvernement moderne*, 118; *Employés, Les*, 151; *Enfant maudit, L'*, 151, 152, 197; *Envers de l'histoire contemporaine, L'*, 52 n, 116, 136, 175, 183, 211; *Epicier, L'*, 142, 185; *Etudes analytiques*, 159; *Etude de femme*, 198 n; *Etudes sur M. Beyle*, 135, 189; *Eugénie Grandet*, 134, 149 n, 164, 183, 185, 186 n, 211, 224; *Falthurne*, 42, 42 n, 43, 43 n, 44, 44 n, 45, 45 n, 48, 51; *Fausse Maîtresse, La*, 121 n, 132, 186 n; *Femme abandonnée, La.* 167, 169, 200, 204–206; *Femme comme il faut, La*, 111; *Femme de province, La*, 145; *Femme de trente ans, La*, 125, 136, 141, 163 n, 168 n, 212–14, 214 n; *Ferragus*, 141, 164, 198 n, 205; *Fille aux yeux d'or, La*, 110, 123,

INDEX

Epée, Charles Michel de l', 18, 156 n
escape mechanism, *see laisser échapper*
especes, 27, 30–31, 35 n
Evans, Henri, 10 n, 66 n
expression, 200–202, 204, 207, 208, 209 n, 223, 223 n, 241, 243, 263–64
exprimer, see expression
Fabre d'Olivet, Antoine, 24 n
faculties of the mind, 30, 30 n, 31, 33, 35 n
Fanger, Donald, 142 n
Fargeaud, Madeleine, 72 n
Fichte, Johann Gottlieb, 24, 46
Flaubert, Gustave, works of: *Bouvard et Pechuchet,* 184 n
Forest, H. U., 3 n
Foucault, Michel, 162 n, 173 n, 219, 219 n, 220 n, 222 n
Frappier-Mazur, Lucienne, 157 n
Fraser, Alexander Campbell, 81 n
freewheeling language, 22, 111, 112 n
Freud, Sigmund, 261
Fromm, Erich, 244 n

Gall, Franz-Joseph, 159, 159 n
Gay-Lussac, Joseph Louis, 71
genius, theme of, 39, 107, 230 n, 263
gesture, 48, 154–56, 156 n, 157–60, 161 n, 161, 162, 162 n, 163, 246 n
Gipper, Helmut, 25 n, 39 n, 107 n, 131 n
Goldmann, Lucien, 219 N, 221 n
Grammaire Générale, *see Port-Royal, La Grammaire*
Greimas, A. J., 225 n
Grenier, Jean, 99 n
Grimsley, Ronald, 34 n, 36 n, 103 n, 104 n, 131 n
Guise, René, 7 n
Guyon, Bernard, 10 n, 45 n, 98 n
Guyon, Jeanne-Marie, 24 n, 28 n, 154, 154 n, 184

Hampshire, Stuart, 37 n, 106 n

Hanska, Evelina, 214, 214 n
Harding, D. W., 68 n
Helvétius, Claude-Adrien, 30 n, 33, 33 n, 35, 35 n
homo duplex, 58
homo parlans, 148, 222
Humboldt, Karl Wilhelm von, 25, 25 n, 39 n, 69, 105–107, 125 n, 131, 134
Hunt, Herbert J., 67, 67 n, 114 n
Husserl, Edmund, 109 n

ideas, collections of, 27, 31–32, 32 n
ideas, innate, 19
idée, theme of, 68, 68 n, 69–72, 72 n, 73, 73 n, 74–78, 78 n, 80–81, 82, 84–88, 89 n, 90–92, 95–101, 113, 117, 153, 178 n, 181, 196, 200, 201, 203, 205–210, 223 n, 225, 242, 243, 254, 262–64
ideology, 104–105
Iknayan, Marguerite, 66 n
improvisation, 116–17, 117 n
incompleteness, theme of, 262–64
inexpressibility, theme of, 47–48, 54, 55, 58, 214
Iser, Wolfgang, 213 n, 215 n

journalism, 133, 173, 244, 250
Juliard, Pierre, 24 n, 33 n

Kant, Immanuel, 24, 46
Knowleson, James R., 156 n

La Chambre, Marin Cureau de, 154 n
laisser échapper, theme of, 50–51, 154, 160–63, 169, 232 n, 241, 262
La Mettrie, Julien Offroy de, 30 n, 33, 33 n
Lancelot, Claude, 17, 17 n, 221 n
language, acquisition of, 102, 104; monetization of, 174–176, 239, 244 n, 251; origins of, 23–24, 102; poetry in, 136, 147
language as power, 6
Laromiguière, Pierre, 118, 118 n
Lavater, Johann Caspar, 7, 156,

INDEX

157, 157 n, 158, 158 n, 159, 159
n, 160, 160 n, 228 n, 229 n
laws, balzacian, 222
Le Breton, André, 42 n
Lebrun, Pierre, 154 n
Lecuyer, Maurice, 132
Lefebvre, Henri, 17 n
Lehmann, A. G., 210 n
Leibnitz, Gottfried Wilhelmn von,
19 n, 22, 24, 208 n
Lemare, Pierre Alexandre, 18
Leonard, S. A., 39 n
Leroy, G., 22 n, 31 n
Lessing, Gotthold Ephraim, 157
lexicons in characterization, 151–
52, 226, 231, 234, 241
Le Yaouenc, Moïse, 66 n
linguistic fit, 149
linguistic freewheeling, 110
linguistic realism, 7
linguistic relativity, 25
Littré, Emile, 15 n
Locke, John, 5–6, 18, 19 n, 20, 20
n, 21–22, 25, 29 n, 30 n, 31, 31 n,
32, 32 n, 34–35, 37, 41, 81–83,
109, 111, 118, 208 n
Lodge, David, 224 n, 226 n
Longnon, Henri, 8 n
Lovenjoul, Charles Spoelberch de,
82 n
Lugli, Vittorio, 7 n
Lukacs, George, 244 n

Maine de Biran, François Pierre
Gonthier, 19 n, 22 n, 27, 32, 36,
36 n, 37, 38, 38 n, 164 n
Malebranche, Nicolas, 29, 29 n, 35,
46
Mallarmé, Stéphane, 84 n, 210 n
Man, Paul de, 100 n
Mandiargues, André Pieyre de,
94 n
Mareschal, Lazare-François, 16,
18, 18 n, 19, 19 n, 26
Martin-Demézil, J., 16 n
Marx, Karl, 34 n, 244 n
materialism, 86
Maupertuis, Pierre-Louis Moreau
de, 31 n, 32, 34, 34 n, 102–103,
103 n, 104 n, 131 n

Mauro, Tullio de, 18 n
May, Georges, 9 n
Mayer, Gilbert, 6 n
McMaster, Juliet, 83 n
mechanism, theme of, 65–66,
70–74, 77–78, 81
memory, 31 n, 65
Merleau-Ponty, Maurice, 69, 69 n,
90, 90 n, 98, 185 n, 225, 261
Mersenne, Marin, 17 n
Miller, J. Hillis, 215 n
mimesis, 224, 224 n
Mitterand, Henri, 6 n
Molière, Jean Baptiste Poquelin,
called, 120
Montaigne, Michel Eyquem de,
120, 154 n
Moore, Will G., 5 n
Moreau de la Sarthe, 156–58, 157
n, 159
Moulinié, Henri, 23 n, 69 n, 162
Mueller, Hugo, 125 n, 134 n
music and language, 48, 52, 52 n,
114–16, 204
Mylne, Vivienne, 172 n

Nacquart, Jean-Baptiste, 159 n
naive realism, 19 n, 20–22, 34, 35
n, 74, 76 n, 77, 80–81, 82–83, 85,
86, 86 n, 89, 91, 95, 98, 99, 120,
170, 173, 203, 205, 207, 212,
214, 219, 235, 251
neologisms, 129, 167–69
norms, linguistic, 130, 130 n, 137,
144–47, 148
Nykrog, Per, 152 n

on, 136–37, 137 n
Oratorians, 16
pathognomonics, 158–60, 206 n
pensée, 68–70, 72 n, 84, 86–101,
103, 113, 117–18, 153, 200, 201,
203, 205, 206, 207–208, 210,
223, 239, 242, 245, 247, 250,
253, 258, 263, 264
perception, 226, 228–30, 238–39,
250, 254, 256–57
Percival, Keith, 18 n
Pfohl, Gerhard, 78 n
physiognomonics, 158–60, 206 n

INDEX

Pierrot, Roger, 210 n, 214 n
Plato, 6
Politzer, Robert L., 23 n, 25 n
Pommier, Jean, 70 n
Pons, Alain, 37 n
Portel, Charles, 16 n
Port-Royal, 16–17, 17 n, 18–19, 21, 26, 30 n, 36, 102, 105, 220–21; *La Grammaire*, 16, 17 n, 33, 36–37, 220; *La Logique*, 220
Posner, Rebecca, 130 n
presentiments, 44, 46, 54, 88, 262
printing, theme of in *Illusions perdues*, 226–27, 234–35, 240, 248
Prioult, Albert, 25 n, 42 n, 45 n, 133 n, 140 n, 157 n
puissance, 27, 28, 28 n, 29–32, 35 n, 43

Rabelais, François, 132 n
Raphaël, Raffaello Santi, 157 n
reader, cooption by narrator, 7, 215, 215 n, 216, 216 n
reader, ignorant, 191–94, 196–98, 207, 226; knowing, 191–93, 199, 207
representation, theory of, 224
Restif de la Bretonne, Nicolas Edme, 171–72
Richard, Jean-Pierre, 88 n, 100 n
ringing, theme of, 165–66
Rodis-Lewis, G., 29 n, 35 n
Roques, Mario, 5 n
Rousseau, Jean Jacques, 23, 23 n, 24, 24 n, 31 n, 35–36, 73, 90, 104 n, 106, 106 n, 115 n
Rudich, Linda, 66 n

Saint-Martin, Louis Claude de, 24 n, 28 n, 154, 154 n, 184
Sartre, Jean-Paul, 34 n, 69 n
Saussure, Ferdinand de, 25 n, 106 n, 219, 221
Scala, Can Grande della, 7
Schilling, Bernard, 240 n, 246 n
Scott, Sir Walter, 133, 133 n
seconde vue, theme of, 61
sensualism, 16, 19, 21–23, 26–27, 36–37, 68 n, 86, 106, 110–13,

117, 117 n, 119–20, 123, 156, 163
Seylaz, Jean-Luc, 76 n, 86 n
signs, eighteenth-century theories of, 222
silence, 208, 213, 233
simulacrum, 223, 223 n, 239, 251
Smith, Colin, 38
Snyder, Georges, 16 n
Spinoza, Baruch, 24, 46
Spurzheim, Johann Christophe, 159, 159 n
Stael-Holstein, Anne Louise Germaine de, 25
staining, theme of, 84–86
Steiner, George, 84 n
Stendhal, Henri Beyle, called, 119 n, 133 n
Sterling, Elwyn F., 9 n
Sterne, Laurence, 82, 82 n, 83, 89 n, 212 n
Stewart, D. H., 8 n
Sullivant, Raymond L., 214 n

Tagliacozzo, G., 18 n
talismanic words, 60, 62–63, 199, 200
Togeby, Knud, 8 n
Turgot, Anne Robert Jacques, 33, 33 n, 34, 34 n, 35, 35 n, 156, 173, 173 n, 175
Turnell, Martin, 261 n

Valéry, Paul, 84 n
Välikangas, Olli, 6 n
Vannier, Bernard, 108 n, 225 n
varnish, theme of, 23 n, 108, 108 n, 109–10, 230–31
veil, linguistic, 44, 47, 52–54, 56, 56 n, 58–64, 69–70, 100, 113, 122, 126, 171, 175, 184, 204, 213–15, 220–21, 258, 262
Verstraelen, Eugene, 69 n
Vico, Giovanni Battista, 23 n, 26 n, 37 n, 106 n
Viertel, John, 24 n
virtuality, theme of, 208, 208 n, 209, 210, 210 n, 211, 212, 213
vocabulary, *see* lexicons in characterization

INDEX

voices, theme of, 45, 53–54, 60–61, 164–65, 240 n, 262
volition, theme of, 67–68, 70 n
volonté, theme of, 67–68
Voltaire, 35, 71

Wais, Kurt, 6 n
Weinberg, Bernard, 225 n
Wells, George A., 26 n
White, Hayden V., 18 n
Whyte, L. L., 68 n
wit, 133, 134, 134 n, 136, 150, 232, 239
Wolff, Christian, 15 n, 46
word as weapon, 177, 178, 179, 180, 180 n, 181, 182, 231–33

word-events, 27, 140 n, 167–88, 189, 230–32, 232 n, 236, 262; condensation of, 168–69; expansion of, 168–70
word game, theme in *Illusions perdues*, 226–27, 229–31, 233, 241, 254–55
words, monetization of, 173, 173 n, 174, 175
words, reification of, 183–85
Wurmser, André, 42 n

Yates, F., 31 n
Yücel, Tahsin, 157 n

Zola, Emile, 71, 71 n

Library of Congress Cataloging in Publication Data

Kanes, Martin.
  Balzac's comedy of words.

  Bibliography: p.
  1. Balzac, Honoré de, 1799–1850—Language.
I. Title.
PQ2185.K3   843'.7   75–2993
ISBN 0-691-06282-X